CRITICAL CONTENT ANALYSIS OF CHILDREN'S AND YOUNG ADULT LITERATURE

In this book the authors describe their strategies for critically reading global and multicultural literature and the range of procedures they use for critical analyses. They also reflect on how these research strategies can inform classrooms and children as readers. Critical content analysis offers researchers a methodology for examining representations of power and position in global and multicultural children's and adolescent literature. This methodology highlights the critical as locating power in social practices by understanding, uncovering, and transforming conditions of inequity. Importantly, it also provides insights into specific global and multicultural books significant within classrooms as well as strategies that teachers can use to engage students in critical literacy.

Holly Johnson is an associate professor at the University of Cincinnati, USA.

Janelle Mathis is a professor at the University of North Texas, USA.

Kathy G. Short is a professor at the University of Arizona, USA.

CRITICAL CONTENT ANALYSIS OF CHILDREN'S AND YOUNG ADULT LITERATURE

Reframing Perspective

Edited by Holly Johnson, Janelle Mathis, and Kathy G. Short

Routledge
Taylor & Francis Group

NEW YORK AND LONDON

First published 2017
by Routledge
711 Third Avenue, New York, NY 10017

and by Routledge
2 Park Square, Milton Park, Abingdon, Oxon, OX14 4RN

Routledge is an imprint of the Taylor & Francis Group, an informa business

© 2017 Taylor & Francis

Library of Congress Cataloging-in-Publication Data
Johnson, Holly, 1956- editor. | Mathis, Janelle, editor. | Short, Kathy Gnagey, editor.
Title: Critical content analysis of children's and young adult literature : reframing perspective / edited by Holly Johnson, Janelle Mathis, Kathy G. Short.
Description: New York, NY : Routledge, 2016. | Includes bibliographical references and index.
Identifiers: LCCN 2016003531 | ISBN 9781138120082 (hardback) | ISBN 9781138120099 (pbk.) | ISBN 9781315651927 (ebook)
Subjects: LCSH: Children's literature—History and criticism. | Young adult literature—History and criticism.
Classification: LCC PN1009.A1 C693 2016 | DDC 809/.89282—dc23
LC record available at https://lccn.loc.gov/2016003531

ISBN: 978-1-138-12008-2 (hbk)
ISBN: 978-1-138-12009-9 (pbk)
ISBN: 978-1-315-65192-7 (ebk)

Typeset in Bembo
by Apex CoVantage, LLC

CONTENTS

Preface   *vii*

1 Critical Content Analysis as a Research Methodology   1
   Kathy G. Short with the Worlds of Words Community

2 The Critical Reading of Children's Texts: Theories,
   Methodologies, and Critiques   16
   Clare Bradford

3 Examining Displaced Youth and Immigrant Status
   through Critical Multicultural Analysis   28
   Holly Johnson and Becca Gasiewicz

4 Using Intertextuality to Unpack Representations of
   Immigration in Children's Literature   44
   *Yoo Kyung Sung, Mary L. Fahrenbruck, and
   Julia López-Robertson*

5 When Entertainment Trumps Social Concerns: The
   Commodification of Mexican Culture and Language
   in *Skippyjon Jones*   61
   Carmen M. Martínez-Roldán

6 "Having Something of Their Own": Passing on a
Counter-Story about Family Bonds, Racism, and
Land Ownership 77
Wanda M. Brooks

7 Representations of Same Sex Marriage in Children's
Picture Storybooks 92
Janine M. Schall

8 Re-Imagining an Alternative Life after the Darfur War:
Writing as Emancipatory Practice 106
Vivian Yenika-Agbaw

9 The Significance of the Arts in Literature:
Understanding Social, Historical, and Cultural Events 122
Janelle Mathis

10 The Right to Participate: Children as Activists
in Picturebooks 137
Kathy G. Short

11 Blurred Lines: The Construction of Adolescent Sexuality
in Young Adult Novels 155
Melissa B. Wilson

12 A Poststructural Discourse Analysis of a Novel Set
in Haiti 169
Deborah Dimmett

13 Connecting Critical Content Analysis to Critical
Reading in Classrooms 185
Holly Johnson, Janelle Mathis, and Kathy G. Short

About the Authors *200*
Index *203*

PREFACE

The primary focus of this book is an exploration of critical content analysis as a research methodology in examining children's and adolescent literature as text. We are interested in procedures for critical content analyses that focus on the critical, on locating power in social practices by understanding, uncovering, and transforming conditions of inequity and locating sites of resistance and change. Our initial interest in this methodology grew out of our needs as researchers for a methodology that would allow us to critically examine texts significant to our work as educators. Unable to find detailed descriptions of this methodology, we worked together as a community within Worlds of Words to develop processes and procedures and try them out within our own research.

Our goal in writing this book is to promote the rigorous analysis of children's and adolescent literature through research processes and procedures that are explicitly discussed in a range of studies, thus giving readers a window into the research process. This transparency of method creates an opportunity for readers to engage with this process in their own literary or critical content examinations. Furthermore, such transparency and rigor positions the literature for children and adolescents as a scholarly pursuit.

These studies also problematize and complicate the concept of cultural representation within literature by utilizing critical content analysis and critical theories. These theories provided a frame for selecting tenets by which to closely examine plotlines, characterization, and assumptions about the known as well as the other. This complicating of literary representation provides readers and researchers with new ways to study literature for young people as well as highlights the need to think about how such literature may be used in classrooms.

Because our mission as a community within Worlds of Words is to build intercultural understanding through literature, the texts we study are global and multicultural literature. Our goal is to make visible the literature of the often underrepresented that has largely gone unexamined in the field. We are concerned with ways of engaging readers, both children and teachers, with these books through critical reading and so we also see the development of critical content analysis as more than a research methodology. The research procedures for analysis offer insights into critical reading strategies that can encourage the development of a critical lens as readers engage with text in classrooms.

In essence, the studies within this text create spaces of opportunity for readers to examine global and multicultural literature in new and critical ways. Readers of these books then have the opportunity to critically examine or reexamine their own assumptions about the scholarly value of children's and adolescent literature and the potential of that literature for expanding their inquiries and perspectives as global citizens.

Overview of the Book

The first section of this book describes critical content analysis as a research methodology. The first chapter represents our current understandings of the procedures and processes involved in critical content analysis and the history of this methodology. The second chapter is based on a presentation by Clare Bradford that was influential in developing our conceptions of critical content analysis as a methodology. Clare is a highly respected literary critic from Australia who has published many articles and several books that we found useful in our attempts to understand critical reading.

The second section of the book includes our individual reports of critical content analysis studies. Given our focus on research methodology, the chapters are written in a research report format and include a fuller description of research procedures than is often found in published studies. Since we are educators, each researcher locates a study within an educational perspective, indicating how the purpose for the study grew out of work with readers and the implications for teachers and students. We invited Wanda Brooks and Vivian Yenika-Agbaw to write chapters because their work has been so influential in our understandings of critical content analysis from an educator's perspective. The rest of the chapters come from members of our community, Worlds of Words.

Because we are part of a community that shares a commitment to intercultural understanding, the books we selected for analysis are titles that reflect a global or multicultural perspective and our research questions reflect this focus as well. We believe that literature can provide an opportunity for children to go beyond a tourist perspective of gaining surface-level information about another culture and work toward the development of intercultural understanding. Literature expands children's life spaces and takes them outside the boundaries of their lives to other places, times, and ways of living in order to participate in alternative ways of being in the world. Readers immerse themselves into story worlds to gain insights about how people live, feel, and think around the world—to develop emotional connections and empathy as well as knowledge. These connections go beyond the surface knowledge of food, fashion, famous people, folklore, festivals, and facts about a country to the values and beliefs that lie at the core of each culture. They also go beyond the mass media emphasis on catastrophe, terrorism, and war that often result in superficial views of the world grounded in fear and stereotypes.

The development of intercultural understanding includes the ability to critically evaluate the misrepresentations and stereotypes of particular cultures that exist within society and so find their way into books, particularly since the majority of literature for children continues to be authored by cultural outsiders. In addition, global books often focus on ways of living that seem far removed from children's immediate experiences and so they can view this literature as "exotic" or "weird," failing to connect in significant ways. The use of culturally diverse literature in classrooms can actually establish stereotypes and misunderstandings unless readers bring a critical stance to this literature.

Knowing how to read the world and the word critically is thus essential to becoming a global citizen. The ability to take such a stance includes researchers who engage in critical content analysis to provide perspectives on the literature used in classrooms. This critical stance is also essential to teachers who select and use books in classrooms and who engage their students in taking on a critical stance.

The third section contains our final chapter in which we reflect on the ways in which the strategies, theoretical frames, and questions used for research can also serve as strategies that teachers and children can use in taking a critical stance as readers. The implications from these research studies relate not just to the specific issues and books that were examined in each study but to the ways in which we work toward critical literacy within teacher education and within elementary and secondary classrooms.

The Worlds of Words community is much larger than the authors reflected in this book and so we want to acknowledge the significance of that thought collective. The ideas and scholarship in this book come out of many conversations over a long period of time, to the extent that we can no longer single out individual contributions to our thinking. Our thought collective functions as a reflective community that facilitates our collaborative thinking and work and provides points of tension that disrupt the commonplace and lead to a reexamination of assumptions about ourselves and the world, thus transforming our work. We invite readers to join this ongoing effort and dialogue.

1

CRITICAL CONTENT ANALYSIS AS A RESEARCH METHODOLOGY

Kathy G. Short with the Worlds of Words Community

Content analysis has frequently been used as a research method to examine children's and young adult literature as texts, particularly within the field of literary studies. Our own interests as educators typically focused on studying the responses of readers to these texts. Over time, however, we found that we needed to critically examine the texts as well and so turned to research methodology textbooks and published studies to find out more about the methodology. After extensive searches and discussions with researchers across disciplines, we realized that the procedures for this analysis are usually not described in detail in published studies and are discussed only briefly in methodology textbooks.

In particular, we are interested in procedures for *critical content analysis* with a definition of critical as a stance of locating power in social practices in order to challenge conditions of inequity. Our struggles to define the methodology and to locate useful analysis procedures brought the authors of this book together. We talked with literary critics who engage in critical content analysis, such as Clare Bradford, and read the work of many literary critics, such as John Stephens, Perry Nodelman, Roberta Trites, and Mavis Reimer. We read critical content analyses by educators who focus on representational issues, power relations, and language as a postcolonial tool, particularly seminal studies by Rudine Sims Bishop (1982) and Joel Taxel (1986). Recent research by educators, such as Vivian Yenika-Agbaw, Wanda Brooks, Patricia Enciso, Carmen Medina, Maria Botelho, and Masha Rudman, was especially helpful. We revisited content analysis within the field of communication to understand the history of this methodology and engaged in our own critical content analyses. In addition, we met as a group over several summers, reading critical content analysis studies and descriptions of the methodology. Finally, we sponsored a study group and several sessions on critical content analysis at annual conventions of the Literacy Research Association to engage in conversations with other researchers (Beach et al., 2009).

These experiences led us to identify processes within critical content analysis as a methodology and to realize that our work as educators influences our approach to critical content analysis. We learned a great deal from literary critics but our intentions as researchers differ in significant ways because of our commitment to, and knowledge of, children, adolescents, teachers, and classrooms. Those differences influence our reasons for selecting a specific research focus, critical theory lens, and set of texts, as well as our reflections on the implications of our research for children as readers. This shift in focus also includes an interest in critical literacy and the ways in which our research strategies can inform classroom practice. The findings from critical content analysis studies of children's texts provide important insights and critical perspectives on specific global and multicultural books that are often used in classrooms. In addition, the strategies and questions we use as research analysis can be adapted as strategies for critical reading by teachers and students.

Our experiences as researchers in the field of education also influence the ways we write about our work, particularly in the use of a research report framework that includes descriptions of research procedures. We admire the ways in which literary critics in children's literature write about their work, often without subheadings, as they weave theory and data together to construct a compelling argument. At the same time, we recognize that we would have difficulty getting our work published in journals for educators, the group of people we want to reach as an audience, using that format. The different expectations between our fields were apparent in a conversation with Clare Bradford after hearing her present on her research methodology. We were excited about her careful and clear description of research procedures and asked why she did not describe those procedures in her published work. Her puzzled response was "It never occurred to me to do that. It isn't something that would be expected or appreciated in literary journals." For us, the opposite is true. Our interest in research procedures, however, goes beyond getting published to include strengthening our analysis strategies and challenging the field to view critical content analysis as a rigorous approach to research of children's and adolescent books as texts.

This chapter provides the contextual frame for this book through a brief description of the history of content analysis and a description of how we have conceptualized and actualized critical content analysis as a research methodology. The following chapters enact this conceptualization through reports of research that include careful descriptions of research procedures and discussions of the findings. The final chapter considers implications of these research analysis strategies for critical literacy approaches in teacher education and K–12 classrooms.

A Brief History of Content Analysis

'Content analysis' is an umbrella term used to indicate different research methods for analyzing texts and describing and interpreting the written artifacts of a society (White & Marsh, 2006). The content of texts are interpreted through coding and identifying themes or patterns, with the actual approaches ranging from impressionistic, intuitive, and interpretive analyses to systematic quantitative textual analyses (Hsieh & Shannon, 2005). Since content analysis involves making inferences from texts to the contexts of their use by using analytical constructs derived from theories or research, researchers adapt content analysis to their research questions and develop a range of techniques and approaches for analyzing text (Krippendorff, 2003).

Although content analysis rose to scholarly prominence in the 1950s in the United States, the method dates back to the 17th century to Western European religious scholars who analyzed newspaper articles for immoral content. In the 18th century, content analysis was used in Scandinavia to examine hymns that were not approved by Lutheran Church officials for possible heresy (Krippendorff, 2003).

Content analysis moved beyond religious affiliations to a more robust and accepted methodology in the 20th century through association with communications studies in the United States. Newspaper readership was flourishing and journalism scholars were interested in exploring the types of news being covered as well as how much space was devoted to each type. This led to *quantitative content analysis* where analysts counted words or inches of column space for particular types of news (Neuendorf, 2002). This quantitative content analysis was adapted to new media that subsequently emerged, including radio, television, film, and, the Internet. While this work was primarily contained in the field of communications and the study of mass media, other fields such as history, psychology, and sociology used variations of this method. For example, the Payne Fund Studies was a large multidisciplinary effort from 1929–1932 to study the effects of movies on children's attitudes and learning.

Content analysis currently includes both quantitative and qualitative approaches. Quantitative approaches are used in fields concerned with mass communications (Neuendorf, 2002), while qualitative content analysis covers methods such as discourse analysis, social constructivist analysis, rhetorical analysis, and textual analysis. Neuendorf (2002), who writes from a quantitative perspective, defines content analysis as a "summarizing, quantitative analysis of messages that relies on the scientific method and is not limited to the types of variables that may be measured or the context in which the messages are created or presented" (p. 10). On the other hand, Krippendorff (2003) sees content analysis as a "research technique for making replicable and valid inferences from the texts to the contexts of their uses" (p. 18). Hsieh and Shannon (2005) note that this approach reflects a focus on "the characteristics of language with attention to the content or contextual meaning of the text" (p. 1278).

Researchers use qualitative content analysis to make inferences from texts and to make sense of these interpretations within contexts surrounding the texts. This analysis involves the close reading of small amounts of texts that are interpreted by the analyst and then contextualized in new narratives. Wilson (2009) gives the example of a researcher "reading" the clothing worn by teens and putting that clothing into different categories representing similar meanings, such as a Goth or hip hop. These categories represent inferred meanings that make sense within the context of a particular group of teens within a particular culture and time period.

Galda, Ash, and Cullinan (2000) argue that the two major strands of research on children's literature as text have been literary analysis and content analysis, each with considerable variation. They point out that although the purposes are similar, the methods differ, with literary analysis describing *what authors do* and content analysis examining *what the text is about*.

Stephens (2015) argues against this opposition, pointing out that literary analysis is based on asking "*What is this text about?*" (p. v) through a theoretical lens and that "any analysis of stylistic devices or narrative patterns is directed towards the interpretation of content" (p. vi). He points out that content analysis is significant because of its focus on literature as representations of human experience and that research involves asking higher-level questions, such as "*How do I determine the significance of what happens here?*" (p. vi), that lead researchers to select particular methodological tools.

In the past, content analyses of children's books were initially quantitative, counting the presence and images of a particular cultural group or phenomena (Galda et al., 2000). Recent research has become qualitative with researchers taking a theoretical position that frames the development of research criteria for text analysis based on an understanding of texts and readings of these texts in the social, cultural, and political contexts in which they are considered (Short, 1995).

Content analysis reflects a hermeneutic, reader-response-oriented research stance and so meaning is not in the text but in the reading event, which is a transaction between an analyst and a text (Rosenblatt, 1938). Texts thus have multiple meanings that are dependent on the analyst's intentions as a reader and the context of the study because the purpose for the reading influences the meanings that are constructed as research findings. Analysts read to draw inferences from texts to apply to the context of the study, thus to make sense of something outside of the text. The texts do not speak for themselves, but are read in order to inform another context (Krippendorff, 2003).

Since content analysis is a stance, one option for researchers is to take a critical stance. What makes a study "critical" is the theoretical framework used to think within, through, and beyond the text, and involves a particular critical theory, such as postcolonialism, critical race theory, or queer studies.

The "Critical" in Critical Content Analysis

Adding the word "critical" in front of content analysis signals a political stance by the researcher, particularly in searching for and using research tools to examine inequities from multiple perspectives. Researchers who adopt a critical stance focus on locating power in social practices by understanding, uncovering, and transforming conditions of inequity embedded in society (Rogers, 2004). This critical consciousness challenges assumptions within thought and in the world that privilege some and oppress others (Willis et al., 2008).

Critical content analysis differs from content analysis in prioritizing a critical lens as the frame for the study, not just as part of interpreting the findings or citing scholarship in a literature review. Some researchers who engage in content analyses use a critical theory to comment on their findings, while in critical content analysis, the researcher uses a specific critical lens as the frame from which to develop the research questions and to select and analyze the texts. A critical approach is based in the intentions of the researcher to transform conditions of inequity and so this stance pervades all aspect of the research process (Willis et al., 2008). Since the researcher takes a political stance based in issues of inequity and power, some researchers believe that this positioning is subjective and unduly influences the research. Freire (1970) argues that all research is political and is always from within the subjective stance of the researcher. Critical content analysis makes the researcher's stance explicit and public to readers of that research.

Critical theory developed out of the work of Kant, Hegel, Marx, and the Frankfurt School, but current theoretical conceptions are traced to Paulo Freire (1970) who states that the world and texts are socially constructed and read through perspectives that differ from one reader to another. Each person conditions or transacts with a specific text in unique ways based on that person's lived experiences, value systems, and cultural understandings (Rosenblatt, 1938). Texts are never neutral as readers can revise, rewrite, and reconstruct texts to shift and reframe meaning (Vasquez, 2012). Texts are also written from a particular perspective to convey particular understandings of the world with the language of the text and the narrative strategies positioning readers toward particular meanings. Because of this positioning of text and reader, the perspectives of each should be questioned. The concept of critical therefore requires a questioning stance when reading the word and the world (Freire & Macedo, 1987).

Typically this questioning stance focuses on social issues involving race/ethnicity, class, or gender, and the ways language is used to shape representations of others who could be similar or dissimilar to the intended audience. The language used can impact the way readers perceive specific groups of people and by extension influence the power those within particular groups may or may not have within a specific society. For instance, women are often portrayed as more sensitive and thus are often held suspect when being considered for powerful roles in the United States.

A critical stance often includes questioning the concept of "truth" and how it is presented, by whom, and for what purposes. Other questions also emerge around whose values, texts, and ideologies are privileged or considered normative. A critical stance focuses on voice and who gets to speak, whose story is told, and in what ways. Groups marginalized on the basis of gender, language, culture and race, and sexual orientation are often the focus of a critical lens (Luke, 2012).

Freire (1970) argues that a critical lens involves critique (questioning what is and who benefits), hope (asking what if and considering new possibilities), and action (taking action for social justice). A critical lens thus moves from deconstruction to reconstruction and then to action. Freire points out that in everyday life many people stop at critique (deconstruction), which often paralyzes them with guilt, unsure about how to take action. In critical content analysis, the focus is on critique, on a critical examination of issues of stereotyping and misrepresentation in literature, a deconstruction of books and the societal issues that are reflected in representations of particular groups of people. Freire makes it clear that we should also be looking for reconstruction, for the ways in which texts position characters as resistant to existing stereotypes and representations in order to develop counter-narratives, and to offer new possibilities for how to position ourselves in the world. Based on critique and hope, researchers take action through publishing their work to a broader audience and engaging with teachers and students in their own critical analysis and use of these texts.

One of our first steps as researchers was to immerse ourselves in critical theories that seemed most relevant to our work, to spend time reading and grounding ourselves in theory. This immersion made it clear that there are many possible critical stances, including poststructuralism, critical race theory, critical feminism, postcolonialism, trauma theory, green theory, Marxism, New Historicism, gender and queer theory, and childism. Reynolds (2011) points out that scholarship in children's literature has benefited from adapting the critical theories used in literary, media, and cultural studies to support investigations based on narratives for children. Which theory is used depends on the research purpose with researchers often combining multiple theories to construct a critical lens through which to analyze text.

Conversations with literary critics indicate that they believe that a strong grounding in theory is one of the differences between content analysis as conducted by educators and their own work. We agree that educational researchers often do not forefront theory, tending to cite rather than to think with theory about their data. One of the major contributions to our thinking about critical content analysis was recognizing the importance of prioritizing theory. We noticed that we tend to quickly locate our studies within a theoretical frame and then immerse ourselves in the data, coming back to that theory in final discussions, but not necessarily thinking about the data *with* that theory as we analyze. Jackson and Mazzei (2012) were particularly useful in pushing our understandings of why thinking with theory about data is important as we moved into defining critical content analysis as a methodology for our own work.

Critical Content Analysis as a Research Methodology

At the broadest level, critical content analysis involves bringing a critical lens to an analysis of a text or group of texts in an effort to explore the possible underlying messages within those texts, particularly as related to issues of power. At a practical level, we developed a shared understanding of the processes that we engage in as researchers in using this methodology, recognizing its flexibility by a researcher within a particular context (see Figure 1.1).

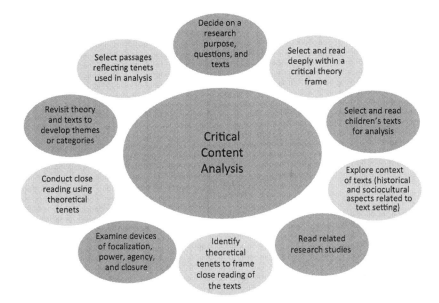

FIGURE 1.1   Elements of Critical Content Analysis

Decide on a Research Purpose, Questions, and Texts

Critical content analysis is embedded in a tension, a compelling interest in exploring texts around a focus that matters to the researcher and, because we are educators, that matters to young people as readers. We research something because our interactions with young people and teachers in classrooms or other contexts have indicated the significance of a particular focus for young people's perceptions of themselves and the world. Sometimes the research questions arise out of our work in classrooms. Interactions with immigrant children led Yoo Kyung, Mary, and Julia to examine novels of immigrant children for representations of their experiences, particularly around agency and "otherness," while Kathy's work on social action in classrooms led to her questions about whether picturebooks portray children taking action in authentic ways. Other times, the questions arise from current events and social media that affect the lives of youth. Janine's awareness of current events around same sex marriage and children's need for expanded perspectives led to her research focus on picturebooks that feature same sex marriage, while Melissa's research focus on sexuality in young adult novels came from her concerns about the negative portrayals of teen sexuality in popular culture and social media.

In any qualitative study, the researcher begins with a tension and an initial set of research questions that are transformed through interactions with the data, in this case with the texts and their interplay within the theoretical frame. With critical content analysis, we find that we begin with a research purpose or focus but often the specific research questions do not emerge until we immerse ourselves in the texts and theoretical frame. At best, we begin with questions that are broad and need to be shaped by immersion in the data and theory.

The selection of texts is based on the purpose of the study and often involves a careful process of researching many different text possibilities before deciding on a specific text or set of texts for analysis. Sometimes the tension relates to a specific set of texts, such as occurred for Carmen Martínez-Roldán and her concerns about the depictions of Latinos and the Spanish language in the popular Skippy-jon Jones series or for Deborah Dimmett in her uneasiness about novels published after the Haitian earthquake. The selection of a specific text can also connect to its potential for insights as occurred for Janelle in selecting a book that integrated poetry, art, and music in powerful ways in order to examine the role of the arts in addressing complex issues and providing a counter-narrative.

Other times, a broad range of texts related to the research focus is gathered from which texts for analysis are selected based on a specific set of criteria. Vivian selected one novel to examine images of war and refugees from a broader set of books, while Holly and Becca gathered a set of novels that reflect displacement and then selected seven for closer analysis. A small number of texts might be selected for in-depth analysis or a larger set of books can be examined to look for patterns rather than engaging in a close analysis of the contents of each book. Botelho and Rudman (2009) engage in critical analysis of large sets of books around social issues.

The first step of analysis is immersion as a reader, rather than as a researcher, in the identified texts. The focus is not to analyze the texts and take them apart but to respond to the whole text as a reader. We find it useful to read each text at least twice, once completely through without stopping before writing a reflection on our initial response. The second reading is still a response to the text but involves making notes as we read, either in the margins or on post-its or in a separate journal, about passages that catch our attention as a reader.

This first reading is in keeping with Rosenblatt's (1938) admonition to allow ourselves to take an aesthetic stance, to immerse ourselves in the experience of the story, rather than standing back to observe the story and get information, a more efferent stance. Much of critical content analysis involves an efferent stance, so we first want to "live within" the experience of that text as a reader—to experience the whole before we start analyzing the parts. Our focus initially is not a critical reading, but a personal response.

Select and Read Deeply within a Critical Theory Frame

Given our research focus and selection of texts, we search for a critical theory or set of theories as well as related sociohistorical and cultural sources. Once these sources are located, a large block of time is spent immersed in reading. This significant immersion into reading about theory and context is a key insight that we gained from literary critics. As educators, we tend to quickly locate ourselves within a theory and spend the majority of time with the data, returning to that theory as needed. Literary critics often spend significant chunks of time reading theory and related sources until a frame for analyzing the books becomes integrated into their thinking as a constant lens through which they interact with their data.

Jackson and Mazzei (2012) argue that researchers are often taught to analyze qualitative data through mechanistic coding that reduces data to themes and does little to capture or critique the complexities of social life. They argue for thinking *with* theory by reading the data while thinking about theory. This movement of "plugging in" and making new connections is a transactional process that creates knowledge out of chaos. Both the data and the theory are essential in this transaction and both are changed to create something new. Theory is used to turn data into something different and data is used to push theory to its limit. They see this complete interweaving of theory and data as a way to move out of the complacency of seeing as we always have and to think with theory in more integral and complex ways.

Our first step of analysis is to select a critical theory or set of theories that seem to have the most potential to provide an effective lens from which to critique the texts based on our research purposes. Some researchers used the same theoretical lens across many studies, focusing on different aspects of that theory as relevant to their work. Clare Bradford, for example, often uses a postcolonial lens for her analyses but selects different aspects of that theory depending on her research focus and combines postcolonialism with other critical theories as needed. Using the same theoretical lens allows a researcher to develop more complex understandings of that theory with each study. Other researchers bring different theoretical lenses to each study, enjoying adding new perspectives to their existing understandings. Still other researchers combine critical theories to develop a lens for their work. Botelho and Rudman (2009) drew from theories such as critical anthropology, cultural studies, political criticism, critical literary criticism, poststructuralism, critical discourse analysis, New Literacy studies, and critical pedagogy to develop what they call a critical multicultural lens to analyze sets of books.

Since we were new to critical content analysis, we initially explored a range of critical theories through books such as *The Routledge Companion to Critical and Cultural Theory*, edited by Malpas and Wake (2013) and *Critical Theory Today* by Tyson (2015), with chapters on different theories. Gillespie (2010) and Tyson (2011) summarize different critical theories and recommend ways of engaging students with these theories. These books provide overviews of critical theories so that we do not just fall back on the theories that are already most familiar to us. These sources allow us to identify theoretical perspectives that might be the best match with our research focus and provide references to pursue for more in-depth understandings of theory. Carmen found that Marxist theories provided an effective framework to examine the socioeconomic ideologies influencing the characters' actions, while Janine found that she needed to combine intersectionality and privilege theories to explore the complex identities of characters in picturebooks involving same sex marriage.

Clare Bradford helped us realize that some of our reading may need to focus on the sociohistorical and cultural context of books. Before analyzing an Aboriginal book, she engaged in extensive reading about Aboriginal culture from an insider's perspective. Vivian researched the historical and modern conflicts in Sudan along with her critical theory lens of intersectionality and third world feminism, while Janelle read about the historical context of all-female bands during World War II as well as interviewed the author and illustrator of a picturebook as a context for her use of New Historicism and social semiotics as a theoretical lens. Wanda notes that she needed to explore the significance of Black land ownership during Reconstruction as well as read interviews and articles by the author to understand her intentions for her work. Deborah Dimmett brought both scholarly knowledge and extensive experiences in Haiti to her poststructural analysis of a YA novel set in Haiti.

Read Related Research Studies

Another body of reading focuses on related studies where researchers analyzed either a similar set of texts or used a related research purpose or theoretical frame. Sometimes other researchers have engaged in critical content analysis or content analysis related to our research focus that informs our findings. Other times researchers have used the same critical theory frame, even though the focus differs, and the ways in which they use the theory to think with their data can inform our research processes. Kathy located several critical content analyses that used the same theoretical lens of childism to examine children's books, while Yoo Kyung, Mary, and Julia located research on immigration-themed children's books, using a range of theoretical lenses. These studies provided useful insights from findings as well as possible theoretical frames and research strategies.

List Theoretical Tenets to Frame the Analysis

We have all experienced reading broadly within a particular theory, resulting in so many different ideas bouncing around inside our heads that those ideas seem haphazard in influencing our analysis. We noticed that literary critics often identified a particular set of theoretical tenets from their reading that were then used to frame their analysis. The additional step of synthesizing our reading of theory into a small set of four to six theoretical tenets that are of most relevance from that theory for our specific research focus and set of texts has sharpened our analysis. Those tenets do not become our categories or themes for the findings that emerge from the analysis, but the tenets provide a clearer lens for reading and analyzing the texts.

Listing the most relevant theoretical tenets for a study provides a way to vary the same critical theory lens for different research studies and foci. In addition, identifying the tenets provides an important opportunity to revisit the research purpose and the research questions to make revisions in the purpose and to shape more specific research questions.

Examine the Texts through Close Reading within the Theoretical Frame

In-depth theoretical and contextual reading provides a more effective and complex frame from which to return to the reading of the children's or adolescent texts that are the focus of the research. Botelho and Rudman (2009) suggest that the initial close readings focus around several broad critical issues that allow the researcher to consider the language of the texts and the narrative strategies related to issues of power from a broader perspective before moving into close analysis of parts.

- Focalization—Whose story is told? From whose point of view?
- Social processes of characters—Who has power? Who has agency?
- Closure—How is the story resolved? What are the assumptions in the story closure?

Carmen began with an analysis of focalization in the Skippyjon Jones books, providing her with important insights into the identities created for characters by the author. Holly and Becca found questions of power relations to be particularly significant for examining the agency of protagonists in their set of immigration books, as did Melissa in her examination of decisions in sexual relationships between males and females.

Engaging in these initial close readings also supports the decision about what unit of analysis seems most productive. That unit of analysis might be interactions or dialogue between a particular set of characters or the actions and thinking of one character. The unit could involve identifying several key incidents or selecting incidents from the beginning, middle, and end of the text or the critical turning point of the text. The unit of analysis will vary with the research purpose and with the characteristics of the texts being analyzed. Because of Melissa's focus on sexuality, she examined excerpts from the novels that focused on discussions and actions around sexuality for male and female characters. Wanda identified chunks of illustrative text that exemplified the critical race theory tenets guiding her analysis and that varied in length from several pages for a compelling incident to a short paragraph of dialogue.

The initial close reading of the text to examine larger issues, such as focalization, social processes, and closure, along with identifying the unit of analysis provides another important perspective from which to revisit and revise the research questions. Adjustments to the research questions grow out of a strong grounding in the theoretical frame and in the texts themselves.

The next readings involve a close examination of the identified units within those texts, moving between the theoretical frame and the texts, initially making many notes and gradually moving toward identifying significant issues, themes, or categories. This analysis often focuses on broad themes or issues that emerge from the interplay of data and theory in an evolving process as described by Jackson and Mazzei (2012). Sometimes, we use constant comparative analysis to organize data from these texts into more discrete categories, documenting emerging themes and evidence from the text and gradually developing these into a focused set of categories to report the findings as Wanda did in her analysis of a novel, going from 24 initial codes to three broad categories. Frequently, however, the data examples from the texts are organized around broad themes or issues rather than discrete categories as occurred for Janelle in her analysis of a picturebook.

Rogers (2004) describes the use of critical discourse analysis as a methodology to analyze children's texts with three levels that merge textual and visual analysis through systemic functional linguistics and social semiotics. She begins by creating a multimodal transcript, carrying out descriptive analysis, examining the grammar of design, and considering the book in context. The multimodal transcript provides a means to look at the book as a cultural text. The descriptive analysis provides a base line description of the book through a word count of each page, a thick description of the images, and a lexical count of key words. The framework of the grammar of design guides an examination of the gestural, spatial, linguistic, and visual designs of the text to look closely at what modes exist and how they are patterned together in ways that privilege some meanings or readings over others.

Rogers (2004) describes the second level as examining each aspect of the systemic functional linguistic framework—genre, discourse, and style. Genre refers to 'ways of interacting,' or the ways in which the textual and visual elements constitute the genre of the book. Discourse refers to 'ways of representing' and involves asking questions about how themes are signified through verbal and visual modes. Style refers to 'ways of being' and includes the elements of visual and textual design that indicate stance, perspective, and affinity. The final level is a consideration of how genre, discourse, and style work together to make meaning.

None of the chapters in this book use this form of critical discourse analysis but we have used these procedures in other critical content analyses and several chapters do include linguistic analysis as part of their research procedures. Carmen did a careful linguistic analysis of the Mock Spanish in the Skippyjon Jones books and Vivian's analysis process included identifying words and phrases that reflected the sociocultural contexts of gender and sociopolitical dynamics of cultural space.

Revisit Theory and Texts

The process of analysis remains flexible and recursive with multiple revisits to theory and texts. Sometimes the need for further reading of theory becomes evident, either within the same theoretical frame or by adding additional theories due to issues arising in the analysis. The units of the text selected for analysis may need to be revisited for further analysis as new themes and issues emerge either from another part of the data or through additional readings. This recursive process of revisiting theory and the data may occur multiple times until the major themes or categories take shape with strong evidence from the texts to support those themes.

Write Theoretical Memos on the Analysis

We find it useful to write theoretical memos for each major theme or category, providing a description of each one based on the professional literature and on the types of examples found in the texts. This definition or explanation of each theme or category is developed by presenting evidence from the texts, citing excerpts and interpretations of those passages as related to the theme, and interweaving theory into those interpretations.

These memos provide the basis from which to write articles and chapters based on the analysis. Our experiences indicate major differences in how the study is shared based on the type of journal to which we plan to submit a manuscript. Educational research journals typically want a research report format focused around research purpose, theoretical frame and literature review, methodology, findings, discussion, and implications, while literary journals begin with a research purpose and then flow into a discussion of the major issues and themes, integrating theory and data throughout the article. Finally, journals that reach out to a broader audience of educators generally focus on sharing key insights from the research and implications for teachers rather than being organized into a research report format. Given the focus of this book on research methodology, we decided to write our chapters using a research report format with an expanded section describing the research methodology within each chapter. The concluding chapter extends the significance of the methodology by relating the various processes to the potential for classroom inquiry and instruction.

Conclusion

Although the processes we have described in this chapter seem logical and step-by-step, the studies we share in this book reflect the many variations of how critical content analysis can play out in actual research. Just as the written curriculum is never the same as the enacted curriculum, our actual enactment of critical content analysis always differs due to our research purposes, texts, and theoretical lens, as well as our own strengths and experiences as researchers. Readers will notice that some aspect of the process described in this chapter was not followed or was greatly adapted in every study reported in this book. We see this variation as a strength of critical content analysis. It is also clear to us that other researchers using critical content analysis will develop their own variations and processes.

The thread that runs throughout all of our work is the willingness to take a critical stance as a researcher. This critical stance is woven throughout our research so that every aspect of the research process is based in thinking through a particular theoretical lens. Acknowledging that all research is political, we believe that critical content analysis adds complexity and depth to the discussion of research methodology. As researchers, we are challenged to explicitly identify our stance and take ownership of our responsibility to critique issues of power and oppression in order to take action in our varied contexts.

References

Beach, R., Enciso, P., Harste, J., Jenkins, C., Raina, S. A., & Yenika-Agbaw, V. (2009). Exploring the "critical" in critical content analysis of children's literature. In K. M. Leander, D. W. Rowe, D. K. Dickinson, M. K. Hundley, R. T. Jiménez, & V. J. Risko (Eds.), *58th yearbook of the National Reading Conference* (pp. 129–143). Oak Creek, WI: National Reading Conference.

Bishop, R. (1982). *Shadow and substance: Afro-American experience in contemporary children's fiction*. Urbana, IL: National Council of Teachers of English.

Botelho, M. J. & Rudman, M. K. (2009). *Critical multicultural analysis of children's literature*. New York: Routledge.

Freire, P. (1970). *Pedagogy of the oppressed*. South Hadley, MA: Bergin & Garvey.

Freire, P. & Macedo, D. (1987). *Literacy: Reading the word and the world*. Santa Barbara, CA: Praeger.

Galda, L., Ash, G. E., & Cullinan, B. E. (2000). Research on children's literature. In M. L. Kamil, P. B. Mosenthal, P. D. Pearson, & R. Barr (Eds.), *Handbook of reading research: Volume III* (pp. 351–381). Mahwah, NJ: Erlbaum.

Gillespie, T. (2010). *Doing literary criticism*. Portland, ME: Stenhouse.

Hsieh, H. & Shannon, S. (2005). Three approaches to qualitative content analysis. *Qualitative Health Research, 15*(9), 1277–1288.

Jackson, A. & Mazzei, L. (2012). *Thinking with theory in qualitative research*. New York: Routledge.

Krippendorff, K. (2003). *Content analysis: An introduction to its methodology*. Thousand Oaks, CA: Sage.

Luke, A. (2012). Critical literacy: Foundational notes. *Theory into Practice, 51*(1), 4–11.

Malpas, S. & Wake, P. (Eds.). (2013). *The Routledge companion to critical and cultural theory* (2nd ed.). New York: Routledge.

Neuendorf, K. A. (2002). *Content analysis guidebook*. Thousand Oaks, CA: Sage.

Reynolds, K. (2011). Introduction to research and theory. In M. O. Grenby & K. Reynolds (Eds.), *Children's literature studies: A research handbook* (pp. 123–127). London: Palgrave.

Rogers, R. (2004). *An introduction to critical discourse analysis in education*. Mahwah, NJ: Erlbaum.

Rosenblatt, L. (1938). *Literature as exploration*. Chicago: Modern Language Association.

Short, K. (Ed.). (1995). *Research and professional resources in children's literature*. Newark, DE: International Reading Association.

Stephens, J. (2015). Editorial: Critical content analysis and literary criticism. *International Research in Children's Literature, 8*(1), v–viii.

Taxel, J. (1986). The Black experience in children's fiction: Controversies surrounding award winning books. *Curriculum Inquiry, 16*(3), 245–281.

Tyson, L. (2011). *Using critical theory* (2nd ed.). New York: Routledge.

Tyson, L. (2015). *Critical theory today* (3rd ed.). New York: Routledge.

Vasquez, V. (2012). Critical literacy. In J. Banks (Ed.), *Encyclopedia of diversity in education* (pp. 466–469). Thousand Oaks, CA: Sage.

White, M. & Marsh, E. (2006). Content analysis: A flexible methodology. *Library Trends*, *55*(1), 22–45.

Willis, A., Montavon, M., Hall, H., Hunter, C., Burke, L., & Herrera, A. (2008). *Critically conscious research*. New York: Teachers College Press.

Wilson, M. (2009). Constructions of childhood in award-winning children's literature. Dissertation, University of Arizona, Tucson.

2

THE CRITICAL READING OF CHILDREN'S TEXTS

Theories, Methodologies, and Critiques

Clare Bradford

The methodological approach scholars take in producing critical analyses of literary and other texts is rarely discussed in the field of literary studies. Publications in this field generally commence with an explanation of theoretical perspectives, the identification of key theorists, and an outline and preliminary analysis of the theories and concepts pertinent to the discussion. From this point the usual practice is to proceed to textual analysis, referring back to the framework of theory and offering a reading of texts in the light of this theory. Often the work of theorists is critiqued in relation to efficacy or explanatory power.

Scholars rarely outline the methodological processes whereby they apply concepts and theories to strategies of textual analysis so as to produce readings of texts. In this chapter, I make explicit the methodologies by which I proceed from concepts and theories to analysis. This chapter is therefore a reflection on research methodology, not a report on research findings, from the perspective of a scholar in literary studies. It is intended to flesh out the "how" of critical analysis of texts by attending to the processes and methods that shape my investigations of children's texts.

Doing Critical Analysis

Critical reading requires that we engage in two processes in tandem. We need both to stand back from a text so as to situate it (top-down) in relation to the historical and cultural forces that have shaped it and the theoretical frames that we draw on; and also (in bottom-up analysis) to examine its linguistic and narrative features. This combination of top-down and bottom-up analysis presents its own difficulties; for instance, when I begin a writing project I often find that I spend so much time thinking about the theoretical and conceptual frames in which I locate a group of texts that the pleasure of playing with ideas takes over and the texts recede into the background. A problem novice scholars frequently encounter is that once they have framed their argument and turn to discuss the texts they have selected, they leave the framing (top-down) concepts behind and fall into the trap of merely describing the texts without returning to and using the top-down ideas they have introduced. My approach to "content analysis" extends beyond discussions of themes and content to the "how" of texts—that is, the language of texts, and the narrative strategies by which they position readers.

To lead into my discussion of critical analysis I use an essay that was published in the December 2009 issue of the journal *International Research in Children's Literature*. I do not imply that this is the only model of how to approach textual critique, but I propose to reflect on the processes and concepts that I brought to the task of writing. My essay is called "Muslim-Christian Relations and the Third Crusade: Medievalist Imaginings," and was submitted for a themed issue of the journal, on "Internationalization, Transculturalism and Globalization: Manifestations in Children's Literature and Film."

The term "medievalist" in the title of my paper refers to the myriad uses of medieval periods, events, characters, fantasy elements (fairies, goblins, dragons), and narratives in contemporary children's literature—that is, everything from Robin Hood to *The Hobbit*, from picturebooks about witches to the castles, warriors, and quests common to video games. In every period people remake the Middle Ages: as a time of filth and ignorance, or of magic, or of a utopian pre-industrial landscape. These remakings are always inflected by the desires and preoccupations of the time and place in which they are formed. It occurred to me as I explored options for my essay that contemporary historical novels set in the Middle Ages often address urgent and contentious questions affecting modern societies by locating them in the distant past.

The question that intrigued me was: How might Muslims and Christians engage with each other while acknowledging and respecting cultural and religious difference? I narrowed down my group of focus texts to three novels set in the period of the Third Crusade (1189–1192): Karleen Bradford's *Lionheart's Scribe* (1999), K.M. Grant's *Blood Red Horse* (2004), and Elizabeth Laird's *Crusade* (2008), all of which track the progress of young English protagonists who go on crusade to Jerusalem and (crucially for my purposes) encounter Muslim people and cultures. The broader context of their adventures lies in the events of the Third Crusade, dominated by the figures of Richard 1 (the Lionheart) of England and Salah al-Din Yusuf (Saladin), Sultan of Egypt and Syria. A brief summary of the three novels is essential to understanding my analysis process:

- *Lionheart's Scribe:* The third book in Bradford's Crusades series, this novel follows the progress of 15-year-old Matthew, an orphan whose father taught him to write. Matthew runs away from his cruel master and stows away on a ship accompanying Richard the Lionheart on his journey to Palestine. He befriends Rashid, the nephew of one of Saladin's advisors, and Yusra, an orphaned girl whom he rescues when the ship captained by her father is sunk by the Lionheart's forces. He is present throughout the siege of Acre and observes the atrocity committed by Richard the Lionheart when he orders the slaughter of 3,000 Muslim prisoners held in Acre. When Lionheart withdraws from Jerusalem, having signed a truce with Saladin, Matthew returns with him to Britain.

- *Blood Red Horse:* The novel follows the fortunes of William, the younger son of Sir Thomas de Granville, who embarks on the crusade with his father and older brother Gavin, as well as his horse Hosanna. In effect this is as much a horse book as an historical novel. Will makes friends with Kamil, the ward of Saladin, and travels with the crusade armies to Jerusalem. Sir Thomas dies in Palestine, and Gavin is seriously wounded, losing one of his arms in battle. William returns to his family estate to discover that he has been made Earl of Ravensgarth.

- *Crusade:* This novel incorporates a doublestranded narrative in which alternate chapters follow the progress of Salim, a Muslim boy from Acre, and Adam, the illegitimate son of a poor woman. When Adam's mother dies unconfessed, he promises to save her soul with dust from the Holy Land, and joins the crusade to reclaim Jerusalem employed as a dog-boy for the local lord, Baron Guy de Bartel. Salim, a merchant's son, is apprenticed to a Jewish physician who is recruited as Saladin's personal doctor. The two boys meet in Palestine and rescue a young English girl who has been kidnapped for the slave trade. Adam discovers that he is in fact the son of Baron Guy de Bartel, who dies during the course of the crusade, bequeathing Adam a castle and land.

For my top-down framing of the essay I drew upon an eclectic mix of theories from postcolonial, critical race, and whiteness studies. Because of my focus on relations between Muslim and Christian protagonists, I consulted sections of Edward Said's classic work *Orientalism* (1978), which examines how the West has produced the East as an object of study. These domains of literary theory have in common an interest in how symbolic codes—such as language and visual arts—are used to construct and maintain systems of power and knowledge. Postcolonial studies focuses on the effects of imperialism on people and places; critical race studies interrogates the seeming naturalness of hierarchies of race; and whiteness studies critically examines how whiteness claims and maintains its power through representation and systemic practices. The three approaches differ in regard to the historical and cultural contexts on which they focus. The ideas that informed my thinking as I researched and wrote included

- notions of otherness (and distinctions between self and other);
- Eurocentrism (the assumption that European values constitute a norm against which non-European values can be measured);
- formulations of time, antiquity, progress, and change;

- distinctions between Orient and Occident;
- intersections of gender and race; and
- discourses of religion.

In preparation for writing the essay I searched through key journals and book publications to locate discussions that draw upon postcolonial theories to inform discussions of medieval and medievalist texts, identifying some important secondary sources, especially Geraldine Heng's *Empire of Magic: Medieval Romance and the Politics of Cultural Fantasy* (2003) and J.J. Cohen's edited collection *The Postcolonial Middle Ages* (2001). While most of the essays in this collection focus on texts produced between 500 and 1500, several deal with contemporary (medievalist) texts, so suggesting lines of investigation. For instance, an essay by Kathleen Davis (2001) discusses an ABC-TV story about the treatment of women under Taliban rule, in which the veiling of women is characterized in terms of a return to medievalism. Davis regards this reference as an instance of neo-orientalism. I also identified discussions on the use of the term "crusade" in contemporary political rhetoric, including Bruce Holsinger's (2008) analysis of how this term and its associated meanings were used to justify the "war on terrorism" and to support rhetorics of savagery and barbarism as applied to Muslim cultures.

Informed by this rich seam of theory and analysis, I began work on the three texts. First I examined their narrative patterns, which broadly adhere to the "home-away-home" schema identified by Perry Nodelman and Mavis Reimer (2003), who maintain that this is the default pattern for most children's texts. In these novels, in which protagonists leave Britain for Palestine and return to Britain at the end, "away" is infused with cultural meanings that pit Englishness against the East and Christianity against Islam. Because so much is made of the dangers of the crusade and the otherness of the East, the return to England and home carries a heightened significance. England and (English) Christianity function as a norm against which other places and cultures are judged.

Another common element in the novels' construction is that their protagonists are all male, boys who are drafted or who volunteer to take part in crusades that function as rites of passage. In two of the novels, *Crusade* and *Lionheart's Scribe*, these boys are Cinderlad figures: poor, friendless, isolated in their world. Two of them (Salim in *Crusade* and Matthew in *Lionheart's Scribe*) have disabilities that limit their participation in warfare. They have much in common with the New Age boys prominent in contemporary fiction for children and young people (Stephens, 2002) who demonstrate qualities of sensitivity and introspection rather than the macho aggressiveness of hegemonic masculinity. The third novel, *Blood Red Horse*, features William de Granville, the younger son of an aristocratic family, and accords with a medieval romance that follows the adventures of an aristocratic hero.

These top-down elements constitute a mixture of discoursal and narrative features including concepts around religion, gender, place, cultural difference, and narrative teleologies. They provided a frame for a bottom-up approach to textual analysis in which I investigated episodes in the three novels when Christian and Muslim characters meet. Stretches of dialogue are often especially telling because they embody power relationships. The narrative strategies of focalization and point of view also repay close attention, since it is through these strategies that readers are positioned to align themselves with protagonists and hence to acquiesce to textual ideologies. The following passage from *Blood Red Horse* (Grant, 2004) introduces the Muslim protagonist, Kamil, who has been adopted into Saladin's entourage:

> Far away in the Holy Land, the muezzin's call bidding Muslims to prayer was being answered by a dark man and a boy, both richly dressed and mounted on high-stepping Arab horses.... The boy dismounted and moved to grasp the bridle of the horse of the older man.
>
> "Ah, Kamil ad-Din," said the man with a smile, "you are always there, before I even have time to look."
>
> The boy flushed with pleasure. "Your Majesty, the great Sultan Saladin," he said, "is like a father to me. I do for you only what I would do for my own father, whose goodness Allah is now rewarding in heaven."
>
> "Always a good answer, too," said the older man, and Kamil was momentarily confused, not knowing if this was a compliment or a rebuke.
>
> *(pp. 2–3)*

The terms "muezzin," "Muslims," "prayer," and "dark" in this passage link ethnicity with religion and with a racialized Muslim identity. The passage occurs eight chapters into the book, following a sequence during which William de Granville has acquired a Great Horse (a steed suited to a squire and future knight) and has adopted the white tunic and red cross of the crusader. Read in the light of whiteness studies, the description of Kamil and Saladin as "dark" inscribes William's whiteness as the norm against which to view an homogenized "Arab" otherness. Not, of course, that William's whiteness is ever mentioned, since as Richard Dyer (1997) notes in *White*, "Other people are raced, we are just people" (p. 1). Another strand of representation is indicated by "richly dressed" and "high-stepping." Said (1978) points out in *Orientalism* that one of the principal contrasts between the West and the Orient in Orientalist writing is that men of the Orient are habitually represented as lovers of luxury, effete, and feminine. There is only a short distance, then, to depictions of Eastern men as slippery and untrustworthy.

The conversational exchange between Kamil and Saladin further enforces a powerful contrast between the English characters and their Eastern others. During the previous eight chapters, William's conversation has been rendered as close to contemporary English. Kamil's, however, is suggestive of antiquity: it is mannered and indirect, studded with formulaic phrases ("the great Sultan Saladin"; "whose goodness Allah is now rewarding"). When Saladin remarks, "Always a good answer, too." Kamil's uncertainty as to what he means suggests that the language of the Orient is opaque, unlike the bluff, straightforward conversational style of the English characters. Drawing on the top-down knowledge I bring to the text, I argue in my essay that Orientalist modes of representation are evident in contrasts between William and Kamil and between Richard the Lionheart and Saladin, which represent Englishness as straightforward, honest, and plain in attire and language, in contrast to an Orient distinguished by subtlety, slipperiness, and a love of luxury. Directed to Western readers, the novel thus affirms that while "we" are easy to understand, "they" are not. More than this, the Orient is associated with an antiquity that stretches back prior to the 12th-century setting of the novel, whereas the Englishness of Will and his friends is not all that different from contemporary Western values and identities.

Among my list of top-down concepts I included "intersections of gender and race." In *Lionheart's Scribe*, such an intersection occurs in a sequence in which the protagonist Matthew saves Yusra, a Muslim girl, from drowning and later falls in love with her. Yusra, who has been incorporated into the household of Lionheart's sister Queen Joanna, can think of nothing but returning to her people. The principal sign of her resistance to the Queen's attempts to convert her to Christianity is her determination to wear the veil: she says, "I must dress like a Muslim woman. Obey the Muslim laws" (Bradford, 1999, p. 188). The top-down knowledge that informed my reading of this episode is the large body of discussion within feminist and critical race studies concerning Western understandings of the veil and its significances. As Davis (2001) points out, media reports on veiled Muslim women frequently use the term "medieval" to represent Muslim culture as "an inert, temporal space incapable of change" (p. 107). Her commentary accords with the depiction of Yusra's incapacity to adapt to a Western, Christian culture. Matthew guides her to Jerusalem, which is held by Saladin following the defeat of Richard the Lionheart. Yusra seeks refuge at the gates of Jerusalem and is taken inside by the guards, while Matthew returns to the English camp. As he wends his way back he hears the Muslim call to prayer, a rather heavy-handed reminder that Yusra is securely locked away in a Muslim culture defined by ancient religious rituals, whereas Matthew is free to move about the world.

In my essay I came to the conclusion that two versions of medieval time exist in the three novels and argue that two medievalisms coexist, "a version of the (Christian) Middle Ages that suggests relationships of continuity between then and now; and a Muslim Middle Ages marked by extreme alterity" (Bradford, 2009, p. 182). To reach this conclusion I drew on the evidence of the novels' language features and narrative strategies, including focalization, symbolism, and conversational exchange. The contrast between the two worlds (Christian and Muslim) enforces the idea that there is no possibility of lasting or intimate relationships between Christian and Muslim protagonists. In this way they model to contemporary readers the sense that the two religions are radically incompatible, and that their adherents are placed on either side of a vast and unbridgeable divide.

This specific example of employing top-down and bottom-up strategies in critically reading texts reflects the general shape of my processes across many different studies. Those strategies vary according to the specific texts, contexts, and purposes for my analysis, particularly when I am analyzing minority texts.

Reading Texts as an Outsider

As a member of a dominant culture (that is, a white Australian living in a nation whose prosperity is built on the destruction of Indigenous cultures), I am powerfully conscious of the fact that I am an outsider to those cultures. This means that I am an outsider also to Australian Indigenous textuality, and that I must approach Indigenous texts in a very different way from how I read the Western texts that lie within the ambit of my experience and training as a scholar. My training in the methodologies and theories of Western scholarship is so central to my repertoire of reading strategies and theoretical understandings that when I read Indigenous texts I frequently experience a sense of destabilization. I say to myself: But how does this text work? What can it mean? My experience of textual unfamiliarity is itself a cue, alerting me to the fact that I am reading a text that originates from a culture different from my own. Although I focus here on strategies for reading Indigenous textuality, much of what I say is applicable to reading the literatures of other minorities.

Western critics often struggle to read minority texts. Just as whiteness is the default way of being in the world for white people, so we are conditioned to believe that Western narrative forms, genres, and conventions are universal norms. However, many Indigenous and other minority groups adhere to quite different ways of creating narratives. In Australian Indigenous cultures, for instance, the concept of "fiction" lies outside traditional modes of narrative. On the other hand, highly complex networks of Dreaming stories exist that deal with the time and place when the Ancestors (sacred beings) traveled across the land, creating landforms, rivers, and forests as well as people and animals, and establishing the Law which governs relationships between people and between people and animals. These Dreaming stories are experienced as true.

Peoples whose stories are orally transmitted habitually combine a variety of symbolic systems, such as art, dance, and song that rely upon the presence of a storyteller and an audience. In the West, in contrast, the introduction of the printing press has led to the experience of reading being imagined as a transaction involving absence and assuming that people are far away from one another (authors, publishers, readers), because the book can be produced in one place and read in another.

Even when they are published as books, the narratives of Indigenous peoples carry the marks of their origins in orality. For instance, it often seems to non-Indigenous readers of Australian Indigenous traditional stories that they begin and end suddenly, without phrases such as "Once upon a time" at the beginning and "They all lived happily ever after" at the end. Indeed, when Indigenous stories have been retold by non-Indigenous people they have generally added such beginnings and endings. Indigenous stories work not as stand-alone individual narratives but as parts of a larger sequence of stories. Thus, audiences would be expected to be already familiar with characters, so that no explanation would be necessary; and because stories were told in particular places with which they had ancient associations, there was no need for descriptions of places. Stories commonly begin with an action or event, in contrast with Western stories that habitually provide a context before introducing action.

The most powerful way to understand Indigenous beliefs and narrative practices is to consult Indigenous people, either firsthand through professional and friendship associations, or by searching out websites developed and maintained by individuals, clans, nations, or tribes, or by reading the work of Indigenous scholars working in anthropology, education, history, literature, and Indigenous studies. Many non-Indigenous postcolonial theorists and critics have produced important work on Indigenous textuality, although it is important to be judicious, selecting authors who do not assume the mantle of experts on Indigenous peoples or speak on their behalf.

In "Ethical Reading and Resistant Texts," Patricia Linton (1999) discusses the experience of "cultural outsiders" (p. 42), those who read the work of minority authors while not belonging to the cultures of such authors. Linton observes that merely because "an ethnic or postcolonial writer hopes to be read by a broad or varied audience does not mean that he or she invites all readers to share the same degree of intimacy" (p. 32). It is common, she says, for cultural outsiders to experience a sense that minority texts incorporate silences and omissions on certain topics and details, so constructing boundaries that alert cultural outsiders to their outsider position. In this way cultural outsiders are reminded that they are not entitled to understand all that there is to know of the worlds of these texts. Linton states that these texts "require a readerly tact that recognizes boundaries and respects them" (p. 43).

Tracking around the Edges

The text I have selected as my focus of analysis is Daisy Utemorrah and Pat Torres's *Do Not Go around the Edges* (1990), an iconic text produced by a revered elder from the Kimberley region of Western Australia. From the moment it was published this book was a cataloguer's nightmare, since it incorporates both a collection of Utemorrah's poems and her autobiography, narrated along the lower margin of each double-page spread. Pat Torres's illustrations constitute the third element of the text, accompanying the poems and forming a border that frames each spread. This diversity of content—poetry, autobiography, visual images—poses a challenge to Western readers accustomed to picturebooks where visual images and verbal text align to produce a narrative.

To make sense of this book I consulted anthropological, historical, and geographical sources for information about Utemorrah and her Worrora clan. Indeed, the book impelled me to attend to the materiality and the locatedness of Utemorrah's text. The first page after the title page presents a photograph and map showing the places significant to Utemorrah: Galanji, her ancestral home; Kunmunya Mission where she grew up; Derby where she and her family were later moved; and Mowanjum where she lived at the time of the book's publication. The italicization of the words Wunambul, Worrora, and Ngarinyin in the map signals that they refer to clans and language groups, not places, and when I researched them I established that these three groups share responsibility for the land and waters of the north-west Kimberley region and that they belong to a system of belief based on the Wandjina, the sacred beings who formed this part of the land. When I turned to the pages of the book, then, I recognized that the Wandjina pattern that frames the lower margin, far from being merely decorative, carries the sense that all that is in the book is built upon the Law and customs established by the Wandjinas, who are represented in many cave paintings and other artwork throughout the region.

The very fact that I needed to do so much research in order to situate this book in relation to geography and cultural traditions heightens the sense of my position as an outsider to the text, its assumptions and meanings. I may access Wandjina images on various Internet sites, and read about the Law they established during the Dreaming, but my access will always be limited to what I can know as an outsider. In these majestic and mysterious paintings I can divine "meaningfulness, but not the meaning itself" (p. 57), as the anthropologist Eric Michaels (1994) observed about the desert sandpaintings by Warlpiri artists which he saw during the 1980s.

The three elements that make up the text—poems, autobiography, visual images—relate to each other sometimes directly, sometimes obliquely. In one double-page spread, for instance (pp. 2–3), the poem "Galanji" is a lament by the speaker for her "far far away" island home; a lament, too, for the ancient traditions and practices associated with Galanji. On the previous page, Utemorrah has explained that she was born in Kunmunya Mission on the Australian mainland, and thus lives her life away from her country, the place that gives her identity and meaning. The autobiographical information on these pages relates to her experience of growing up on the mission and going to church, concluding with "When I was five I went to school; I had to face it" (p. 3). Utemorrah's language is so understated, so bald that "I had to face it" stands out for its articulation of fear or even dread. In a situation where Utemorrah and her family have been wrenched away from their island home and forced to live in the mission, the school is an alien place. Later in the book, Utemorrah refers to the time when she must leave her family permanently: "I thought I was stepping to another world" (p. 12). This negotiation between Indigenous and white cultures, religions, and languages is inescapably part of Utemorrah's experience, involving hurt and pain but also enabling her to contribute to the survival of her people and language.

The last double-page spread in the book instantiates this complexity as the poem "Our Mother Land" again laments the loss of the past, "buried under the ground." At the same time Utemorrah explains, "I help with the language to make it live again" (p. 28). Steadfastly holding on to her languages and traditions, she asserts Indigenous survival by maintaining language. In the gaps between poetic and autobiographical discourses, between words and pictures, a Western audience can glimpse something of the chasm between then and now, home and not-home, Indigenous and non-Indigenous, that permeate the lived experience of Utemorrah and her people. The book both invites and withholds, in a way that is very common in minority textuality, where what is most precious is hidden from those outside the minority culture.

Conclusion

When mainstream readers approach minority texts they are normally required to do more work in order to understand them, since they are situated outside the systems of belief that inform such texts. The work required to conduct critical analysis of texts from a reader's own culture is of a different kind and offers a wide range of possible frames of reference. If I had selected other frames of reference for my discussion of the historical novels I studied for my essay on medievalism, I would have reached quite different conclusions. If, for instance, I had decided to read the novels in the light of masculinity studies, I would have drawn on theorists such as R.W. Connell, who have tracked shifts in conceptualizations of masculinity over time, and I would have consulted other work on masculinities in children's literature, notably John Stephens's edited collection *Ways of Being Male* (2002). It is of course possible to combine theoretical perspectives; thus, another angle might have been a study of representations of girls and women in the texts. This approach would have required more reading in feminist and orientalist studies, since the novels incorporate European and Arabic female characters. Although I investigated the historical contexts of the novels, I did not seek to identify how closely the novels approximated history, because I believe that this is a dead end in the analysis of historical fiction, which does not deal in facts but selects and orders historical events and personages for moral purposes.

I do not believe that textual analysis can ever be conducted "objectively," since we bring our ideologies and value systems to the texts we read. In the field of literary studies it is now usual for writers to use first person and to be explicit about their views of texts and textual ideologies, rather than hiding behind the indefinite pronoun "one" or resorting to "we," which implies an unproblematically unified readership. Nor are quantitative strategies particularly helpful in themselves; thus, I might have counted the proportion of male to female characters in the three novels, or carried out a quantitative survey of members of different social classes. This would have taught me very little, because fiction works on its readers through language, which is central to the promotion of values and ideologies. Even if I were able to show that 70% of characters in the novel *Crusade* came from the lower classes, this in itself would not indicate that the book interrogates classism or foregrounds the relationships between the classes.

Examination of the language of texts (sometimes referred to as "close reading") is thus central to effective critical analysis. If I chose to consider how class is treated in *Crusade* I would need to consider which events or sequences carry the most importance; who is involved in them; how power relationships work; which protagonists function as focalizing agents. This could only be achieved through an examination of language, taking in any or all of the following:

- what is selected, what is omitted;
- mode: whether narrative, descriptive, or argumentative;
- narrative processes: narrator(s), point of view, character focalization;
- overt and implicit ideologies;
- order in which events and actions appear;
- how long episodes and narratives take (duration);
- relationships between narrative elements (characters, places, etc.);
- how setting is represented (time, place); and
- symbols, intertexts, allusions.

(Based on Stephens, 1992, p. 18)

Because no two readers bring to a text exactly the same repertoire of knowledge, reading history, tastes, values, and personality, every reading of a text is different, even though there will often be similarities across readings because texts rely on a degree of consensus among readers. There are cultural differences, too, in the way scholars approach texts, since methods of analyzing texts relate to scholarly practices that stem from and are informed by cultural values. It is vitally important that researchers are conscious of the methodologies they adopt and aware of their strengths and shortcomings. They also bring their own values, preconceptions, and political views to research. Critical reading does not comprise a body of rules or strategies, but is always situated and contingent, calling on us to be alive to how texts for children position their readers, the ideologies they advocate, and the worlds they imagine.

References

Bradford, C. (2009). Muslim-Christian relations and the Third Crusade: Medievalist imaginings. *International Research in Children's Literature, 2*(2), 169–191.

Cohen, J. J. (Ed.). (2001). *The postcolonial Middle Ages.* New York: Palgrave.

Davis, K. (2001). Time behind the veil: The media, the Middle Ages, and orientalism now. In J. J. Cohen (Ed.), *The postcolonial Middle Ages* (pp. 105–122). New York: Palgrave.

Dyer, R. (1997). *White.* London: Routledge.

Heng, G. (2003). *Empire of magic: Medieval romance and the politics of cultural fantasy.* New York: Columbia University Press.

Holsinger, B. (2008). Empire, Apocalypse, and the 9/11 premodern. *Critical Inquiry, 34*(Spring), 468–490.

Linton, P. (1999). Ethical reading and resistant texts. In D.L. Madsen (Ed.), *Post-colonial literatures: Expanding the canon* (pp. 29–44). London: Pluto Press.

Michaels, E. (1994). *Bad aboriginal art: Tradition, media and technological horizons.* Minneapolis: University of Minnesota Press.

Nodelman, P. & Reimer, M. (2003). *The pleasures of children's literature* (3rd ed.). Boston: Allyn and Bacon.

Said, E. (1978). *Orientalism.* London: Routledge & Kegan Paul.

Stephens, J. (1992). *Language and ideology in children's fiction.* London: Longman.

Stephens, J. (2002). "A page just waiting to be written on": Masculinity schemata and the dynamics of subjective agency in junior fiction. In J. Stephens (Ed.), *Ways of being male: Representing masculinities in children's literature and film* (pp. 38–54). London and New York: Routledge.

Children's Literature References

Bradford, K. (1999). *Lionheart's scribe.* Toronto: HarperCollins.

Grant, K. M. (2004). *Blood red horse.* London: Penguin.

Laird, E. (2008). *Crusade.* London: Macmillan.

Utemorrah, D. & Torres, P. (1990). *Do not go around the edges.* Broome: Magabala.

3

EXAMINING DISPLACED YOUTH AND IMMIGRANT STATUS THROUGH CRITICAL MULTICULTURAL ANALYSIS

Holly Johnson and Becca Gasiewicz

> I will always be a stranger everywhere. With my parents, I am too American. With Americans, I am a spectator with my nose pressed against their window-panes, watching their weird rituals and rites of passage, never quite understanding them completely. A little chunk of me will always be a stranger.
>
> (Andreu, 2014, p. 98)

Andreu's teenage character resides as a stranger within her psychological and social homeland. Argentinian by birth but American by undocumented immigration, she keeps aspects of herself hidden from others. To do otherwise is too dangerous. Similarly, English practices designed to impart literary knowledge to the young frequently confer immigrant and illegal status to controversial content within classroom landscapes. Critical literacy and close reading are often practices that remain dangerous strangers to one another within the same academic homeland.

As the United States becomes increasingly more diverse, a variety of classroom texts have become more readily available to meet the needs of our multicultural society. Yet, literary theories that address the importance of diverse literature remain largely absent in the curricular standards mandated at local and national levels. Privileging the need for "close reading of texts," a return to or renewed dedication to New Criticism has largely marginalized theories that question relationships of power, identity, or privilege. Such theories also address the context within which narratives are produced or consumed—context that remains outside the reading of the text when more traditional literary analysis is utilized. When bound to literary theories that address only the world of the text and not the text's connection to the world, the development of critically literate young people remains illegal and secret, often viewed as irrelevant, or dangerous.

Given this gap in knowledge about how to read a text, young people seldom wrestle with critical questions of literary representation, cultural authenticity, and political and social power. One promising literary theory, however, combines both the mandate for close reading and the necessity of a critical stance toward texts. Critical multicultural analysis (CMA), as developed by Botelho and Rudman (2009), is an important tool for text analysis that compels readers to examine representations of power, authenticity, accuracy, and the sociopolitical and historical context present in a narrative. In this chapter, we demonstrate the potential of critical multicultural analysis through our examination of young adult literature that addresses issues of displacement and immigration within the current context of American society. We first discuss CMA as a theoretical framework and its relationship to close reading. After sharing how CMA functions as a tool of literary analysis in the practice of reading young adult literature, we share our findings and the potential of CMA for educators.

Theoretical Framework

The legitimacy of critical multicultural analysis as a framework for teaching and reading literature is essential to this study. Treating the terms "critical" and "multicultural" as separate but complementary aspects of investigating literature, Botelho and Rudman (2009) assert that "all children (young and old) have the capacity to be critical multicultural readers" (p. 11). CMA as a theoretical stance starts with the contention that all pieces of literature are historical and cultural artifacts that reveal representations of power and the interplay of race, class, and gender found within their generative societal contexts. Thus, "an analysis of power relations must play a decisive role in how we read children's literature" (p. ix) in classroom settings. *Critical* demands reading beyond the text to make connections between the local and global and the personal and political and to consider the imbalance of power within a society as part of historical context. Language is important as the tool that shapes perceptions and social processes. *Multicultural* attends to the varied histories within a society and acknowledges the dynamic and fluid nature of cultural experience within the unequal access to social power experienced by some groups within a society. These considerations reveal the need for "the construction of spaces in which to examine issues of diversity and social justice by problematizing children's literature" (p. 33), which aligns with Moynihan's (1988) contention that "stories told or written for children are often indicators of the dominant values within a society" (p. 9).

Drawing from theoretical foundations that include critical literacy (Comber & Simpson, 2001) and cultural studies (Hall, 1996), CMA is also informed by critical theories such as Cummins's (2000) work on the dialogical, Rudman's (1995) social issues approach on gender and heritage, and Nieto's (2004) work on multicultural education that is antiracist and grounded in social justice. Reader response theory (Rosenblatt, 1978) and feminist analyses that question and problematize texts also undergird this approach to literary analysis. CMA recognizes the need for readers to interrogate the treatment of certain groups within texts as the codification of reality frequently emulated by literature. Regardless of the setting or the genre of a text, relationships—and often metaphors concerning human relationships—represent the author's historical context from which the text springs. Thus, where and with whom power is located and how it is negotiated and exercised or constructed and reconstructed are fundamental questions to be asked by readers. Asking readers to move beyond the narrative to address its construction, assumptions, and the context of publishing and power relations in their society, CMA is "literary study for social change" (p. 33). In essence, the process provides a philosophical shift for teaching literature, constructing curriculum, and taking up issues of diversity and social justice. CMA problematizes children's literature, offers a way of reading power, explores the complex web of sociopolitical relations, and deconstructs taken-for-granted assumptions about language, meaning, reading, and literature.

Every theory comprises tenets by which to view or conduct analysis—in essence, what to look for in the literature. Based on our research interests, the following tenets from CMA were most salient for our analysis of selected books on displacement:

- the placement of agency;
- the assumptions of who holds power and status in the ending of the text; and
- the representations of those who fall outside the U.S. dominant norm.

Literature Review

Critical multicultural analysis has been used to explore what a text is about, examining not only what authors do but the content of the text itself. Through the use of CMA as both theory and analysis, we were able to address the questions of what it is authors and texts do. Other researchers have employed this methodology in similar studies.

Zaria Malcolm and Ruth McKoy Lowery (2011) explored representations of the Caribbean in children's literature, arguing that multiple cultural groups from the region immigrate to the United States. How those cultural groups are presented and for what reasons are thus important questions for teachers to ponder. In another study, Lamme, Fu, and Lowery (2004) examined how immigrants were portrayed in picturebooks, finding that difficulties faced by immigrants are seldom represented, thus producing narratives that seem simplistic with smooth transitions into new lives and situations.

Elizabeth Clifford and Maya Kalyanpur (2011) examined 20 young adult novels presenting immigrants' experiences, finding that a "hybrid" reality of combining a home culture and the new American culture affords a way for young adult protagonists to fit into the new culture as well as the adolescent culture of their new home. They further assert that the fitting into a new culture as a result of immigrating is not a single phenomenon, but a life-long process. What needs to be noted, however, is that cultural groups are often pressured to fit into a larger mainstream culture, and coming to the United States is no different. Moves within U.S. political and economic arenas have the expectation that cultural groups need to "Americanize."

Finally, Amy Cummings's (2013) work on the portrayal of undocumented migration across the U.S.–Mexico border in 11 young adult novels found that many of the novels create a sympathetic portrait of youth who cross the border. These particular novels highlighted the convoluted issues involved with such journeys. Through reading such works, readers may have a more ethical and empathetic stance toward such moves by those represented in these narratives.

Research Methodology

In addition to serving as a theoretical stance in literary study, critical multicultural analysis is a method of analysis that allows readers to engage deeply with a text by looking closely at language and at character relationships to power and to each other. CMA also scrutinizes the ending of novels as a way of positioning readers and the residual themes readers take from the narrative. As the framework for our study, CMA provided a way for us to enter into examining several young adult novels with the intent to examine the representations of characters who immigrated to the United States. We selected a set of books written for grades 7–12 that encompassed a variety of perspectives, authorial locations, and geographical regions of the world. Following the suggestions by Botelho and Rudman (2009), as well as our own knowledge of global literature, we used the following questions to guide our examination of seven narratives that constituted our displacement text set:

1. In what ways do these texts portray the respective cultures represented in the narrative?
2. How are issues of identity and power enacted within the narratives?
3. What do these texts suggest about current U.S. culture and the status of immigrants?

Selecting Texts that Reflect Displacement

> To be rooted is perhaps the most important and least recognized need of the human soul.
>
> (Weil, 1987, p. 41)

To select a set of young adult books, we had to first define displacement and use that definition to select texts. After reading and researching concepts of displacement, we worked with Kibreab's (1999) assertion that "people identify themselves with territories where their entitlements emanate from belonging to a society, which occupies a geographically bounded physical space" (p. 408). Displacement thus occurs when people are uprooted from their territories or countries of origin and forced into refugee status. Cohen and Deng (2012) posit that internal displacement is the forced removal of a population from their homes with the end result of remaining destitute and vulnerable within their own countries. Often displacement is the result of environmental events such as tsunamis and earthquakes, or as a result of political events including armed conflict and cultural cleansing. Black, Arnell, Adger, Thomas, and Geddes (2013) theorize that displacement is a type of migration that is long term and based on extreme events. Involuntary displacement is a denial of the fundamental right to remain or belong to a place where safety is expected and there is no external pressure to forcibly remain or leave a territory or country. Displacement also includes the possibility of escaping persecution, human indignity, or insecure economic conditions (Kibreab, 1999). The Jewish and Kurdish Diasporas were based on a lack of a particular homeland over centuries, while other movements such as those of American Indians are internal displacements, and still other migrations involve the forced removal of peoples for a range of reasons.

We embraced these definitions for our study, recognizing that populations of diaspora are those that have been displaced across the globe as a result of specific events or situations, leading to similar results to the identities of those displaced. Those who hold refugee and immigrant status may inhabit deplorable states of being, especially if the host society assumes there are "natural places from which people derive their identity," and those who have origins outside that geographical space are strangers or non-members, and therefore "other" (Kibreab, 1999, p. 387). We wanted to explore the situations of those who are often considered "other" in our study of novels about young adults who have migrated to the United States as a result of forced displacement from their home countries.

Based on our concept of displacement, we looked through the texts we had gathered on refugee experiences and selected seven for this study. Our criteria included:

- fictional narratives or fictionalized accounts of actual events;
- narratives that covered cultural groups from a variety of places across the globe, but eventually ended up in the United States;
- narratives containing authentic reasons for displacement and immigration to the United States; and
- narratives with representations that matched our definition of displacement.

Our text set consisted of *Ask Me No Questions* (Budhos, 2006), *A Step from Heaven* (Na, 2001), *Home of the Brave* (Applegate, 2008), *Never Fall Down* (McCormick, 2012), *Inside Out and Back Again* (Lai, 2011), *Trafficked* (Purcell, 2012), and *The Secret Side of Empty* (Andreu, 2014).

As a frame for discussing our analysis, brief summaries of these books are provided:.

- *Ask Me No Questions* (Budhos, 2006). The challenges Muslims face in the United States following September 11, 2001, are presented through the story of 14-year-old Nadira, whose family emigrated from Bangladesh and reside in New York City on expired visas. The family constantly struggles with their citizenship status and becoming legal, but then her father is detained at the Canadian border. A major turning point in their family, this event makes life more difficult for Nadira, who must negotiate both coming of age and her illegal status.

- *A Step from Heaven* (Na, 2001). Young Ju Park, whose family immigrated to the United States when she was five, realizes as she grows into adolescence that maybe America is not the wonderful place she was promised. The adjustments needed to acclimate to a society and culture unlike their own are more than their family can handle. Young Ju finds herself neither solely Korean nor truly American, and must learn how to develop her own sense of self embracing both cultures.

- *Home of the Brave* (Applegate, 2008). Kek, a young adolescent, survived the Sudanese War and feels guilty for not only living when the rest of his family was lost, but living in a vastly different culture than his own. Learning to live within the United States while also learning English, Kek must negotiate his feelings about his African culture with his experiences in a new country.

- *Inside Out and Back Again* (Lai, 2011). Hà immigrates to the United States with her three older brothers and mother after the Vietnam War. Her acclimation to American culture is difficult as she learns to adjust to the language, food, and alienation she experiences as a refugee.

- *Never Fall Down* (McCormick, 2012). Addressing the violence of the Khmer Rouge in Cambodia during the 1980s, Patricia McCormick collaborated with survivor Arn Chorn-Pond to tell his story. Arn is conscripted into the Khmer Rouge, but always looks for a way out. He eventually crosses the border and is brought to the United States by an aid worker.

- *The Secret Side of Empty* (Andreu, 2014). Monserrat Thalia, aka M.T., is an undocumented immigrant from Argentina. Entering her senior year, M.T. is at the top of her class academically and a hard-working soccer player, but knows her status will stand in the way of her chances to continue her education. Unable to share her situation with her friends who are applying for colleges and making future plans, she withdraws from the activities she loves.

- *Trafficked* (Purcell, 2012). The story of human trafficking from Moldova to Los Angeles is told through Hannah, who immigrates as a nanny, convinced this offers the perfect opportunity to support her family at home. She discovers, however, that she must first pay back her plane ticket and documentation costs. Living in fear that she is not known and will not be missed if something should happen, Hannah must figure out a way to claim her freedom.

Conducting Critical Multicultural Analysis

To conduct our study we began by meeting every three weeks with others who had expressed an interest in CMA. At first, the group met to discuss the academic text by Botelho and Rudman (2009), but then added selected pieces of global literature to read and analyze. We read four novels that helped us construct the theme of displacement and gave us the opportunity to construct categories of analysis based on the tenets of CMA: *Home of the Brave* (Applegate, 2008), *Never Fall Down* (McCormick, 2012), *Funny in Farsi* (Dumas, 2004), and *Under the Mesquite* (McCall, 2011). As a larger interpretive community, we discussed our individual responses and constructed categories of meaning from each text in conjunction with the guidelines outlined for conducting critical multicultural analysis. Upon completion of one round of reading and discussion, the two of us continued with a second set of seven narratives, dropping *Under the Mesquite* and *Funny in Farsi* for texts more relevant to our formalized definition of displacement.

Data Sources

We collected a variety of data to answer our questions. Data sources included the seven narratives, our discussions of the texts, and the notes we individually took as we went through the texts. In addition, we highlighted areas that reflected the CMA tenets' addressing of power, gender, race, class, and culture as well as instances of language that seemed especially salient to the movement within the novels. We also considered the end of each novel as a way of examining the positioning of readers in respect to the outcome of the characters' plight.

Data Analysis

Botelho and Rudman (2009) propose a shift in thinking in moving "reading and writing away from an exclusively cognitive model which positions literacy as an internal, individual, psychological act, to literacy as a sociocultural, multiple, and political practice" (p. 44). In our analysis we employed this model. Although we initially read each text independently, we collaboratively interpreted, analyzed, and questioned the elements of the text as well as the interpretations we constructed. As we read more texts with a displacement theme, our discussions and the analysis of each subsequent text became more engaging and meaningful.

CMA asserts that specific areas of analysis that should be considered when reading texts are the following:

- the social construction of culture, race, class, and gender (pp. 260–261);
- narrative endings and whether those endings provide a solution or leave the problem or situation open for questioning (p. 262);
- the historical and sociopolitical conditions found within the text (p. 262), in our case, the cause for displacement and relationships of power.

In our analysis, we embraced these suggested themes for examining the texts while also leaving ourselves open to other themes that we constructed from our particular text set. We recognized the potentials of these themes for a deep examination that could develop readers, both teachers and students, who are more analytical and empathetic in knowing how to closely read the text and the world of the text.

Our analysis began by working in an interpretive community (Fish, 1980). Using the suggested areas of analysis from Botelho and Rudman (2009), we established four categories for scrutiny. First, was *Characterization and Issues of Agency*, which included examining (1) who has agency within the text and how it is manifested, (2) how characters are represented in respect to race, class, gender, and (3) power relationships among the characters through an analysis of the position of adults, support networks, and how the character is "saved" from their destitution and often "refugee" status. The second category was *Positionality of Authors and Readers*, in which we examined the author's relationship to the culture being presented in the text as well as assumptions about authorial (Rabinowitz, 1998), actual, and implied readers (Iser, 1978). The representation of homelands and the United States also fell into this category. *Language and Text Structure Implications* was the third category, in which we noted language usage, structure, and format. And finally, the context of *Displacement* and reasons for it was our fourth category. This category also included how the book ended in respect to displacement. We saw overlapping elements of all these categories as they conditioned each other.

We created a cross-comparison matrix addressing each area of analysis to more clearly see, understand, and track our analysis and category construction. We kept careful notes about each theme at our meetings and gained greater inter-rater reliability through working together, reflecting our assertion that CMA allows for close reading of a text across readers who have determined themes or lenses in which to view the work.

Findings on Representations of Displacement and Immigration

Characterization and Issues of Agency

In our analysis of characters, we first examined the agency of the protagonist in order to examine power relationships within the narratives. The main character in each story faces a difficult situation and we wanted to explore how the characters managed those situations, with or without help, and from whom help is given. In *Trafficked* (Purcell, 2012), Hannah is trapped by fear and abuse as a slave inside a house in a suburban Los Angeles neighborhood. She has no real way to find help, but must save herself. Resisting the demands of her employers, she befriends a neighbor as she takes out the garbage after dark each week. This friendship is essentially what saves her in the end. Kek, in *Home of the Brave* (Applegate, 2008) negotiates a way to bridge his old world with the new by learning English and working with a local farmer. Há must battle bullies in her school in *Inside Out and Back Again* (Lai, 2011), while Arn must find a way to survive and escape the Khmer Rouge in *Never Fall Down* (McCormick, 2012). These examples show the agency and power that these young characters display in order to survive. Since all are immigrants, their actions to survive through both immigration and adjustment in the United States show great resiliency.

The issue of who helps them survive, however, and in what manner required a closer look at each text. The characters find support from family and often a friend to help them navigate their situations, yet this support is often male. Hannah is helped by her male neighbor; Kek is aided by a relief agency whose representative is male; Há's relief from bullies comes through her brothers; and Arn is brought to America through a relief organization whose representative and foster family is dominated by male presence. Thus, upon closer scrutiny, while the characters all show agency, their "salvation" comes through a masculine presence. The two stories of female characters who are undocumented immigrants (*Ask Me No Questions* and *The Secret Side of Empty*) contain protagonists who "rescue" themselves. Nadira persists despite the ramifications of deportation and stands up for her family in court, while M.T. perseveres by leaving her home, which is not supportive, finding a support system, and getting into a community college. Concurrently, the DREAMers law is passed which will allow her to gain citizenship.

The role of adults, education, support networks, and salvation all seemed pertinent to each narrative. As noted, all have support networks that facilitate the protagonists' salvation and survival in varying degrees. Ironically, these networks play against the American mythology of individuals "pulling themselves up by their bootstraps." The role adults played across texts also varies. In *Never Fall Down* (McCormick, 2012), *Home of the Brave* (Applegate, 2008), and *The Secret Side of Empty* (Andreu, 2014), adults are supportive but passive. The family in *Ask Me No Questions* (Budhos, 2006) is very close and the adults play a significant daily role, while in *A Step from Heaven* (Na, 2001) and *Inside Out and Back Again* (Lai, 2011) the mothers are present and supportive, but Young Ju's father is an abusive alcoholic and Há's father has passed away. The adults in *Trafficked* (Purcell, 2012) are not Hannah's parents, and the adults she lives with are abusive and instill fear in her; they are not role models, guides, or any type of support.

Education is present in each text except *Trafficked* (Purcell, 2012). Depending on the text, school is a place to learn, a place to become enculturated, a place to exceed, and a place of fear. The role of school is particularly complex in *The Secret Side of Empty* (Andreu, 2014) because M.T. is successful academically, yet she is faced with the question of what comes next as her legal status weighs heavily upon her. She tries to maintain her composure as her classmates and close friends plan for a future at college and ask about her plans. In this text, further education is portrayed as the way to a better life, a life M.T. hopes to achieve and deeply desires.

In respect to the protagonists, we also considered how race is represented, the socioeconomic status of the main characters, and in what juxtaposition to their friends, and how gender is enacted, particularly within the family structure. In many of the texts, males held the power within the family structures, both in decision making and financial responsibility. In *The Secret Side of Empty* (Andreu, 2014), M.T.'s father controls their house with an iron fist. He is the only one who works and makes most of the decisions. Because M.T.'s family is not legal, her father makes very little money, however, M.T. attends a school that is upper middle class and her friends are part of families with strong mothers. In comparing the narratives, each family is represented as in need of economic aid, or has family members—typically males—who work long hours or in jobs that are of lower-class status. Examining this aspect of how immigrants are represented allows readers to read beyond the text to examine how immigrants and refugees are represented in other media.

Positionality of Authors and Readers

A critical piece of our analysis process was to consider the author's relationship to the culture represented in the text, and how that relationship might impact narrative authenticity. We read the texts and noted nuanced uses of language in dialogue as well as descriptions of the characters' homeland and their feelings about their new country. The authorial positions ranged from actual experiences to family stories to research on the culture. Thanhha Lai lived in Vietnam during the war and moved to Alabama, which is codified in *Inside Out and Back Again* (Lai, 2011). In contrast, Katherine Applegate, the author of *Home of the Brave* (2008), had not been to Africa and did not claim to have had an experience with Sudanese refugees. One text felt more real, while the other addressed a current issue, yet the authenticity of representations of the cultures, characters, languages, and homelands of each story were impacted by the author's relation to the culture.

Just as authors are positioned through the use of language and detail, readers are also positioned. Through our analysis, we considered how readers might be positioned through each text, and noted that frequently the protagonists were written as sympathetic characters, which positions readers to feel the plight of the characters and their situations. This positioning thus addresses an implied reader stance (Iser, 1978) requiring reader dispositions and values that match the intent of the text rather than positioning readers as authorial readers (Rabinowitz, 1998), which would require *actual readers* to attempt to enter the author's ideal audience. The difference in these two types of readers is the use of language in conjunction to the work of the reader. While both types of readers are hypothetical, implied readers are those the author specifically has in mind when writing. Authorial readers create a more persuasive text in an attempt by the author to convince readers to think like the author. Thus, one audience is assumed (implied) and the other is being courted to join the author in the author's thinking. Neither of these audiences fully accommodates actual readers whose thoughts will join with the author during their reading of the text.

In *Ask Me No Questions* (Budhos, 2006), *A Step from Heaven* (Na, 2001), and *The Secret Side of Empty* (Andreu, 2014), the adolescent characters are at the mercy of decisions not of their making, thus creating narrative situations that might resonate with adolescent readers, an implied stance the author assumed about adolescents. In *Home of the Brave* (Applegate, 2008) and *Never Fall Down* (McCormick, 2012), the main characters are refugees, and as such, out of sync with their new surroundings. Through the use of language and text structure, the authors close the distance between reader and character in order to pull actual readers into empathic feelings about refugees, thus creating a more authorial stance.

The representation of each character and their homelands was also considered under the category of positionality. Kek from *Home of the Brave* (Applegate, 2008) was represented as naïve in comparison to American counterparts, while Há was perceived as smart, but weak. Nadira and Hannah are frightened, as more powerful others paralyze their movements. M.T. and Arn, while strong characters, must keep the truth of themselves hidden, often seemingly betraying their own sensibilities. In respect to homelands, all are considered more dangerous, less organized, and less important in comparison to the United States, which is portrayed as safe and welcoming, even as each character struggles through the difficult acclimation process to make America his or her homeland. This connection to homeland, while present in most of the texts, was considered the past with America the future.

This mythology of the United States persists in the literature even as most immigrants feel a stronger tie to their homelands and the importance of that homeplace than what is presented in the narratives (Kibreab, 1991). CMA provides the space for younger readers as well as researchers to explore the representations of characters and their positions in juxtaposition to the reality of the world. The reality is that not all immigrants are destitute, in need of aid, believe that the United States is their future, or unattached to their homelands as an influence on who they are as people within American society.

Language and Text Structure Implications

In our analysis, we thought it important to consider the genre of the text, the language used, and the text structure. *The Secret Side of Empty* (Andreu, 2014), *Ask Me No Questions* (Budhos, 2006), *A Step from Heaven* (Na, 2001), and *Trafficked* (Purcell, 2012) are all written as novels, which can create a distance between narrator and reader; *Home of the Brave* (Applegate, 2008) and *Inside Out and Back Again* (Lai, 2011) are written in poetic verse, which suggests a more oral language structure, and thus a more intimate text whereby the narrator is speaking to the reader. *Never Fall Down* (McCormick, 2012) is written as a narrative, but in broken English—the language Arn might use if telling the story orally, which also creates a closer bond between narrator and reader. The author justified her choice of using broken English through her extensive hours interviewing Arn and, wishing to maintain authenticity, wanting his "voice" to be present in the text.

In most of the narratives, English is used entirely with only minimal use of the home language. This reliance on English leads to questions about the authenticity of the texts, which often rely on the nuanced language of home culture. More authentic language usage, especially in cases of immigrant status where English is being learned as part of the protagonists' displacement, would allow readers to better experience the protagonists' acquisition of English as well as understand the importance of their home language. When a language other than English is used, it is typically one word with context clues that make the word meaning obvious. Other times the use of English is naïve, even after the protagonist had been in country for a period of time. In *Home of the Brave* (Applegate, 2008), the main character Kek uses "snowflake" but not "oven," which he consistently refers to as a "cooking machine." Kek also flies to the United States in a plane, which is still a "flying boat" at the end of the book. No justification for these word choices was apparent in the text.

Displacement as Context

The context of each story is displacement. Each narrative is the unfolding of what caused the move to the United States and what happened to the protagonists after their arrival in the United States. In *Never Fall Down* (McCormick, 2012), *Inside Out and Back Again* (Lai, 2011), and *Home of the Brave* (Applegate, 2008), the main characters are displaced because of war or violent conflict. *The Secret Side of Empty* (Andreu, 2014), *A Step from Heaven* (Na, 2001), and *Trafficked* (Purcell, 2012) are all present-day examples of those who travel to the United States following the "American Dream"; hoping to be better off economically. *Ask Me No Questions* (Budhos, 2006) is also present day, but focuses on the challenges undocumented immigrants, particularly Muslims, have faced following September 11, 2001. Each context is slightly different, but many of the obstacles are similar.

Examining the ending of each book led us to the second category we constructed under the theme of displacement. All of the books end with hope, as is often the way young adult novels in the United States conclude. The United States is seen as a safe place, a place of welcome, and a place of hope. While we have already addressed our concerns with these endings in this text set about displacement and immigrant youth, there is another read on these endings, particularly in considering what they suggest about the protagonists' homelands, and the residual effect these representations have on readers in respect to the countries represented in these narratives. What do these texts suggest about the world and issues of power on a global level? And just how detrimental can this type of thinking be on youth who do no critical thinking beyond the text?

Discussion

> She recognized in Kelsey [the character] the nationalism of liberal Americans
> who copiously criticized America but did not like you to do so; they expected
> you to be silent and grateful, and always reminded you of how much better
> than wherever you had come from America was.
>
> (Chimamanda Ngozi Adiche, *Americanah*, 2014)

Our findings suggest that there are a number of issues to address when reading
about those who fall outside the mythological "American" lifestyle—in literary
texts or life. The texts within our study portrayed those who appear to desire
inclusion into a mythological norm. None of these stories attempted to forefront
the importance of the homeland or culture of the protagonists, nor were the
protagonists interested in returning home. There is a reification of the homelands
as permanently dangerous, which lacks authenticity and accuracy. Further danger
resides in the representation of those from other cultures who have been displaced
and what readers may think of the actual human beings whose lived experiences
include circumstances of displacement.

As noted by Clare Bradford in Chapter Two, critical reading requires readers to distance themselves from a text to see how it has been shaped historically
and culturally as well as to view it closely to examine its linguistic and narrative
features so as to see what rhetorical devices the author may have used in referencing the characters and situations within the text. Upon examination of these
books as a set we found that being a refugee or displaced person is not an envi-
able situation even as the texts we analyzed attempt to bring hope to each of the
situations within the narratives. In many respects, younger readers may embrace
two sentiments: (1) unfamiliarity or lack of experience and connection with the
protagonists, and (2) how much better life is in the United States. Both of these
sentiments can be dangerous.

When juxtaposing the situations within the texts with the sentiments found
in the media about immigrants and issues of language, the United States may not
be a safe place for many who have attempted to find refuge within its borders as
depicted in these texts. In addition, when experiences from stories are so different
from adolescents' lives, they have difficulty embracing those alternative realities
as authentic, and thus have little opportunity for accommodating such situations
into their worldviews. These misrepresentations can lead to lack of empathy or
understanding of those who have come to the United States with the promise
of a better future. The characters within the text set all feel displaced, and each
book has the potential of gaining reader understanding and empathy with guided
efforts by the teacher or a cultural insider. Only one narrative actually portrays
the United States as a difficult place to be, and that is *Inside Out and Back Again*
(Lai, 2011), which shows the bullying that Há experiences at school. Without
critically examining how the United States actually responds to immigrants, adolescent readers may be left with feelings of how wonderful the United States is

without acknowledging that there are times when specific groups of people are not welcome, and for reasons that are not accurate or aligned with the image of opportunity.

Displacement is becoming more and more a matter of fact on a global scale that includes members of American society rather than only individuals or cultural groups who fall *outside* the norm. Perhaps we should look more closely for texts that reflect the global *reality* of displacement, movement, and immigration of which America is a part rather than suggesting the United States is *the* answer and the arrival place that promises safety and salvation for the world, a difficult situation in which any country could position itself. And while the United States is a powerful country that is generous with its aid to those around the world, we further recognize that only by reading outside the text do we come to understand the mythology that American citizens embrace about that generosity with little acknowledgment of how that power might be perceived.

Conclusion

Nancy Larrick's (1965) article about "all the whiteness of children's literature" created awareness about the need for diversity within children's literature, yet little has been accomplished in publishing novels that represent the varied cultural narratives that make up the global story. And thus, the question of representation of cultures outside the U.S. dominant norm remains. Examining the plight of refugees as they enculturate as well as how they are treated within U.S. society brings literature to life for adolescents, not something only to be read about in a book. Furthermore, an analysis of the author's craft and intent brings into view the political issues of books and representation—whose story gets told, in what way, and for what purpose.

Critical multicultural analysis is an area of research in need of further exploration, but more important, of further practice within classrooms. CMA asks readers to consider not just the stories and characters, but to also conduct an analysis of the power relations as they relate to the "trends of what gets written, illustrated, and published" (Botelho & Rudman, 2009, p. 2) and for what reasons. This lens recognizes a systematic loop that exists between writers, publishers, and readers, and analyzes the ways in which published works have the ability to influence representations of the world, which should be scrutinized for relationships of power in conjunction with race, class, gender, and culture. Furthermore, CMA has the potential to address the call for close reading while also giving young adults opportunities to develop critical literacy skills and strategies.

Botelho and Rudman (2009) suggest, "An analysis of power relations must play a decisive role in how we read children's literature, [CMA] invites readers to think about the interplay of race, class, and gender in books" (p. ix). It is our hope that young people will be encouraged to begin or continue dangerous conversations

about representations of gender, race, class, and power in literature written especially for them as a way of questioning such relationships within the wider world.
To do so requires closely reading, not just the texts, but their responses to those
texts and to the world as well. Displacing such conversations with young people
creates a context that can develop an inauthentic and inaccurate sense of the
world and those who live—and move—within it.

References

Adiche, C. N. (2014). *Americanah*. New York: Anchor Books.
Black, R., Arnell, N. W., Adger, W. N., Thomas, D., & Geddes, A. (2013). Migration, immo-
bility and displacement outcomes following extreme events. *Environmental Science &
Policy, 27*, S32–S43.
Botelho, M. J. & Rudman, M. K. (2009). *Critical multicultural analysis of children's literature:
Mirrors, windows, and doors*. New York: Routledge.
Clifford, E. & Kalyanpur, M. (2011). Immigrant narratives: Power, difference, and repre-
sentation in young-adult novels with immigrant protagonists. *International Journal of
Multicultural Education, 13*(1), 1–20.
Cohen, R. & Deng, F. M. (2012). *Masses in flight: The global crisis of internal displacement*.
Washington, DC: Brookings Institution Press.
Comber, B. & Simpson, A. (Eds.). (2001). *Negotiating critical literacies in classrooms*. New York:
Routledge.
Cummings, A. (2013). Border crossings: Undocumented migration between Mexico and
the United States in contemporary young adult literature. *Children's Literature in Educa-
tion, 44*(1), 57–73.
Cummins, J. (2000). *Language, power, and pedagogy: Bilingual children caught in the crossfire*.
Clevedon, ME: Multilingual Matters.
Fish, S. (1980). *Is there a text in this class?: The authority of interpretive communities*. Cambridge,
MA: Harvard University Press.
Hall, S. (1996). Who needs 'identity'? In S. Hall & Paul du Gay (Eds.), *Questions of cultural
identity* (pp. 1–17). Thousand Oaks, CA: Sage.
Iser, W. (1978). *The implied reader: Patterns of communication in prose fiction from Bunyan to
Beckett*. Baltimore, MD: Johns Hopkins University Press.
Kibreab, G. (1999). Revisiting the debate on people, place, identity and displacement. *Jour-
nal of Refugee Studies, 14*(4), 384–410.
Lamme, L. L., Fu, D., & Lowery, R. M. (2004). Immigrants as portrayed in children's picture
books. *The Social Studies, 95*(13), 123–130.
Larrick, N. (1965). The all-white world of children's books. *Saturday Review, 48*(11), 63–65.
Malcolm, Z. & Lowery, R. M. (2011). Reflections of the Caribbean in children's picture
books: A critical multicultural analysis. *Multicultural Education, 19*(1), 46–50.
Moynihan, R. (1988). Ideologies in children's literature: Some preliminary notes. In
B. Bacon (Ed.), *How much truth do we tell the children: The politics of children's literature*
(pp. 8–14). Minneapolis, MN: Marx Educational Press.
Nieto, S. (2004). *Affirming diversity: The sociopolitical context of multicultural education* (4th ed.).
Boston: Pearson.
Rabinowitz, P. (1998). *Before reading: Narrative conventions and the politics of interpretation*.
Columbus, OH: Ohio State University Press.

Rosenblatt, L. (1978/1994). *The reader, the text, the poem: The transactional theory of the literary work*. Carbondale, IL: Southern Illinois University Press.

Rudman, M. (1995). *Children's literature: An issues approach* (4th ed.). New York: Longman.

Weil, S. (1952/1987). *The need for toots: Prelude to a declaration of duties towards mankind*. New York: Ark.

Children's Literature References

Andreu, M. (2014). *The secret side of empty*. Philadelphia, PA: Running Press Kids.

Applegate, K. (2008). *Home of the brave*. New York: Square Fish.

Budhos, M. (2006). *Ask me no questions*. New York: Simon Pulse.

Dumas, F. (2004). *Funny in Farsi: A memoir of growing up Iranian in America*. New York: Random House.

Lai, T. (2011). *Inside out and back again*. New York: HarperCollins.

McCall, G. (2011). *Under the mesquite*. New York: Lee & Low Books.

McCormick, P. (2012). *Never fall down*. New York: Balzer & Bray.

Na, A. (2001). *A step from heaven*. New York: Speak.

Purcell, K. (2012). *Trafficked*. New York: Viking.

4

USING INTERTEXTUALITY TO UNPACK REPRESENTATIONS OF IMMIGRATION IN CHILDREN'S LITERATURE

Yoo Kyung Sung, Mary L. Fahrenbruck,
and Julia López-Robertson

Readers' attitudes and views on cultural groups different from their own are impacted by reading and responding to global literature. However, simply reading this literature does not guarantee positive changes in perceptions. In fact, inadequate discussions and undisputed perspectives can reinforce misunderstandings, stereotypes, biases, and prejudices; a danger we have observed firsthand in our classes when students discuss global and multicultural literature.

We are particularly interested in representations of people and experiences in immigration-themed literature. Lowery (2000) emphasized the need for positive representation of immigrants because readers' perceptions can directly influence their relationships with people. She purposefully used "representation" in her study citing Giroux (1994) that representation is a way of understanding "the past through the present in order to legitimate and secure a particular view of the future" (p. 47).

Immigration-themed literature creates a common ground that brings different voices together and gives children the opportunity to create their own images and ideas of immigrants. This is particularly important for us as we think about teachers interacting with immigrant children from various global contexts in their classrooms. Teachers and students alike need to be aware of how immigrant experiences are portrayed in children's literature, both for the sake of immigrants and for those children attempting to understand the immigrant experience. Given the significance of this body of literature for teachers and students, we engaged in a critical content analysis of a set of immigration-themed books through the lens of postcolonial studies.

Theoretical Framework: Postcolonialism and Colonialism

Stories about transitioning from one place to another often tell about struggles, hardships, and obstacles. Immigrants contend with language, ethnic, and cultural differences as they make their way across borders. Being targeted as "Other" because of these differences adds to the hardships that immigrants are already experiencing. Because of their unique experiences, immigrants' stories are perceived by readers as different from general stories of relocation, such as moving from one place to another within the same country. We interpret this perception of difference related to immigration as "a privileged position in contemporary discourses" (Smith, 1988, p. 28) and so viewed postcolonialism as a lens that would allow us to examine the embedded power issues in immigration-themed literature. Postcolonialism refers to "a self-consciousness on the part of emerging people of a history, a culture, and an identity separate from and just as important as those imperial 'masters'" (McGillis, 2000, p. 23).

Although colonialism is often understood as the historical imperialism of European countries, postcolonialism is not restricted to historical relevance and includes a mindset of the Other as the colonized. Within colonialism, colonizers from "advanced" civilizations are in a dominant position over or above those who have been colonized. Through our own transactions with immigration-themed children's literature, we believe that these novels are replete with postcolonial narratives that foster mental images of dominance over immigrant, migrant, and refugee people.

McGillis (2000) notes that a postcolonial critic infers stated and unstated ideas about the Other. Because immigrant populations in the United States are often associated with specific cultural groups along with negative stereotypes of national origins and social status, immigration-themed children's literature can reinforce global Othering. These associations reinforce the postcolonial mindset and perpetuate readers' hierarchical sense of dominance over immigrant characters.

Postcoloniality is an embedded social attitude for constructing knowledge about Others who immigrate to the United States that creates a dichotomy of 'us' and 'them'. Tuner (1983) notes, "the way we talk about other people is the central problem of all human interaction and one of the constitutive debates with the social sciences" (p. 132). Immigrants are considered one hegemonic group for the purpose of Othering even though they comprise many diverse groups of people.

Using postcoloniality as a theoretical lens for our study, we adopted two tenets to frame postcolonialism for our analysis. The first tenet involves resisting, denying, and even mocking the postcolonial mindset by the characters in stories. There are numerous children's literature studies that incorporate a postcolonial critique; however few studies use resistance to frame the analysis. The second tenet is the attitude of overcolonizing immigrant children. We examine the literature for instances where immigrant children are portrayed as naïve or innocent, due to their dual identity of child and immigrant.

Literature Review

Researchers have used content analysis and critical content analysis to examine themes of immigration and migration in children's literature. Son and Sung

(2015) used an Orientalism theoretical frame to analyze the representation of Korean Americans in 31 picturebooks published in the United States for children. Through critical content analysis, they found that the relationships between protagonists and parents, *halmonis* (grandmas), grocery store owners, peers, and teachers played a role in helping construct bicultural identities of Korean American children. Further, critical findings revealed the prevalence of Orientalism, "the discourse of power" (p. 62), through the portrayals of the relationships of Korean Americans.

Though they did not employ a critical theory, Wee, Park, and Choi (2015) used content analysis to explore cultural hierarchies in the representations of Korean cultures in 33 picturebooks published in the United States for children. Their findings showed a majority of the picturebooks used in their study (25 of 33) featured immigration stories. Insufficient representations of contemporary Korean cultures are problematic as the books leave readers with a surface-level understanding and appreciation of the culture. Picturebooks were also the focus of Yi (2014) who used content and thematic analysis to study Korean immigration experiences in 14 picturebooks. She identified five themes: English-language-acquisition difficulties, assimilation through name changing (Korean names changed to American names), language mediation, family separation, and positive experiences post-immigration.

Cummins's (2013) study of 11 young adult (YA) novels featuring undocumented Mexican migrants revealed an almost exclusive focus on migrants illegally crossing the Mexico/U.S. border. Overrepresentation of undocumented Mexican migrants' lives fostered what López and Serrato (2001) call empathetic outreach. Empathetic outreach is not a critical theory per se, but a conceptual framework that guides the analysis of a study to findings that are critical. Findings from this study revealed adolescent readers developed empathetic responses to border crossing narratives of undocumented immigrant adolescents.

Tuon (2014) used narrative and historical analyses to examine *Inside Out and Back Again* (Lai, 2011), one of the immigration-themed novels in our study. Tuon explored resistance and accommodation in Há's experiences as a refugee in the United States. Many researchers, including Cummins (2013), Hope (2008), and Liang, Aimonette, and Galda (2009), recognize refugee experiences as the result of forced migration and thus conducted critical studies on refugee issues as distinct from other immigrant stories. Liang et al. (2009) discovered refugee-themed novels convey a shared message that America is a safer, less violent country than other places where extreme acts of violence occur more frequently.

Though content analysis studies of immigration-themed children's and adolescent literature conveyed some levels of critical discussions, others did not use a critical theoretical framework. This lack of critical frame may reflect seldom challenged assumptions (by readers, authors, and researchers) that immigrants are eager to leave their homeland for the promise of a better life in a new country and that immigrating to a new country is not without difficulties. It may also reflect a widely accepted assumption that people who immigrate to another country will inevitably encounter Othering. Critical theories like postcolonialism can bring awareness to unchallenged assumptions found in immigration-themed children's and adolescent literature.

Research Methods

Our research is grounded in critical content analysis but within that methodology we searched for strategies that would support us in analyzing our selected group of texts. The tool that we found particularly generative is intertextuality, "the elaboration of a text in relation to other texts" (Frow, 1986, p. 152). Wilkie-Stibbs (2004) notes three types of intertextuality in children's literature: texts of quotation (texts that allude to other literary and non-literary works), texts of imitation (texts that parody or paraphrase the original), and genre texts (texts that use recognized clusters of literary conventions). We interpreted immigration-themed literature as genre texts. Despite varying portrayals of immigrants' experiences, immigration-themed literature has common literary themes, such as crossing borders, encountering discrimination, learning a new language, and hoping for a better future. Because immigration literature has its own distinct conventions, we consider these books as genre texts for this analysis.

According to Allen (2000), novels relate to each other "so intertextuality is woven text from the thread of the 'already written' and the 'already read'" (p. 6). Barthes (1975) argues readers find ways of integrating intertextuality into the primary text when readers see distinctly different textual voices.

Hiramoto and Park (2012) use intertextuality as a methodological framework to conduct media studies, stating that intertextuality is "a tool for exploring the semiotic processes that underlie the way in which the media negotiate and reinscribe the complex relationships of identity" (p. 2). Wahl (2012) uses intertextuality to analyze popular visual media in television and film, while Hiramoto (2012) uses it as a tool to explore heterosexual normativity in anime. These studies investigate issues in pragmatic, sociolinguistic, and linguistic anthropological research in which intertextual distances constitute an interpretive framework. Most establish an anchoring work or cornerstone media piece to serve as an intertextual frame to study other texts.

Immigrant-Themed Children's Literature

We selected four award-winning immigration-themed novels for our study, specifically focusing on books which highlighted a female character's immigration experiences to the United States. The novel *Inside Out and Back Again* (Lai, 2011) served as the cornerstone novel of our study, our anchor text, since this was the book that challenged us initially to think differently about immigration-themed children's literature. We chose this novel because of its unique portrayal of the main character's immigration experience to the United States. We read this novel closely and engaged in multiple discussions to develop our interpretations and understandings of the messages about immigration conveyed through the main character's experiences.

To conduct our critical analysis using intertextuality we selected three additional immigration-themed novels to read in comparison to our cornerstone text. The additional novels were selected for two reasons. First, they remained in our memories long after we had read them because of the tensions and connections we made while we read each one. Second, these novels are well-known award-winning novels that are widely read.

- *Inside Out and Back Again* by Thanhha Lai (2011) is the winner of the 2012 National Book Award for Young People's Literature and a 2012 Newbery Honor book. Há and her family board a ship to leave Saigon in 1975, right before the war reaches the city. Há's father, a soldier, has been missing for several years, so Há's mother decides to immigrate to the United States, rather than France, believing her children will receive a better education in America. The family settles in Alabama where racial tensions create hardships. Há endures bullying, resistance, and low academic expectations at school. New and strange foods, customs, and language make Há homesick for Vietnam. Despite these hardships, she gradually learns English and develops friendships with peers who respect her. Even though Há and her family are often treated unjustly, many community members act with kindness and provide support.
- *Esperanza Rising* by Pam Muñoz Ryan (2000) is a well-known immigration book that has won many awards and prizes, most notably the 2002 Pura Belpré Award and the 2001 Jane Addams Award. Esperanza Ortega lives a privileged life on her family's vineyard in Mexico. Each year the harvesting of the grapes coincides with her birthday celebration, but her birthday also signifies a turning point in her life when her beloved Papá is found dead. Set in the late 1930s, Esperanza and her mother must deal with Mexican laws pertaining to land ownership which do not allow a widowed woman to own property. Rather than accept the marriage proposal of one of Papá's step-brothers, Mamá and Esperanza immigrate to the United States, fleeing their privileged lives to the glaringly different world of migrant farm workers in California during the Great Depression.
- *A Step from Heaven* by An Na (2001) is the winner of national awards including the Asian Pacific American Award for Literature for 2001–2003 and Michael L. Printz Award in 2002. Four-year-old Young Ju and her family emigrate from South Korea to Mi Gook (America). Adjusting to life in Mi Gook is initially difficult for Young Ju. She must learn English without support, her father is abusively strict, her mother is victimized by domestic violence, and her younger brother, Joon, becomes a rebellious teen. However, despite the constant tension and drama, Young Ju excels academically and becomes an excellent high school student. Through Young Ju's journey,

readers experience the challenges immigrants experience growing up bicultural in the United States.

•   *Call Me Maria* by Judith Cofer (2006) has received four awards including Honorable Mention by Américas Award for Children's and Young Adult Literature in 2004. Maria's father grew up in the barrio in New York City and moved to Puerto Rico where he met and married Maria's mother. Longing for the barrio, Maria's father lives in sadness on the island. Refusing to leave Puerto Rico but realizing the sadness that has overcome her husband, Maria's mother suggests that he move back to the barrio. Maria is given a choice of whether to stay on the island or move to the United States with her father. Having always dreamed of attending an American university, Maria moves with her father. Written with poems sprinkled amid vignettes, the book tells the story of Maria and her move from Puerto Rico to New York City; the move from island girl to barrio girl.

Collectively, these novels feature young female protagonists who immigrate to the United States. Two of the novels are historical fiction, *Inside Out and Back Again* and *Esperanza Rising*. The other two novels, *A Step from Heaven* and *Call Me Maria*, are contemporary realistic fiction. Though the dominant language of these novels is English, each includes words, phrases, and sentences from the protagonist's home language. Three of the novels target readers ages eight and older. Only *A Step from Heaven* targets readers 12 years and older.

Using Intertextuality to Think Critically

We noticed when we read immigrant-themed children's literature we empathized with the characters, especially the children, whose fate seemed to hold countless circumstances that left them destitute. We expected to experience similar feelings when we read *Inside Out and Back Again* (Lai, 2011). That was not the case, however. Hà's experiences as a female immigrant in the United States differed from the experiences of the main characters we had read about in the other novels. These differences prompted us to think about the ways intertextuality might be used as a methodology for critical analysis. We decided to explore our thinking through a postcolonial lens asking:

1. How are transnational immigrant female protagonists represented in children's literature?
2. How does intertextuality influence our mental images, assumptions, and representations about immigrants?

Our analysis occurred in three phases: (a) our memory of reading the novels, (b) thinking intertextually about the novels, and (c) critical discussions on intertextual assumptions. This depiction of our analysis tells how the phases seem to unfold logically as we began recalling our memories of the novels. After talking about our memories, we made connections from the cornerstone novel *Inside Out and Back Again* to each of the other novels. As we discussed our connections, our conversations shifted to themes that we identified as assumptions about immigrants in children's literature.

Our Memories of the Novels

We began our analysis by recalling memories from our previous readings of these novels. As our discussions focused on specific details about each novel, we noted our thinking (see Table 4.1). Initially, the memories related to demographics of the characters (e.g., age, number of siblings). Eventually our memories turned toward moments in the stories where we had tensions and connections. For example,

TABLE 4.1 Memories of Events from Novels

Title	Our Memories
Inside Out and Back Again	Poor
	Three brothers
	Father, a soldier, has gone missing during the war
	No knowledge of English language
	Criticizes English language
	Interacts with peers who have mixed racial backgrounds
Esperanza Rising	Wealthy in Mexico, poor in U.S.
	No siblings
	Father was murdered
	Sheltered by adults
	No knowledge of English language and wants to learn
	Interacts with farm-labor Mexicans and Latino Americans
	Becomes a migrant field worker
	Empowered by mom and Abuelita
A Step from Heaven	Poor
	One brother
	Strict, abusive parents
	No knowledge of English language and wants to learn
	Extremely naïve
	Victim of gender-favoritism by family
	American best friend
	Excels academically
Call Me Maria	Poor
	No siblings
	Parents are separated, living in different U.S. regions
	Limited knowledge of English language, wants to learn
	Interacts with Mexican and Indian immigrants in barrio
	Eager for U.S. education
	Loves music by Celia Cruz, Felipe Rodriguez, and others
	Loves to dance

Yoo Kyung remembered her uncomfortable reaction to *A Step from Heaven* when she realized the Korean word of *Uhn-nee* (sister) was inaccurately used in the book.

Our conversation shifted after Yoo Kyung shared that the predominately monolingual English-speaking students enrolled in her university courses expressed frustration about not having English translations of the Spanish words in *Call Me Maria*. Hoping to push our thinking, we shifted our discussion from memories about each novel to connections between the cornerstone novel, *Inside Out and Back Again*, and the other novels.

Thinking Intertextually

Our second phase began with a conversation in which Yoo Kyung pointed out Há's strong sense of agency at the beginning of *Inside Out and Back Again* and how it grew throughout the novel. For example, Há remained loyal to Vietnam. Even though Há knew the dangers of returning to live in war-torn Saigon, she states that if given the choice she "would choose wartime in Saigon over peacetime in Alabama" (Lai, 2011, p. 195). Há's strong sense of agency is also evident during lessons at school after the teacher instructs classmates to clap for her efforts to count to 20 and say the alphabet in English. Angry, Há tells readers she "already learned fractions and how to purify river water" when she lived in Vietnam (p. 283).

We questioned the agency of the protagonists in the other novels. We agreed that the protagonists' sense of agency became stronger by the end of the novels but only after enduring the hardships experienced during and after immigrating to the United States. Although we found excerpts from the novels where the protagonists compared life in the United States with life in their home countries, we could not find excerpts where protagonists longed to return home or wanted others to know about the grandeur of the people, landscape, and culture of their homeland. For instance, Maria writes poems about her life in America and some of the difficulties she and Papi endure in *Call Me Maria*, but does not discuss a desire to return to Puerto Rico.

We returned to *Inside Out and Back Again* to identify the ways in which this book provided a different portrayal of the immigrant experience. We noted that while cultural assimilation is often viewed as a solution to the issues and problems of immigrants, requiring them as "Others" to adjust and assimilate, Lai doesn't portray Há as the subject of assimilation. From Há's point of view, she is the Self and her Alabama community is the Other. Há resists the audience's expectation that her family as Vietnamese refugees are grateful to relocate in the United States and maintains a love and preference for her own country. She resists portrayals of her family as poor and unable to enjoy good food and quality clothing, she does not view English as holding status over her own language, and she avoids isolation through developing relationships based in respect, not pity. Há's resistance to being viewed as "Other" invited us to think critically on how views of self and the Others are often portrayed in books on immigrants.

Critical Discussions on Intertextual Assumptions

Throughout our third phase we explored notions of "self" and "Others" in the novels. We discussed the ways distorted perceptions of immigrants including stereotypes, biases, and prejudices support Othering. As a result of our discussion, we identified four themes from the novels that reflect assumptions about immigrants—language barriers, socioeconomic status, community members, and beliefs about childhood. In Table 4.2, we use paraphrased passages from the novels to support our thinking about the assumptions; thus relying on the actual text that readers encounter in the novels. The passages represent examples of intertextual connections across the four novels beginning with our cornerstone novel *Inside Out and Back Again.*

We discussed the negative implications of these assumptions about immigrants. For example, we noted that language barriers limit employment opportunities and advancement. Despite being well-educated, Esperanza and her mother in *Esperanza Rising* must take low-paying jobs in order to survive. As female migrant workers they will most likely live as lower SES citizens. And while we believe that one's quality of life is not based solely on income, we recognize that poverty has a rippling effect due to the impact on health care, educational opportunities, living conditions, and the way one is perceived and treated in society.

The four assumptions that resulted from our discussions had pushed our thinking. We used what we had learned to create thematic categories for the final phase of our study in considering these themes through the critical lens of postcolonial analysis.

Themes through a Postcolonial Lens

Postcolonial criticism helped us see connections among the domains of our experiences of looking for Otherness. For our analysis, we interpreted immigrants to the United States to be colonized and citizens of the United States to be colonizers within the frame of a postcolonial mindset. Thus, borrowing from Tyson (2006), we assert the colonizers (Americans) see themselves as the embodiment of what a human being should be, the ideal "self." A closer and more critical examination of the assumptions revealed four intertextual themes across the four novels:

1. exotic homelands and lifestyles;
2. challenges to home and family structures;
3. learning a new language; and
4. colonizing the childness of immigrants.

These categories represent the experiences of immigrants as "they cross political, linguistic, cultural, religious and social frontiers, which evokes images, prejudices and stereotypes about Others in particular, even dramatic clarity—ideological importance of migration literature" (Blioumi & Beller, 2007, p. 366).

TABLE 4.2 Intertextual Connections in the Genre Texts

Assumptions	Inside Out and Back Again	Esperanza Rising	A Step from Heaven	Call Me Maria
Language Barriers	She makes me learn rules I've never noticed like a, an, and the, which act as little megaphones to tell the world whose English is still secondhand. (p. 166)	Esperanza could hear them talking in English, the words hard and clipped, as if they were speaking with sticks in their mouth. (p. 100)	The teacher points to her lips and says, "Laanchu." Then she is eating from the empty bowl again. (p. 31)	I have a thick accent; it makes people in school think I am not good in English. (p. 28)
Socioeconomic Status	What I don't love: pink sofas, green chairs, plastic cover on a table, stained mattresses, old clothes, unmatched dishes. All from friends of Cowboy. (p. 126)	Esperanza felt anger crawling up her throat. "Mama, we are living like horses! How can you sing? How can you be happy? We don't even have a room to call our own." (p. 103)	I tilt my head down in shame, look at the worn, shaggy orange rug that was too cheap to pass up at a garage sale. (p. 81)	Not much money because my mother is a teacher and that made us middle-class, what they call blue collar life here. (p. 17)
Community Members	Eggs explode like smears of snot on our front door. "Just dumb kids," says our Cowboy. Bathroom paper hangs . . . from our willow. A brick shatters the front window landing on our dining room table. (p. 162)	"Look, there they are!" said Alfonso, pointing out the window. "My brother, Juan, and Josefina, his wife. And his children, Isabel and the twins. They have all come." (p. 85)	I see gone girls whispering to each other. I have never seen so many different colors of hair. (p. 29) The whole neighborhood will think we are stranger than we already look. (p. 54)	Doña Segura is nearly blind, but she embroiders like an angel in patterns her fingers remember. When she calls out a color, *amarillo, azul, verde, rojo*, one of her grand-daughters threads her needles. (p. 42)
Beliefs about Childhood	They chase me. They yell "Boo–Da, Boo–Da" at me. They pull my arm hair. They call me Pancake Face. They clap at me in class. And you want me to wait? Can I hit them? (p. 215)	I will even show you the beautiful doll my papa bought me, if you will teach me how to pin diapers, how to wash. (p. 120)	Well, you are here now and you can become a Mi Gook girl. Here, try this drink. Everyone in Mi Gook loves ko–ka ko–la. They drink it like water. (p. 26)	I will go with Papi. I will explore a new world, conquer English, become strong, grow through the concrete like a flower. (p. 14)

Exotic Homelands and Lifestyles

Each novel begins with exotic descriptions of food, fashion, festivals, and/or facts. In the cornerstone novel, *Inside Out and Back Again*, Lai (2011) invites readers into the exotic world of Saigon with an introduction of the Lunar New Year, "Tết 1975: Year of the Cat." Readers learn that Tết is a special day of celebration when Vietnamese people eat sugary lotus seeds and rice cakes, and wear new clothing (from undergarments to outerwear). The author uses authentic Vietnamese names for characters in the story and vivid descriptions of plants like papaya trees. Adding to the image of Vietnam as an exotic place is the interspersement of Vietnamese language throughout the English text. For U.S. readers the festival, food, Vietnamese names, and physical setting are unfamiliar and therefore likely to be perceived as exotic.

Like Lai, Ryan (2000) begins *Esperanza Rising* with a festival, ¡La Cosecha! (Harvest) and with discussions of other cultural festivities, like Quinceañeras. Ryan includes a rich description of Esperanza's home, El Rancho de las Rosas, to help readers understand the setting of the story. Characters have Spanish names and like the text of *Inside Out and Back Again*, the main character's home language, Spanish, is interspersed throughout the predominately English text.

In *A Step from Heaven*, Na (2001) describes Young Ju's Korean homeland in exotic terms by having Young Ju's parents compare Korea to the United States and her loving grandma stay in Korea. Na's characters romantically describe life in Mi Gook (America) as the land of opportunity and happiness. They believe that anyone can succeed in Mi Gook. Young Ju's family celebrations focus on new possibilities in Mi Gook rather than Korean culture. In fact, festivals and food-centered Korean events rarely occur in the novel. Instead, a collective Asian identity is projected more strongly than a Korean identity. For example, Young Ju's mother works at a Japanese restaurant where Young Ju meets the Japanese cook, Grill Woman. Young Ju describes her mother and Grill Woman's conversations as "a language of mixed and chopped Korean and Japanese, glued together with pieces of English" (p. 62).

Cofer (2006) in *Call Me Maria* builds exoticism into the description of Maria including her clothing and her family. Cofer describes Maria as a proud native Puerto Rican who cares deeply about her Puerto Rican identity. Maria's home in Puerto Rico is a place of celebration. In one scene, Maria enters the kitchen, telling readers, "I am wearing my mambo costume, I have painted my face like a clown's, lots of red lipstick and thick blue eye shadow. I climb up on a chair; Mami's red Mexican skirt is dragging on the floor" (p. 6). They live in a *cabana* and Mami drinks *café con leche*. Maria wants to learn Mambo. Abuela and Papi disagree about life in Puerto Rico. Abuela recalls it as a place of "*La familia, los amigos, el amor*, that's what mattered" (pp. 92–93). Papi thinks, "On my screen was the same world I see on our TV here: drugs, guns, angry people, and violence. Only difference the bad news was in Spanish" (p. 93). This binary perspective shows Puerto Rico as an exotic yet tough place to live.

Many narratives begin with an introduction of the setting and characters; however, we question the exotic nature of the descriptions in these books. The authors' approach of incorporating festivities and objects that can only be described in Spanish, Vietnamese, or Korean language enhances the exotic sense of each character's homeland. Descriptions of the landscape romanticize a homeland where life was happy and trouble-free. As the stories continue, readers learn that life as an immigrant is filled with obstacles and challenges. When authors contrast memories of an exotic homeland with a difficult life in a new country, they inevitably draw a sympathetic response from readers. Othering is enhanced, especially for U.S. readers who often compare diverse cultures and experiences (Other) to their own culture and experiences (self). Their view of their own culture as the norm against which other cultures are negatively compared remains unchallenged.

Há does challenge the assumption that refugees are happier in the United States because America is richer, safer, and more beautiful than their home countries. When her teacher shows photos of Vietnam that only depict the chaotic war zone as if those images define all of Vietnam, she comments, "She's telling the class where I am from." Images of her own everyday life come to mind and she says, "I would choose wartime in Saigon over peacetime in Alabama" (p. 195). Her pride in her own country resists American labels of inferiority.

Challenges to Home and Family Structures

In each of the four novels, challenges to home and family structures provide a catalyst for the decision to immigrate to the United States. In *Inside Out and Back Again*, readers learn the ways the encroaching war has impacted the family's way of life, especially since Há's father, a soldier, has been missing for over nine years. Impoverished and most likely widowed, her mother must raise Há and her three brothers alone in Alabama.

Esperanza's home and family structure changed dramatically in *Esperanza Rising* after the sudden death of her father. Before his death, Esperanza and her family lived a life of luxury and wealth. After his death, Esperanza's mother is expected to marry her deceased husband's cruel brother and so abandons nearly all of their possessions in order for her and Esperanza to immigrate to California. Esperanza begins her immigration journey as a poor child of a widowed mother seeking a better life in a new country.

Asian American stereotypes are reinforced in *A Step from Heaven* by portraying Young Ju as a model-minority; a historically formed stereotype of Japanese and Chinese Americans as well-behaved minority citizens that has become a collective stereotype of Asian Americans (Lee, 2007). Young Ju excels academically and obeys her parents despite living with a stubborn, abusive father and passive mother "who lives solely to guide her children's education," a stereotype that "serves the rhetoric of traditional family values espoused by neoconservatives" (Lee, 2007, p. 11). Young Ju passively participates in situations at the beginning of the novel with her compliant personality mirroring stereotypical Asian characteristics.

When Maria's parents separate in *Call Me Maria*, she decides to live with her Papi in New York City, as he seems to need more support. Maria feels lonely and disconnected from him in the United States, noticing that he connects with people in the barrio, but not with her. Because Maria's parents are separated and no longer talk to each other, Maria's Abuela decides to visit her in New York City. Papi doesn't get along with Abuela and tensions arise. Maria's family structure is not quite complete.

The authors' portrayals of immigrant families suggest that tensions, conflicts, abuse, sadness, and despair are common characteristics of immigrant families. This depiction separates readers from the characters and fosters a sympathetic response for readers through feelings of pity for immigrants and a sense of superiority for their own way of life. One example of resistance to this pity is when Há questions the poor quality of the donations given to them by sponsors. She comments that even in Vietnam where her family had little, they celebrated birthdays with smaller portions of good food, indicating that living in poverty does not reflect an inability to enjoy the finer things in life.

Learning a New Language

Language becomes a way for Há in *Inside Out and Back Again* to interact with and develop relationships with community members. Rather than creating a barrier, language helps Há develop her sense of identity and belonging. Weedon (1987) explains Há's actions noting, "Language is the place where actual and possible forms of social organization and their likely social and political consequences are defined and contested. Yet it is also the place where our sense of ourselves, our subjectivity, is constructed" (p. 21). Há demonstrates for readers how learning English from her neighbor, Miss Washington, serves as a mediator in their relationship. After Miss Washington uses a new word, *delicious*, in a question, "Was your lunch delicious?," Há responds "*I eat candy in toilet*" (Lai, 2011, p. 180). Shocked, Miss Washington responds, "*What?*" Miss Washington is unaware that students are bullying Há at lunchtime so she hides in the restroom to eat. Há thinks Miss Washington is shocked because she omitted the article "the" in her answer. Há thinks, "I realize my mistake. '*Oh, the toilet*'" (p. 180).

After immigrating, Esperanza in *Esperanza Rising* receives no English-language instruction and is desperate to learn English as a means to better her circumstances and future. She feels no sense of agency which may be due to her privileged childhood where she was accustomed to having things done for her.

Of the four protagonists, Young Ju in *A Step from Heaven* has the most difficulty with the English language. When she started school in the United States, she was very sensitive to the sounds of the English language, negatively impacting her ability to communicate and amplifying her struggle to adjust to life in the United

States. Young Ju's home language frequently appears in her narratives especially when she uses accented Pidgin English with specific forms of address [i.e., Gomo (aunt), Uhmma (mother), Apa (father)].

Maria in *Call Me Maria* observes how people in New York City speak Spanglish. Although the language does not appear to be correct Spanish, she learns to accept it. Similar to Há, Maria has a strong sense of agency as a second-language speaker; "I have a thick accent; it makes people in school think I am not good in English. But I know more words than many native English speakers because I need words to survive" (p. 28). Maria is determined to learn to communicate in English.

Each of the protagonists has varied experiences acquiring English. Há is explicitly taught English and uses the experience to mediate her relationships and to help develop her identity. Esparanza, Young Ju, and Maria are motivated to learn English; however, their motivation to learn grows out of necessity to survive in the United States. The authors' decision to create characters desperate to learn English in order to survive the United States perpetuates notions that all people living in the United States must learn to speak English if they want to succeed. After reading these novels, readers could believe that all immigrants want and need to learn English, that all immigrants must become proficient in English to succeed, and thus, that English-only mandates and laws are justified.

Again, only Há is shown actively resisting the view that English holds status and power over her own language. She critiques the English language as illogical, commenting that "whoever invented English should have learned to spell" (p. 177) and that her American teacher needs to listen for "the diacritical mark" (p. 141) to pronounce her name.

Colonizing the Childness of Immigrants

Colonialism can also be used to critique adults' perceptions of immigrant children. Nodelman (1992) argues that literature published specifically for children may, in fact, mirror adults' ideas about children. Nodelman ties postcolonial interpretations to cultures and children, stating, "Children's literature is highly reflective about sociological phenomena that can be accounted for in terms of the operational characteristics and structural principles they share with other social activities" (p. 117). In particular, children are often portrayed as naïve and inferior to adults in their understandings and actions.

As the youngest of four children and the only girl, Há's naïveté is magnified through her interactions with her three brothers in *Inside Out and Back Again*. At the same time, her insightfulness to gather information from her surroundings is realistically portrayed. She demonstrates a competent portrayal of childness through her increasing sensitivity about the changes in her community and her awareness of tensions, worries, and even anxiety.

As an only child with no siblings, Esperanza interacts with other children for the first time in the migrant camps in *Esperanza Rising*. The portrayal of her innocence and naïveté reflects the shock of her new, unfamiliar living conditions but also seems somewhat exaggerated. Esperanza believes that her family is still wealthy and will eventually move to a big house with servants. She also appears sheltered from externally influenced social knowledge. For example, when Marta, a girl at the migrant camp, talks about the people coming together to strike in protest of their living conditions and wages, Esperanza is completely unaware of what she is talking about.

Young Ju's life in the United States centers on interactions with her teacher and family members in *A Step from Heaven*. The portrayal of her innocence and naïveté seems exaggerated in her portrayal as unable to differentiate an airplane from a bus, lack of familiarity with Coca Cola, and belief that Mi Gook is heaven where her grandpa lives. Like Esperanza, she is also sheltered from externally influenced social knowledge.

In *Call Me Maria*, Maria, an only child with no siblings, interacts with other immigrant teenagers who live in her apartment complex. She is not sheltered like the other protagonists, something we attribute to the fact that 15-year-old Maria is older than the other protagonists. Há and Esperanza are around 10 years old, and Young Ju is four years old at the beginning of the story.

Ryan's novel, *Esperanza Rising*, draws partly from her grandmother's immigration experiences, while Na's novel, *A Step from Heaven*, "draws on past emotions but not the story of my life" (Michael, n.d., p. 2). It is possible that these authors meant to reflect social prejudices against Korea and Mexico in their books; however, we believe readers will find it difficult to believe that Esperanza cannot bathe herself and that Young Ju has never tasted Coca Cola, thus perpetuating images of "self" and "Other." In this case, readers (self) might see themselves as more knowledgeable and independent while viewing immigrants (Others) as uneducated and naïve children.

Conclusion

Stories have the power to shape the thinking of readers about people, places, events, and circumstances. Critical theories like postcolonialism and methodologies like intertextuality can help readers uncover and examine the ways texts create and perpetuate images of "self" and "Other." Critical theories provide a framework for thoughtful discussions that challenge the stereotypes, biases, and prejudices that contribute to collective attitudes about immigrants and immigration experiences. Intertextuality serves as a methodology to help readers notice and grapple with their inner tensions when they think deeply and critically about the context of similar texts and read across those texts.

Our study of immigration-themed novels brought us to two conclusions. First, we noticed that immigration-themed children's literature has evolved over time as a result of a growing global community. In our study, the immigrant-themed narratives published between 2000 and 2006 raised awareness about culturally and linguistically diverse populations in the United States in relation to familial and historical backgrounds of immigrants. Missing from these novels is a post-colonial critique of unchallenged assumptions about immigrants and immigrant experiences. In 2011, readers meet Há in *Inside Out and Back Again*, who asserts a postcolonial critique of unchallenged stereotypes, biases, and prejudices toward immigrants like herself. No longer is the global community too expansive and disconnected to know these misconceptions. Social, economic, and political inter-connected global wholeness is now a reality of daily life. Therefore, postcolonial-ity embedded in children's and adolescent literature continuously challenges the global community to become more sensitive to the needs of citizens.

Second, we found that through the act of reading literature with an eye on intertextual connections, pathways were opened to connect story elements includ-ing characters, contexts, themes, authorship, and genres across multiple novels. These intertextual connections provide readers with opportunities to challenge stereotypes, biases, and prejudices embedded in literature. Providing children with opportunities to read literature and discuss their intertextual connections and tensions with each other and with someone who will challenge their thinking can create a critical lens. Through intertextual discussions, children can critically strengthen their thinking about and understandings of contexts found in cultur-ally and linguistically responsive children's and adolescent literature.

References

Allen, G. (2000). *Intertextuality*. New York: Routledge.

Barthes, R. (1975). *The pleasure of the text*. New York: Hill and Wang.

Blioumi, A. & Beller, M. (2007). Migration literature. In M. Beller & J. Leerssen (Eds.), *Ima-gology: The cultural construction and literary representation of national characters: A critical study* (pp. 365–370). Amsterdam, NL: Rodopi.

Cummins, A. (2013). Border crossings: Undocumented migration between Mexico and the United States in contemporary young adult literature. *Children's Literature in Education, 44*(1), 57–73.

Frow, J. (1986). *Marxism and literary history*. Cambridge, MA: Harvard University Press.

Giroux, H. (Ed.). (1994). *Living dangerously: Identity politics and the new cultural racism*. New York: Routledge.

Hiramoto, M. (2012). Anime and intertextualites: Hegemonic identities in *Cowboy Bebop*. In M. Hiramoto (Ed.), *Media intertextualities* (pp. 57–70). Amsterdam: Benjamins.

Hiramoto, M. & Park, J. S. (2012). Media intertextualities: Semiotic mediation across time and space. In M. Hiramoto (Ed.), *Media intertextualities* (pp. 1–10). Amsterdam: Benjamins.

Hope, J. (2008). "One day we had to run": The development of the refugee identity in children's literature and its function in education. *Children's Literature in Education, 39*(4), 295–304.

Lee, S. (2007). *Unraveling the "model minority" stereotype: Listening to Asian American youth*. New York: Teachers College Press.

Liang, L., Aimonette, B., & Galda, L. (2009). The refugee experience in books for adoles-cents. *Journal of Children's Literature, 35*(2), 59–68.

López, T. A. & Serrato, P. (2001). A new Mestiza primer: Borderlands philosophy in the children's books of Gloria Anzaldua. In T. Edwards & E. D. Wolfe (Eds.), *Such news of the land: U.S. women nature writers* (pp. 204–216). Hanover, UK: University Press.

Lowery, R. M. (2000). *Immigrants in children's literature.* New York: Peter Lang.

McGillis, R. (2000). Introduction. In R. McGillis (Ed.), *Voices of the other: Children's literature and the postcolonial context* (pp. xix–xxxii). New York: Routledge.

Michael, W. (n.d.). Teachers notes. *A step from heaven.* Sydney: Allen & Unwin.

Nodelman, P. (1992). The other: Orientalism, colonialism, and children's literature. *Children's Literature Association Quarterly, 17*(1), 29–35.

Smith, P. (1988). *Discerning the subject.* Minneapolis, MN: University of Minnesota.

Son, E. H. & Sung, Y. K. (2015). The journey of U.S. Korean children: (Re)constructing bicultural identities in picture books. *The Dragon Lode, 33*(2), 52–65.

Tuon, B. (2014). Not the same, but not bad: Accommodation and resistance in Thanhha Lai's *Inside Out and Back Again. Children's Literature Association Quarterly, 39*(4), 533–550.

Turner, B. S. (1983). Accounting for the orient. In D. MacEoin & A. Al-Shahi (Eds.), *Islam in the modern world* (pp. 9–26). Lahore: Publishers United.

Tyson, L. (2006). *Critical theory today.* New York: Routledge.

Wahl, A. (2012). The global matastereotyping of 'Hollywood dudes': African reality television parodies of mediatized California style. In M. Hiramoto (Ed.), *Media intertextualities* (pp. 31–56). Amsterdam: Benjamins.

Wee, S. J., Park, S., & Choi, J. S. (2015). Korean culture as portrayed in young children's picture books: The pursuit of cultural authenticity. *Children's Literature in Education, 46*(1), 70–87.

Weedon, C. (1987). *Feminist practice and poststructuralist theory* (2nd ed.). New York: Wiley-Blackwell.

Wilkie-Stibbs, C. (2004). Intertextuality and the child reader. In P. Hunt (Ed.), *International companion encyclopedia of children's literature* (pp. 352–361). New York: Routledge.

Yi, J. H. (2014). "My heart beats in two places": Immigration stories in Korean-American picture books. *Children's Literature in Education, 45*(2), 129–144.

Children's Literature References

Cofer, J. O. (2006). *Call me Maria.* New York: Scholastic

Lai, T. (2011). *Inside out and back again.* New York: HarperCollins.

Na, A. (2001). *A step from heaven.* New York: Speak.

Ryan, P. M. (2000). *Esperanza rising.* New York: Scholastic.

5

WHEN ENTERTAINMENT TRUMPS SOCIAL CONCERNS

The Commodification of Mexican Culture and Language in *Skippyjon Jones*

Carmen M. Martínez-Roldán

Several years ago, a librarian brought a picturebook to a class on Latino literature, asking for my opinion. The book was full of references to Mexican culture and the Spanish language. The librarian, self-identified as Caucasian and a resident of the southwestern United States, felt something was wrong with the representation of Mexicans but could not name the problem. The book, *Skippyjon Jones in the Doghouse* (Schachner, 2005), received the 2004 E.B. White Read Aloud Award by the Association of Booksellers for Children for its universal appeal as a great book to read aloud and applauded for its use of Spanish expressions. The main character is a Siamese cat named Skippyjon Jones who speaks with a Spanish accent and wants to be a Chihuahua dog. Wearing a mask and cape and describing himself as "the great sword fighter," like the Spanish TV character El Zorro, Skippyjon Jones embarks on an adventure to rescue Chihuahuas who ask for his help during a difficult situation. The librarian's question marked the start of my inquiry into the series of books about Skippyjon Jones. The series presents educators and researchers with tension, as it has great popularity and claims pedagogical intentions, while reproducing stereotypes of Latinos, their language, and culture.

This study contributes to discussions of socioeconomic issues impacting the production of children's literature, highlighting the relationship between economic forces and the books available to children (Hade & Edmonson, 2003; Taxel, 2010; Zipes, 2001). One concern addressed in these discussions pertains to how the process of commodification, for which something is valued for its monetary worth, plays a role in the kinds of books available for children. The negative consequences of the commodification of literature, which affects the production of children's literature in general, are magnified in books that incorporate characters and experiences from groups that have been traditionally underrepresented, such as Latinos. For instance, in 2014, of the 3,200 multicultural books received at the

Cooperative Children's Book Center, less than 59 were written or illustrated by Latino authors/illustrators and less than 66 were about Latino characters and/or experiences. This small number is of concern as one in four students (24.7%) in the U.S. public educational system is of Latino background (Fry & López, 2012) and the books written about Latinos and by Latino authors are not growing at the same rate as the population. Because of the limited number of books addressing Latino experiences, understanding issues of availability and, more important, issues of representation as impacted by the commodification of literature becomes critical.

This chapter focuses on Judy Schachner's popular series Skippyjon Jones as an example of the negative consequences of the commodification of literature that focuses on characters and experiences of underrepresented groups. The study uses critical content analysis to examine what is at work in the production of these books that promotes their popularity. Following the process of thinking with theory (Jackson & Mazzei, 2012), I use a Marxist framework, which addresses how capitalist economies work in order to uncover the ways in which Mexicans and their language are treated as commodities in the stories to enhance their marketability. My analysis indicates that the capitalist ideology of commodification is reflected in the Skippyjon Jones series and products through the author's use of the Spanish language and Mexican characters as commodities for entertainment and marketing purposes, overlooking problems with the ways Mexican culture is represented.

Theoretical Perspectives: A Marxist Framework

Marxist theory has been used in education to analyze children's and young adolescent literature in order to understand the socioeconomic ideologies influencing characters' behaviors and the ways that literary works support or challenge oppressive ideologies (Tyson, 2011). In Tyson's analysis, a Marxist framework exposes the ways oppressive ideologies, or shared belief systems, such as classism and capitalism, foster a socioeconomic hierarchy that grants enormous wealth and power to a relatively small number of people at the top of the socioeconomic ladder and prevents a large number of people from escaping poverty (p. 112).

A key process characterizing these socioeconomic capitalist processes is described through the concept of "commodification." Marx was concerned with the ways in which capitalist modes of production treat human activity and people's work as commodities. Within a Marxist perspective, work is described as a fundamental human activity, "a definite form of activity of . . . individuals, a definite form of expressing their life" (Marx & Engels, 1970, p. 42); however, this activity, through which individuals not only subsist but transform society, is treated and redefined in capitalist economies as a commodity. The product of an individual's work does not belong to the individual anymore; it has been objectified and appropriated by the capitalist for its potential to be commodified, in other words, for its worth in money, for its exchange value. Not only has people's relation to their work been altered but also how people relate to each other and to things to the extent that, as Tyson (2011) indicates, everything can be defined in terms of its worth in money; everything can also be owned or bought. The capitalist ideology of commodification prioritizes economic transactions over social concerns. When making the most money becomes a virtue, an ethics of greed may develop, leading to the exploitation of the worker (Marx & Engels, 1970; Tyson, 2011).

Scholars have analyzed the implications of the capitalist ideologies of commodification for the book publishing industry (Hade & Edmonson, 2003; Taxel, 2010; Zipes, 2001). One of the points highlighted in that collective work is the fact that most of the industry is dominated by a few megacorporations and multinational companies and this domination has changed the publishing business. For instance, Taxel (2010) calls attention to the dramatic shift in the way books are conceived, commissioned, produced, and sold. When the bottom line is what drives production, other criteria such as the literary quality of the books, social concerns, and the representations of ethnolinguistic groups take a back seat or are not considered. The potential of literature to engage readers in learning about their worlds and about themselves, to connect with other human beings or to reflect on larger matters of life are given less weight than the book's ability to sell.

The strategies through which commodification takes place include the capitalist processes of branding and synergy. Branding (of an author's or a product's name) aims at creating a meaning that transcends a product and aims to attract children as consumers to any product that carries the brand's name (Hade & Edmonson, 2003). Synergy is the process through which a series of products create the opportunity for the brand to be consumed in different ways, so that books are not valued just by themselves but by the number of products they can inspire (Taxel, 2010). This process aims to attract the young consumer not just to the book, but to the toys that come with the book, the video, the movie, and the artifacts associated with the brand. The dominance of this process fosters a view of children as consumers and of happiness as possessing things rather than children as readers. A question to ponder for those concerned with children and literature is the extent to which the reading experience of young children is mediated through marketing and what is lost in that process (Taxel, 2010; Zipes, 2001).

While Marxist theory has been interpreted by some as promoting economic determinism, it is a theory of hope on human agency and on people's capacities to change and transform their circumstances (Venable, 1945). Therefore, discussions about the role of capitalist ideologies in children's development as readers should not ignore the potential for agency on the part of children or the adults who promote children's engagement with literature. Opening up spaces where this agency can develop requires the ability to engage in uncovering and understanding how these processes operate in the production of children's literature and their role in shaping young children's values and perceptions (Taxel, 2010).

Using concepts from Marxist theory to interpret Alice Walker's (1973) *Every Day Use*, Tyson (2011) shows how the capitalist ideologies of competition, commodification, the American Dream, and rugged individualism frame an interpretation of the portrayal of an African American female character who escapes poverty. Dee is portrayed as a competitive character, concerned about social status, who commodifies everything and everyone and sees herself as an American Dream success story. Her adherence to these capitalist ideologies damages her relationships with others. The American Dream has not been available to her mother and sister who have worked hard. Unlike Dee's character, their portrayals invoke the reader's sympathy. In this way, it could be argued that the story invites the reader to reject capitalist ideologies.

While not explicitly claiming a Marxist framework, critical analyses of Harry Potter (Zipes, 2001) and the Curious George series (Hade, 2001) as cultural products focus on these as marketing and capitalist phenomena. Such analyses highlight the negative effects of the commodification of literature and the treatment of child readers as consumers, a concern in line with a Marxist framework. The analysis presented in this chapter builds on and extends this work.

Methodology: Critical Content Analysis

Through this critical content analysis I aim to gain insights into the question: What is at work in the production of the Skippyjon Jones books that promotes their popularity? More specifically, I examine the questions of: How do the literary elements in the series, particularly the author's use of language and the illustrations, come together to produce a particular view of Mexicans and their language? What images are conveyed through such representations? I approach this work acknowledging my location as a Latina educator concerned with issues of representation of minoritized groups in children's literature. In what follows I am explicit about the various analytical tools used in my analysis, which helped to both distance myself from data and look more closely at it.

For my initial analysis, I primarily used Botelho and Rudman's (2009) strategies for critical multicultural analysis. I analyzed the focalization of the story in one of the picturebooks, *Skippyjon Jones in the Doghouse* (2005), followed by an analysis of interactions among characters. This process involved microanalyses of language. For the analysis of language, I identified loaded words and used Barrera and Quiroa's (2003) categories for examining the use of Spanish words in English books, focusing on the semantic fields of kinship, culinary, and ethnographic terms.

After a microanalysis of the text, Botelho and Rudman (2009) propose to do a critical reading across texts and an examination of the historical and sociopolitical forces contributing to the construction of the texts, such as how the prevailing dominant ideologies about race, class, and gender are (or are not) reflected in the text. Thus, I introduced into the analysis four additional books from Schachner's series: *Skippyjon Jones* (2003); *Skippyjon Jones in Mummy Trouble* (2006) and

Skippyjon Jones . . . Lost in Spice (2009), both from the middle period of the series (the series spans 2003–2012 thus far); and *Skippyjon Jones Class Action* (2011). I then focused on the sociopolitical contexts reflected in the stories. Findings of the analysis focusing on *Skippyjon Jones in the Doghouse* (2005) documented the presence of Mock Spanish in the series, which worked to stereotype Mexicans and their culture (Martínez-Roldán, 2013).

The findings of that first analysis invited further exploration of what might be at work in the series to promote its popularity. I continued my exploration relying on critical content methods as described by Bradford (see Chapter Two) who proposes (a) a top-down approach that situates the text in relation to the historical and cultural forces that have shaped it and, especially important, the theoretical perspectives we draw on, and (b) a bottom-up analysis, similar to Botelho and Rudman's (2009) microanalysis of the text to examine linguistic and narrative features.

My familiarity with the series suggested that a Marxist perspective, with its critique of capitalism, particularly the concept of commodification, offered great potential to unpack what might be at work in the series. Central to this analysis were the following concepts that relate to a major tenet in Marxism literary criticism, namely, the relation of literature to the social and economic history within which the text has been produced (Williams, 1977):

- capitalism: a system in which almost everything—every object, every activity, every person—can be defined in terms of its worth in money (Tyson, 2011, p. 113);
- commodification: the process through which individuals' work, things, and ideas become commodities (are valued for their worth in money) in capitalist economies (Marx & Engels, 1970);
- appropriation: the process through which the ruling class or capitalists collect the value of individuals' work for its potential to be commodified (Marx, 1997). In cultural anthropology, the concept includes symbolic resources such as linguistic appropriation in which words are commodified and become properties with their meanings and uses determined by their owners (Hill, 2009, p. 158).
- branding and synergy: these two concepts provide specifics as to how commodification is promoted. Hade and Edmonson (2003) describe them as two of the processes through which a series of products create the opportunity for a brand to be consumed in different ways. Branding means to create a meaning that transcends any product. A synergy occurs when a brand is pushed into a new line of products (pp. 138–139).

These concepts or theoretical tenets from Marxism were the lens that I used to analyze Schachner's series, particularly two books: *Skippyjon Jones* (2003) and *Skippyjon Jones Class Action* (2011). I selected these two books, hoping that the span of eight years between their publication would help elucidate to what extent the concept of commodification holds explanatory power to understand what is at work on the texts and on the series' production. As part of this analysis, I also studied book-related products used to merchandise the series.

Findings on Commodification in *Skippyjon Jones*

I started by analyzing how characters are depicted in the texts through the identities created for them. The protagonist of the series is a Siamese cat that can be described as a "white" character who speaks with a Spanish accent. On the other hand, the dogs are assigned characteristics that reference a Mexican identity. They are introduced as "a mysterioso band of Chihuahuas" (Schachner, 2003) and described as Chimichangos. They have Spanish names, such as Don Diego, Poquito Tito, Alfredo, Rosalita, Tia Mia, Montezuma, Pato Ganso, and Julio.

The dogs are further characterized in *Skippyjon Jones Class Action* (2011) and in other books as *"poochitos"*—an Anglicization and diminutive of the Spanish noun "pochos." "Pocho" refers to a culturally Americanized or assimilated Mexican residing in the United States, or an American of Mexican descent, who speaks Spanish with an accent characteristic of North Americans (Anzaldúa, 1987; Maciel, 2008). It became institutionalized as a pejorative label until *Chicano* began to replace it in the late 1960s (Maciel, 2008, p. 276). The Chicano civil rights movement helped reinterpret the pocho identity and rehabilitated pochos' language as a legitimate mode of speaking and writing; traditionally, however, *pochismos* carried the stigma of marginal citizens (Sánchez, 2011). Nevertheless, whether pochismos are seen as positive or negative, the language used by the Chihuahuas in the series misrepresents pocho language and Mexican Americans' linguistic practices and does not correspond to the literary bilingualism used by Chicano authors to represent their bilingual communities.

The author's profuse use of Spanish and Spanish-like words, for apparently humorous purposes, also serves to create particular identities for Skippyjon Jones and the Chihuahuas. The following excerpt from *Skippyjon Jones* (2003) illustrates the author's borrowing or, in Marxist terms, her appropriation of elements from the Spanish language, so characteristic of the series. [I add clarifying notes in brackets; brackets with ellipsis signal omission of text]:

> "HOLY GUACAMOLE!" exclaimed Skippyjon Jones. "What was that?"
> [He looks at his image in a mirror, which reflects a dog.]
> Then, using his very best Spanish accent, he said "[. . . .] I AM A CHIHUAHUA!" [. . . .] After he put on his mask and sword [. . .], Skippyjon Jones began to sing in a *muy, muy* soft voice [represented in the audio version using the music of El Jarabe Tapatío]:
> "My name is Skippito Friskito. (clap-clap)
> I fear not a single bandito. (clap-clap)

My manners are mellow,
I'm sweet like the jell-o,
I get the job done, yes indeed-o." (clap-clap)

Skippyjon Jones meets the Chihuahuas on a lonesome desert road, far away in old Mexico, and the following dialogue develops, starting with Skippyjon Jones's surprise:

> "¡Ay, *caramba!* Who goes there?" Then the smallest of the small ones spoke up. "Why the maskito, dude?" asked Poquito Tito. "I go incognito," said Skippito. "Do you like rice and beans?" asked Pintolito. "*Sí*, I love mice and beans," said Skippito. "He might be the dog of our dreams," whispered Rosalita. "Perhaps," said Tia Mia.

A comparison of the number of Spanish words between the first publication and later ones shows an increase. As illustrated in Table 5.1, in *Skippyjon Jones* (2003) there are 71 uses of Spanish words, using a corpus of 35 different words; out of the 71 references, 35 involve 9 name-related words; while in *Skippyjon Jones Class Action* (2011) there are 85 references to Spanish words, using a corpus of 44 words; out of the 85 references, 27 involve 7 name-related words. That is, the number of references to Spanish and the number of Spanish words have increased from the 2003 publication to the 2011 book. The use of Spanish words has become a major characteristic of this popular series.

The use of upside-down exclamation marks and accent marks or diacritics has also increased, although the latter has not been integrated successfully, as the following examples illustrate. What should be "incógnito," a word stressed in the third-last syllable, appears as "incognito" (Schachner, 2003) (a word stressed in the second-last syllable). This could have been a purposeful omission of the diacritic to highlight the use of the "ito" ending for rhyming purposes as the lack of diacritic moves the accent from the syllable "cog" to the syllable "ni," which is closer to "ito." What should have been "suerte" (luck) appears as "suérte" (Schachner, 2011). While the strong syllable is identified correctly, the word does not need the diacritic given that it is an acute word that ends in a vowel. For a series that is marketed as an educational tool to learn Spanish, this usage should be of concern for teachers. In an online guide for teachers, Schachner (2012) describes her stories as opportunities to teach and learn Spanish:

> Each of my adventures are *ay caramba, mucho fun* but they're educational too! Instructing elementary poetry, Spanish or language lessons? . . . No problem, dude! Each story provides *mucho* material that will easily fit into your curriculum.
>
> *(para. 2)*

TABLE 5.1 Sample of Spanish Words Used in the Series *Skippyjon Jones*

Skippyjon Jones (2003)	*Skippyjon Jones in the Doghouse* (2005)	*Skippyjon Jones Class Action* (2011)
adios★	abuelo	amigos
amigos	amigos	¡Andele!★
¡Ay Caramba!	bozo	barrenas
buenas	burrito	beso
burritos	casa	¡Queso Cabeza!
el	cha-cha-cha	chico(s)
fiesta	cinco	de
frijoles	dramatica★	el
gracias	el	escuela
GUACAMOLE	fanatica★	estoy
hola	frijoles	frijoles
incognito★	gracias	gatito(s)
loco	gozo	grande
los	hola	hambre
mis	jalapeño	hombre
muchachitas	la	lana
muy	loco	libros
noches	los	los
piñata	mango	mareado
¿por que?★	mira	mucho
quiero	muchas	muchachos
sí	muchos	mezquino
siesta	perrito(s)	mochila
vamos	poco	muy
yo	Poochos	planeta
	por que★	plátano
	rumba	perro
	sí	perritos
	tango	sí
	tortilla	suérte★
		también
		taza
		tengo
		trofeos
71 references, corpus of 35 words, 9 name-related words	80 references, corpus of 41 words, 10 name-related words	85 references, corpus of 44 words, 7 name-related words

Note: Characters' Spanish names are not included in the table. An asterisk after the word indicates that a diacritic mark is missing or misplaced.

However, from a pedagogical point of view, the lack of accuracy and attention to diacritics is not as worrisome as the author's appropriation of Spanish morphology for incorporation into English words to make them sound Spanish, in the process, altering the Spanish pronunciation, writing, and often the meaning of Spanish words.

Linguistic Appropriation

The grammar elements most used in the series for the creation of Spanish-like words are the suffixes *-ito* and *-ita*, which in Spanish create a diminutive. There are 43 instances of grammar affixations in the 2003 story (in a corpus of 14 words) and 46 instances in the 2011 (in a corpus of 17 words). There is also addition of the masculine and feminine gender suffixes *-o* and *-a*. Table 5.2 provides examples from three books.

Such linguistic appropriation via the affixation of Spanish grammatical elements is a tactic used mostly by monolingual speakers of English, as part of what Hill (2009) calls "Mock Spanish." Hill describes Mock Spanish as an example of the strategy of incorporation, whereby members of a dominant group expropriate and appropriate desirable materials and symbolic resources from subordinated groups. This appropriation illustrates the change in relationships Marx referred to between privileged groups and marginalized (mostly working-class) groups. Specifically, Mock Spanish "borrows Spanish-language words and suffixes, assimilates their pronunciation to English (often in hyperanglicized or boldly mispronounced form), and changes their meaning, usually to make them humorous or pejorative" (Hill, 2009, p. 134).

The effect of this process is to assign positive qualities to white individuals and undesirable qualities to the language donors in a social system that is segmented according to color or designated minorities. Some of the positive qualities assigned

TABLE 5.2 Examples of Mock Spanish through Affixation of Spanish Grammar Elements

Skippyjon Jones (2003)	Skippyjon Jones in the Doghouse (2005)	Skippyjon Jones Class Action (2011)
bandito	attica	bug-ito
BANGITO!	birdito	bull-ito
Blimpo	Booble-ito	comme-cito
buzzito	Crispito	doubt-ito
CRASHITO!	(Polka) Dot-ito	(The Mona) Fleasa
eato	Friskito	Friskito
Friskito	heckito	hydrant-ito
indeed-o	hootito	indeed-o
maskito	jumbolito	Pinto Lito
mysterioso	mamalita	poochitos
Pintolito	poochitos	poof-ito
POP-ITO!	purr-ito	reader-ito
Skippito	sciatica	Skippito
Yippito	sirrito	snack-ito
	Skippito	shiver-ito
	SNAP-ito	strike-ito
	Yee-HAW-ito	tazalita
43 references, corpus of 14 words	52 references, corpus of 17 words	46 references, corpus of 17 words

to whites through their use of Mock Spanish are sense of humor, playful skill with a foreign language, authentic regional roots, and an easygoing attitude toward life. Some of the undesirable qualities assigned to people of color are laziness, language disorders, and mental incapacity. Thus, people of color are assigned an identity that restricts them to the lowest sectors of regional and national economies. In other words, Mock Spanish is a way of speaking that whites do not understand as racist, but which works to reproduce negative stereotypes of people of color, in this case, members of historically Spanish-speaking populations in the United States (Hill, 2009, p. 119).

One main strategy used in Mock Spanish is the affixation of Spanish grammatical elements, such as the definite article "*el*" and the masculine gender suffix "*o*," added to English words to give them a new semantic flavor, ranking from jocularity to insult. Examples include "much-o," "no problem-o," and "el cheap-o." As Hill (2009) indicates, the "el–o" frame can be used for any reference that the speaker or writer wishes to locate within a jocular colloquial register, and suffixation with "o" can proliferate through an utterance or text (p. 139). Most users of Mock Spanish are unaware of their participation in this racist practice, which is part of a larger system; this covert racist discourse is covert and invisible for most whites but not for Latinos, many of whom can immediately recognize it when they hear or see it in writing.

Hill (2009) argues that there is a sub-variety of Regionalist Anglo Spanish, whereby individuals use a few Spanish items to signal a regional identity as an "old timer" in the Southwest. She clarifies how such usage includes sincere, as opposed to mocking, uses of Spanish greetings and other expressions. While such usages are still appropriations, they suggest positive images of Spanish speakers as warm and courteous, in contrast to the Mock Spanish usages of the same items (p. 131). In Schachner's books, the Chihuahuas are referred to by the narrator or Skippyjon Jones as "*amigos*" [friends]. In the 2011 story they are further referred to as "los chicos," and "los muchachos," signaling a warm and affective relationship between Skippyjon Jones and the Chihuahuas. One question is thus whether her use of Spanish is closer to the variety of Regionalist Anglo Spanish described by Hill rather than Mock Spanish.

To recognize Schachner's (2003) linguistic appropriation as Mock Spanish, the language needs to be analyzed within the context of the entire book including the illustrations. While her use of Mock Spanish assigns positive qualities to Skippyjon Jones and to the author, such as a sense of humor and playful skills with a foreign language—the identity of a desirable colloquial persona that is informal and easygoing (Hill, 2009 p. 128)—critical content analysis requires the analyst to ask about the kinds of images of Chihuahuas in the books and the kinds of identities assigned to the "Mexican" characters through the use of language.

The most evident image of Mexicans is conveyed through the choice of the Chihuahua dog to represent Mexican characters. This racist stereotypical image of the Chihuahua dog, also used by Taco Bell and Disney to commodify Mexicans, caused much controversy and was interpreted by a sector of the Mexican American community and the Latino community overall, as well as by critical scholars in the field, as fostering racist stereotypes about Mexicans, yet author Schachner still decided to use it. Moreover, in guidelines for teachers distributed by Scholastic to promote the book at a conference for teachers, the dogs were introduced as "a roving band of Mexican Chihuahuas," a play on words that brings to mind an image of Mexicans as robbers and bandits.

Throughout the series, the Chihuahuas trick Skippyjon Jones into solving problems for them, an image that builds on the stereotype of Mexican Americans as treacherous (Hill, 2009). They also appear in Schachner's (2003) book as taking a siesta once they recruit the help of Skippyjon Jones. The picture in which they are sleeping has the illustration of a blurred saguaro with a Mexican hat under it, suggesting the offensive image that Mexicans call "El Pancho" (the man sleeping, leaning against a saguaro cactus, and his face covered by a hat) (Hill, 2009, p. 172), a well-known stereotype of Mexican Americans and Spanish speakers as lazy procrastinators.

Some of the Spanish words used in the picturebooks are culinary terms. The Chihuahuas are described as eating "typical" Mexican food, such as tortillas, guacamole, burritos, and frijoles (beans), "red beans, black beans, Boston baked . . ." (Schachner, 2003). In fact in *Skippyjon Jones in the Doghouse* (2005), one of the characters is called "the beaner." In addition, the expressions "Holy jalapeño!," "Holy guacamole!," "Holy frijoles!," and "Holy HOT tamales!" are overused in the series. Describing Mexicans and "Mexican" food in this repetitive and superficial way does not capture or convey powerful nuances of Latino experiences; rather, the culinary words function as clichés that misrepresent Mexicans and their culture (Barrera & Quiroa, 2003).

Linguistic appropriation through Mock Spanish has the potential to reshape the meaning of words and in this case how they can be written. Schachner's creation of words such as "tazalita" instead of "tacita" (a small cup) and "mysterioso" instead of "misterioso" are among many examples found in her books. The word "mysterioso" builds on the reader's knowledge of cognates. The use of cognates (words in two languages that share the same meaning and are written similarly) is a strategy that can support bilingual learners' literacy and biliteracy development; however, the ways it is used in the series can lead to confusion, given that not all cognates are real ones, they may look like cognates but mean something totally different.

The disregard for the grammar of Spanish and the stereotypes conveyed by the books about Mexican Americans and Latinos in the United States appear overshadowed by the humorous effect of the language. The "playful" use of language is clear not only in the "funny" rhymes but also in the author's appropriation of the music of *El Jarabe Tapatío* (the Mexican Hat Dance), a feature of Mexican culture, which has become a main characteristic of the series. The Mexican Hat Dance is overused in all the picturebooks from the series, which can be better appreciated in the audio versions of the books. Just in *Skippyjon Jones Class Action* (2011) the music of the Mexican Hat Dance is used not once but three times. Unfortunately, by making a parody of this traditional Mexican song, the author trivializes aspects of Mexican life that have deep meaning for many Mexican communities.

In sum, the use of Mock Spanish in the stories and of stereotypical cultural references, along with the illustrations, create caricatures and stereotypes of Mexicans and Spanish-speaking people in the United States. White speakers who have been confronted with Mock Spanish are often unaware of the negative effects of Mock Spanish, including the white teachers who represent most of the teaching force in the United States (Hill, 2009). In fact *Skippyjon Jones* appeared as one of teachers' preferred picturebooks in a survey conducted by the National Education Association in 2007. The book was listed in the 11th place, a prime example of how difficult it is for cultural outsiders, as Bradford reminds us in Chapter Two, to understand the worldviews and experiences of minoritized groups. Such selection reflects a lack of familiarity with the history of subordinated groups in the United States.

Moreover, by narrowly focusing on the pleasurable aspects of the reading experience, teachers—whether cultural outsiders or insiders—can overlook the normative power of whiteness and fail to identify stereotypes. In addition, the use of a Marxist framework that highlights the role of commodification in capitalist societies leads me to propose that another factor mediating the popularity of these books may relate to two important capitalist strategies employed by Dutton Children's Books and other publishers, namely, branding and synergy.

Branding and Synergy

The name "Skippyjon Jones" has become a brand and so the publishing company is taking advantage of the series through the strategy of synergy. Through this strategy the children or the customer can consume the Skippyjon Jones brand in different ways, increasing the bottom line of the company. What started as one book became a series and a look at the products based on the Skippyjon Jones brand reveals the creation of additional multimedia products. The books are promoted through Webisodes, in which parents, teachers, and children can get a taste of the series online, as a marketing strategy to sell the books.

Skippyjon Jones (2003) has also been transformed into a musical for children by TheatreworksUSA, which describes it as "an enchanting musical about unleashing your powerful imagination and following your dreams." Based in New York, this theatre group has received multiple awards and has a good reputation for providing access to theatre for students and family audiences nationwide, including underserved communities. Schools can bring their students to see the musical, paying a lower price. The musical, recommended for grades K–4, is sold to teachers for its potential to make curriculum connections. Unfortunately, the theatre company failed to acknowledge the problematic representations of Mexicans in the story.

There are also multiple products associated with the Skippyjon Jones brand, such as the drawing kit *Skippyjon Jones Keepin' Busy Kit* for ages 3 and up, published in 2014 by Grosset and Dunlap, a division of the Penguin Young Readers Group and a trademark of Penguin Group (USA). While manufactured in China, Judy Schachner retains the copyright. It sells for $16.99 in the United States and $18.99 in Canada. In the front, the box shows Skippyjon Jones's drawing of a group of cross-eyed and cockeyed dogs, as in Schachner's (2005) book. One of the mini board books (originally published by Dutton Children's Books) is a counting book that also includes Mock Spanish in the expressions "Ay, caramba!," and "oocho mucho poochos!" Again, the lack of number congruence between the adverb "mucho" and the noun "poochos," the overpronunciation and alteration of the Spanish words *ocho* and *pocho*, and the use of the well-known expression "Ay, caramba!," just for fun, point to the commodification of Mexicans and their language for entertainment and marketing purposes. Such commodification is disguised by calling the potential customer 'friend' in "Let's color, amigos!" The word "amigos"—used on the crayon box and a salient term in the series—serves to create a relationship with the audience and to disguise the economic transaction as a personal relationship. The kit also targets a potential customer interested in bilingual learning, as each crayon inside the book has the color written in English and Spanish, hinting that it is a resource for bilingual learning.

The linguistic appropriation and Mock Spanish characteristic of the series is salient in all components of the kit. All the press-out pieces to assemble start with the following introduction: "INSTRUCTION-ITOS!" accompanied by many words ending in "ito." The affixation of the Spanish suffix "ito" to English words is central to the branding of the series, leading to the commodification of Mexican language and culture that the Dutton publishing company, as part of Pearson, a megacorporation, exploits for business purposes. The marketing divisions of megacorporations know how to sell an idea, privileging entertainment while mediating cultural meanings, in this case, making caricatures of the Spanish language, of Mexicans, and of aspects of Mexican culture.

It is ironic that the linguistic resources denied to Latino children through English-only legislation, which severely limit bilingual programs, contribute to the wealth of a white author and megacorporations. In fact, Hill (2009) argues that this simultaneous suppression of Spanish for Latinos and appropriation of Spanish by whites suggests that what is at stake is white privilege, "their right to control the symbolic resources of Spanish and shape these to their own purposes" (p. 126).

Discussion

A Marxist perspective enables us to reflect on the socioeconomic factors impacting the kinds of books available for children in classrooms and libraries. Specifically, attention to the dangers of commodification helps us understand how entertainment trumps social concerns in the production of books such as *Skippyjon Jones*.

The Skippyjon Jones series does not have pedagogical value as far as learning about culture and language, given the misrepresentations of Spanish and the stereotyping of Mexicans. The fact that such misrepresentations are overshadowed by the humor of the stories makes it even more critical for teachers to pause, to acknowledge their position and ideologies in order to respect Latinos' experiences, and to plan how to discuss these texts, already available in many classrooms, with their students.

Taxel (2010) argues childhood has become a key moment in the formation of consumers with children as a primary target for global capital (p. 483). A major concern these books raise for teachers and educators is the series' potential to develop children as consumers more than as thoughtful readers who can engage aesthetically to reflect on the human experience through literature. I share Hade and Edmonson's (2003) concerns "that the desire to find entertainment, intellectual fulfillment, and spiritual well-being will become confused with a desire to accumulate branded, material possessions, that what it means to be human for children is how much stuff can they consume" (p. 140).

Moreover, while other books and series can also lead to this treatment of children as consumers, the Skippyjon Jones series is especially problematic because it is promoted as educational and because the books work against the development of intercultural understanding. Intercultural understanding allows children to see others, especially marginalized groups in the United States, as dignified persons deserving respect and to value the richness and complexity of cultures different from our own. Finally, the books are problematic because the author has tapped into a body of literature about a group that is underrepresented and whose authors, as cultural insiders, are working hard to represent the variety of experiences within a non-homogenous Latino community. To inject stereotypical representations into these efforts, while accumulating worth by doing so, can only be explained as an expression of white privilege in a capitalist society.

When a white author deliberately chooses to develop her writing agenda and business around the representation of minoritized and Indigenous communities, that author has a social responsibility. Analyzed within the historical context of colonization and linguistic repression of Spanish-speaking and Indigenous groups, the appropriation of their language and culture as commodities can be read as another expression of colonizing efforts. Vélez-Ibáñez (1996) notes that the history of Anglo–Mexican relations has often been defined by this imposed commodity identity, which has influenced how Mexicans are perceived by others (p. 7). Mexicans have fought hard against such commodification; they have created political and cultural organizations including voluntary associations, labor unions, cultural movements, and household mechanisms to accommodate and resist the larger economic and political processes of commodification in a search for cultural place and space (p. 7). The Skippyjon Jones series reinforces this commodity identity.

Conclusion

A Marxist perspective to critical content analysis invites us to read texts against the social and historical contexts in which they are produced. It also compels us to think about human agency and thus to reflect on what can we do to question and resist books' potential commodification of others. As Taxel (2010) asserts, the future of children's literature may be determined in great part by how authors, editors, and publishers resist escalating pressures to commodify literature.

Children actively make meaning and are not passive recipients of others' ideological efforts; however, texts, especially if sanctioned by teachers and librarians, can shape children's ideas about others and about themselves. Promoting series such as Skippyjon Jones and its related products in primary classrooms without addressing issues of representation may perpetuate the texts' stereotypes of Mexicans and other Latinos while encouraging consumerism. Such positioning compromises the development of critical and reflective capacities in young readers to engage with other human beings and to understand the growing diversity and complexity of our society (Hade & Edmonson, 2003).

Critical content analysis strategies can support teachers' efforts to create contexts that support children's development as thoughtful readers; readers who question how others and themselves are positioned, ignored, or misrepresented in the literature. Students can ask questions, such as: What kinds of relationships are developed among characters in a particular text and between the reader and the literature? What is the definition of success in a story? What ideologies are promoted or critiqued through the description of the characters and the consequences of their actions? To facilitate this process, we all have the responsibility as educators to acknowledge our location and ideological beliefs when reading.

Encouraging reading for pleasure and entertainment is an important aim for educators. Disregarding social concerns for the sake of entertainment, however, jeopardizes the potential of literature to support the development of what Maxine Greene (1995) richly describes as social imagination, an imagination to envision and to work for a better world.

References

Anzaldúa, G. (1987). *Borderlands/La frontera: The new mestiza*. San Francisco, CA: Aunt Lute.

Barrera, R. B. & Quiroa, R. E. (2003). The use of Spanish in Latino children's literature in English: What makes for cultural authenticity? In D. L. Fox & K. G. Short (Eds.), *Stories matter: The complexity of cultural authenticity in children's literature* (pp. 247–265). Urbana, IL: National Council of Teachers of English.

Botelho, M. J. & Rudman, M. K. (2009). *Critical multicultural analysis of children's literature: Mirrors, windows, and doors*. New York: Routledge.

Fry, R. & López, M. H. (2012). Hispanic student enrollments reach new highs in 2011. *Pew Research Center Hispanic Trends*. Retrieved from http://www.pewhispanic.org/2012/08/20/hispanic-student-enrollments-reach-new-highs-in-2011/

Greene, M. (1995). *Releasing the imagination: Essays on education, the arts, and social change*. San Francisco, CA: Jossey-Bass.

Hade, D. (2001). Curious George gets branded: Reading as consuming. *Theory into Practice, 40*(3), 158–165.

Hade, D. & Edmonson, J. (2003). Children's book publishing in neoliberal times. *Language Arts, 81*(2), 135–143.

Hill, J. H. (2009). *Everyday language of white racism*. Maiden, MA: Wiley-Blackwell.

Jackson, A.Y. & Mazzei, L. A. (2012). *Thinking with theory in qualitative research: Viewing data across multiple perspectives*. New York: Routledge.

Maciel, D. (2008). Pocho. In J. Kinsbruner & E. D. Langer (Eds.), *Encyclopedia of Latin American history and culture* (2nd ed., Vol. 5, p. 276). Detroit, MI: Charles Scribner's.

Martínez-Roldán, C. M. (2013). The representation of Latinos and the use of Spanish: A critical content analysis of *Skippyjon Jones*. *Journal of Children's Literature, 39*(1), 5–14.

Marx, K. (1997). *Capital: A critique of political economy, Vol 1*. (Marxists Internet Archive). Retrieved from https://www.marxists.org/archive/marx/works/1867-c1/index.htm

Marx, K. & Engels, F. (1970). *The German ideology: Part I with selections from parts two and three and supplementary texts*. New York: International Publishers.

National Education Association. (2007). *Teachers' Top 100 books for children*. Retrieved from http://www.nea.org/grants/teachers-top-100-books-for-children.html

Sánchez, M. E. (2011). *Pocho en español*: The anti-*pocho pocho*. *Translation Studies, 4*(3), 310–324. doi:10.1080/14781700.2011.589654

Schachner, J. (2012). Teachers. *Skippyjon Jones' Closet: For Teachers*. Retrieved from http://www.skippyjonjones.com

Taxel, J. (2010). The economics of children's book publishing in the 21st century. In S. Wolf, K. Coats, P. Enciso, & C. Jenkins (Eds.), *Handbook of research on children's and young adult literature* (pp. 479–494). New York: Routledge.

Tyson, L. (2011). *Using critical theory: How to read and write about literature* (2nd ed.). New York: Routledge.

Vélez-Ibáñez, C. G. (1996). *Border visions: Mexican cultures of the southwest United States*. Tucson: The University of Arizona Press.

Venable, V. (1945). *Human nature: The Marxian view*. New York: Knopf.

Williams, R. (1977). *Marxism and literature*. Oxford, UK: Oxford University Press.

Zipes, J. (2001). *Sticks and stories: The troublesome success of children's literature from Slovenly Peter to Harry Potter*. New York: Routledge.

Children's Literature References

Schachner, J. (2003). *Skippyjon Jones*. New York: Dutton.

Schachner, J. (2005). *Skippyjon Jones in the doghouse*. New York: Dutton.

Schachner, J. (2006). *Skippyjon Jones in mummy trouble*. New York: Dutton.

Schachner, J. (2009). *Skippyjon Jones . . . lost in spice*. New York: Dutton.

Schachner, J. (2011). *Skippyjon Jones class action*. New York: Dutton.

6

"HAVING SOMETHING OF THEIR OWN"

Passing on a Counter-Story about Family Bonds, Racism, and Land Ownership[1]

Wanda M. Brooks

During my years as a middle grade teacher and now as a researcher, the novels of Mildred Taylor have remained close by my side. Searching for multicultural literature to share with my then largely White, suburban sixth graders to more recent encounters facilitating book clubs with urban youth, Taylor's historical fiction stands the test of time and context. Initially, I chose Taylor's novels to offer readers windows through which to view the historical past of African Americans. Her highly regarded books such as *Roll of Thunder Hear My Cry* (1976) and *The Friendship* (1987) beautifully depict pivotal time periods in U.S. history including the Great Depression and the emerging Civil Rights Movement. A few years ago, while researching and co-facilitating a book club for African American seventh graders reading *The Land* (2001) by Taylor, my focus differed. In choosing this novel, the teacher and I aimed to provide a less well known narrative about the African American experience for students who already possessed deep experiential as well as acquired knowledge of their history and culture. Arguably, *The Land* provides a counter-story to commonly read fiction as well as nonfiction about the years of Reconstruction. The youth who read this novel enthusiastically agreed that Mildred Taylor's powerful writing offered them a perspective rarely imagined, shared, or read.

Throughout this chapter, I analyze *The Land*, a recipient of the 2002 Coretta Scott King Author Award. Given that the significance of Black land ownership during the period of Reconstruction gets addressed in few historical young adult books, this chapter offers a close reading of a storyline that authenticates experiences of countless mixed-raced individuals who lived during the Reconstruction era. Moreover, as a descendent of a comparable family history (my great-great grandfather received land in North Carolina bequeathed in a will by his White biological father and owner), both personal and scholarly reasons compelled me to study this novel.

I begin by situating *The Land* and its author within a tradition of historical fiction written by and about African Americans. Following this, I describe the research methodology with a focus on the critical content analysis used to examine the novel. Next, I present findings informed by using critical race theory (Ladson-Billings & Tate, 1995; Lynn & Adams, 2002) as an interpretive tool to examine the ways Taylor embeds meanings of land ownership into the novel. In particular the following themes emerged: (1) inspiration and adoration, (2) entitlement and privilege, and (3) freedom and security. The concluding section considers the importance of applying critical race theory to content analysis of historical fiction for young adults. Suggestions regarding how to effectively incorporate the African American young adult historical fiction genre within today's classrooms are also offered.

Literary Traditions and the Craft of Mildred Taylor

Since the inception of African American children's literature, its writers have often selected themes addressing discrimination or racism and overcoming their impact by obtaining literacy/education, enacting forms of protest as well as maintaining family or community solidarity (Bishop, 2007; V. Harris, 1997). This thematic tradition surfaced within a number of genres but perhaps most prominently within historical fiction. Beginning in earnest during the 1970s, these accounts recontextualized and often challenged past representations of racism or conveyed alternative depictions of African Americans through the voices of triumphant men and women who surmounted oppression (Bishop, 2007). Literary honors bestowed on books depicting African American life frequently go to historical fiction narratives (e.g., see Coretta Scott King awardees). Currently, this genre maintains its place as one of the most published, popular, and awarded of the past three decades. With respect to the genre at large, a plethora of historical fiction novels continue to be included within language arts, reading, and English curriculum. Along with *The Land*, a short list of well-known African American historical fiction (middle grades and young adult) that currently stands as favorites in Grades 4–8 include: *The Watsons Go to Birmingham—1963* (Curtis, 1995), *Fallen Angels* (Myers, 1988), *Anthony Burns: The Defeat and Triumph of a Fugitive Slave* (Hamilton, 1988), and *The Glory Field* (Myers, 1994). Additionally, *One Crazy Summer* (2010) by Rita Williams-Garcia, *Elijah of Buxton* (2007) by Christopher Paul Curtis, *Copper Sun* (2006) by Sharon Draper, and *Day of Tears* by Julius Lester (2005) make up more recent historical fiction CSK author awards for 2011, 2008, 2007, and 2006, respectively. Each of the aforementioned novels focuses on discrimination or institutionalized racism.

Writing within the African American children's literary tradition, Mildred Taylor's respectability as an accomplished writer can be measured, in part, by the caliber of her accolades. Among others, she was awarded the prestigious John Newbery Medal for *Roll of Thunder Hear My Cry* in 1976. Bader (2002) has called the stories about the Logans the seminal family saga of the second half of the twentieth century: one closely paralleling the "all American" Laura Ingalls Wilder books that popularized and endeared many readers to the little house in the big woods. Further, teachers and scholars have found Taylor's writing worthy of discussion and examination (Martin, 1998).

Despite Taylor's success, it is also important to point out that her work does incite controversy. As late as 2006, novels about the Logan family were banned in school districts across the country. Opponents from all ethnic backgrounds have argued that the racial violence and use of historicized language in some of Taylor's books take away from their literary quality and instructional appropriateness. As a result, before reading Taylor's historical fiction with children, teachers in one school district must be trained on how to introduce and present the novels to young readers (*School Library Journal*, 2004). Well aware of the opposition, in a "Note to the Reader" found in *The Land* (2001), Taylor defends her art:

> All of my books are based on stories told by my family, and on the history of the United States. In my writing I have attempted to be true to those stories and the history. . . . Although there are those who wish to ban my books because I have used language that is painful, I have chosen to use the language that was spoken during the period, for I refuse to whitewash history. The language was painful and life was painful for many African Americans, including my family. I remember the pain.
>
> *(unpaged)*

Notwithstanding the opposition, the publishing industry and countless school systems enthusiastically endorse Taylor's narratives.

The Land constitutes the prequel book within a series of seven about several generations of a southern African American family named the Logans. The Logans lived from the late 1800s to the 1960s. The novel describes Paul-Edward Logan's initial attempts to purchase land once he and his best friend Mitchell leave the former plantation of Paul-Edward's White father. Prior to their departure, readers learn about the inception of the Logan family, which includes Paul-Edward's multiracial sister, Cassie, and mother of American Indian and African ancestry named Deborah. As a woman once enslaved and raped, Deborah Logan bore two children for her "owner." At the same time, she also raised his three White sons. Paul-Edward and his older sister grow up largely unaware of the racial tensions persisting outside of their father's family. They are in many ways treated just as their White sibling counterparts. However, throughout the novel's progression, and primarily when Paul-Edward becomes a teenager and then a young man desiring to acquire acres of land, he learns firsthand of bigotry and oppression as well as the racialized life he must lead. Despite being afforded opportunities denied to his recently emancipated African American peers, such as gaining literacy and apprenticing in a trade, Paul-Edward could not escape the confines of his ethnicity.

In interviews, Taylor has explained that tales about the Logans derived from her own experiences and memories of Mississippi (Moss, 1996). Included throughout the series of books are pieces of wisdom passed on from her father and representations of the love extended to her from family members across generations. As a writer, Taylor chooses to situate her books in a personalized legacy that differs, in part, from non–African American and even other African American authors. One aim of the Logan saga includes presenting readers with a rival portrait of African American life. Taylor (1977) has "recounted not only the joy of growing up in a large and supportive family," but also her "own feelings of being faced with segregation and bigotry" ("Acceptance" par 3). According to Davis-Undiano (2004), Taylor presents herself to readers as "a writer always working fundamentally on behalf of her community" (p. 2). As one of only 3% of stories about Black life rendered by an African American writer in the year 2002, this storytelling perspective brings forth a particular nuance, authenticity and ring-true-ness that might not come through otherwise. Bishop (2007) asserts the following about writers who maintain a purpose-driven tradition of storytelling:

> African American literature has been a purposeful enterprise, seldom if ever art for art's sake. . . . Across genres, in poetry, picture books, and contemporary and historical fiction, Black authors and artists have created a body of children's literature that 1) celebrates the strengths of the Black family as a cultural institution and vehicle for survival; 2) bears witness to Black people's determined struggle for freedom, equality, and dignity; 3) nurtures the souls of Black children by reflecting back to them, both visually and verbally, the beauty and competencies that we as adults see in them; 4) situates itself through its language and its content, within African American literary and cultural contexts; and 5) honors the tradition of story as a way of teaching and as a way of knowing.
>
> *(p. 273)*

Perhaps to maintain integrity as a writer of historical fiction, Taylor relies closely on the stories passed onto her by family members. Consequently, the trueness of her fiction seems to resonate with contemporary readers. As an introduction to Taylor receiving the Neustadt Prize for Children's Literature, literary scholar Dianne Johnson (2004) explains:

> Every genre has its place and its value. The genre of historical fiction, of which Mildred Taylor is a master, will always be important in sadly ahistorical times. The particular era of which much of Taylor's writing is situated— the American Civil Rights Movement in its broadest configuration—seems like ancient times to contemporary children. So work like hers becomes more and more important as time passes. In truth though, Mildred Taylor's

writing is timeless; in a most profound way, it is bound neither to date nor place because she writes not only about American civil rights but about human rights and the human spirit. She is the consummate storyteller, and few are her equal as literary artists.

(p. 1)

Despite historical settings, Johnson insinuates that Taylor's body of work and, thus, the strong literary tradition of historical writing from a number of African American authors, remain critically important for present-day readers. Similarly, critical race theory begins to answer the question of how historical fiction, although offering perspectives on the past, might offer its readers valuable insight to historicize contemporary race relations.

Critical Race Theory

Critical race theory (CRT) is a multidisciplinary epistemology typically situated within legal studies that places race at the center of analysis (Bell, 1995). According to Lynn (2006):

One of the more crucial aspects of this discourse is the persistent use of narratives and legal cases as exemplars for telling stories about racial injustice. This approach has led to the development of educational research and theory that not only foreground race but that place it at the center of the stories of those who occupy liminal spaces in an inherently unjust society.

(p. 116)

CRT consists of a number of key conceptual tenets or approaches including: (1) racism's impermanence in American society, (2) interest convergence, (3) microaggressions, and (4) counter-storytelling (Lynn & Adams, 2002). Increasingly, tenets of CRT have been recognized within the educational community as conceptual tools that enable researchers to examine the role race plays in a variety of school related phenomena such as school funding, curriculum representations, teacher expectations, and ability grouping (Ladson-Billings & Tate, 1995; Lynn & Adams, 2002). One example of the relevancy of CRT within the context of studying children's literature includes the historical and long-standing exclusion or devaluation of books written by people of color from the literary canon. Almost two and a half decades ago, Violet Harris (1990) highlighted this phenomenon by arguing, "Few texts written by African Americans or other people of color are designated classics, even though many exhibit extraordinary literary merit, expand or reinterpret literary forms, or provide a forum for voices silenced or ignored in mainstream literature" (p. 540). Arguably, curricular and canonical debates such as this continue to be influenced by matters of race.

Although still infrequent, a few studies have relied on CRT as a theoretical framework when examining children's literature. Franzak (2003) applied CRT to an analysis of a young adult book, *Tears of a Tiger* (Draper, 1994). Regarding her rationale for choosing this theory to better understand Draper's novel, Franzak (2003) addressed the importance of "the ability to examine the construction of racial privilege and oppression as played out in the texts our students encounter" (p. 54). Citing a similar rationale for applying CRT, McNair (2008) examined historical and contemporary stories for children written by and about African Americans. The purpose of the McNair study was to conduct a comparative analysis of *The Brownies' Book*, one of the first periodicals created primarily for Black children during the Harlem Renaissance, and contemporary African American children's literature written by Patricia McKissack. The research results indicated that both bodies of work challenged dominant perspectives via counter-storytelling, were committed to social protest, and depicted literacy as important. These scholars found CRT useful perhaps because critical and cultural critiques are necessary when interpreting literature created and produced within the racialized macro system of our society. In an acceptance speech for the Alan Award, Mildred Taylor (1998) acknowledges the central role of race in her stories by saying, "My stories might not be 'politically correct' so there will be those who will be offended, but as we all know, racism is offensive. It is not polite, and it is full of pain" (par 7–8).

Methodology

The following research question guided this critical content analysis: How does a counter-story about Reconstruction get depicted in a well-regarded African American young adult novel? The primary data source consisted of the novel, *The Land*, written by Taylor in 2001. To gain insight about the narrative and, in particular, the writer's aims, I also reviewed websites about Taylor, interviews she has given about her work, as well as published articles about her body of writing. To prepare for my own close readings, I immersed myself in a wide range of background and informational texts about the Reconstruction Era with a focus on better understanding the circumstances of land ownership by mixed-raced (often newly emancipated) individuals.

Analysis

Michael Patton (1990), an expert in qualitative research methodology, defines content analysis as "the process of identifying, coding, and categorizing the primary patterns in the data" (p. 381). As an approach to Taylor's novel, I conducted critical content analysis both undergirded and analytically guided by a critical race theoretical frame. This critical content analysis allowed for a purposefully guided inductive examination of reoccurring patterns in the literature that brought forth thematic (rather than numerical) representations of the data. I also incorporated prolonged engagement with the text; I read and reread the novel multiple times to progress through several stages of coding (Glesne, 1999).

Coding Process

Although a number of tenets make up CRT, three tenets in particular were useful for the analysis of Taylor's novel. I contend that these tenets can be extended to the analysis of young adult historical fiction at large. These tenets guided my lens for coding. The first tenet describes the medium of counter-storytelling; the second tenet addresses property ownership in the United States and the privileging of Whites as a racial group; and the third tenet, which is possibly the most debated, takes into account the continued manifestation of racism in contemporary society.

As a tenet of CRT, counter-stories consist of the accounts African Americans share to voice and validate their life circumstances. Leading theorists of CRT as applied to education, Ladson-Billings and Tate (1995) note that counter-stories allow for the "psychic preservation of marginalized groups. . . . Historically, storytelling has been a kind of medicine to heal the wounds of pain caused by racial oppression" (p. 53). Counter-stories respond to racism and its dominant ideology by calling into question normative depictions of everyday living that ignore or discount structural barriers to equality faced by people of color. Although usually documented through oral narrative, I identify counter-stories as they materialize through the pens of writers and the characters personified in novels. In its entirety, then, *The Land* represents a counter-story told by the protagonist Paul-Edward Logan. This character-driven approach to counter-stories corresponds well with scholars who argue that, "CRT has roots in the African American literary tradition, drawing much of its flair from the poets, writers and artists of the Harlem Renaissance or other storytellers from communities of color who dared to be openly critical of America's racist past" (Lynn & Adams, 2002, p. 89).

The next tenet of CRT applicable to an analysis of historical fiction explicates the role of property rights in U.S. society and its relationship to Whiteness. According to Cheryl Harris (1993), during the late 1700s:

> The hyperexploitation of Black labor was accomplished by treating Black people themselves as objects of property. . . . Similarly, the conquest, removal and extermination of Native American life and culture were ratified by conferring and acknowledging the property rights of whites in Native American land. Only white possession and occupation of land was validated and therefore privileged as a basis for property rights. These distinct forms of exploitation each contributed in various ways to the construction of whiteness as property.
>
> *(p. 1716)*

As Harris explains, the privileges tied to being born White in America eventually materialized as levels of status among certain ethnic groups emerged. At the onset, Blacks were literally owned as property, but when the practice of slavery was abolished, other ways of maintaining status and privilege were enacted by some Whites. This tenet is particularly applicable to the analysis herein because the underlying conflict in *The Land* highlights the issue of who has the right to own land. Indeed, representations of land and how it is tied to economic stability, voting, and democracy as well as nourishment and health show up repeatedly in historical fiction. In this analysis, the ownership of land as property is foregrounded although the term "property" is both literally and metaphorically understood in critical race scholarship (C. Harris, 1993).

The third applicable CRT tenet addresses institutionalized racism in U.S. society. Delgado and Stafacic (2013) argue that racism is normal, not aberrant in American society. For this reason, racism can appear natural and ordinary, as opposed to abnormal. Because debates about racism's endemic and, "perhaps even permanent" (Lynn & Adams, 2002, p. 88) nature go on, historical fiction such as *The Land* offers possibilities for analyzing the antecedents and perpetuation of this phenomenon across time.

The tenets of CRT served as a theoretical guide that narrowed the chunks of texts I analyzed. I searched the novel (375 pages in length) for examples and evidence of a counter-story related to land/property ownership and racism or discrimination. I passed through the text line by line, and my unit of analysis consisted of chunks of illustrative text that exemplified the selected CRT tenets. In some instances, then, a compelling incident in the book (perhaps 2–3 pages long) received a code and in other instances a brief dialogue between two characters received one. This phase of the process resulted in approximately 24 codes. During the next phase of the process, I consolidated those codes into somewhat broader categories. These categories represented the same concepts coded, but I gave them a different name. The new list of 11 included each unique category only one time. In this respect, this stage of the coding could be loosely defined as a combination of axial coding and selective coding (Strauss, 1999). I then searched further for other patterns of overlap that could be subsumed under a broader conceptual representation. Those 11 categories were further reduced (but conceptually merged and expanded) into three broad thematic categories that serve as the structure for the findings. Additionally, the findings coincided with the arc of the novel (mapping onto the protagonist's evolution and maturation as the storyline progresses).

Findings on Race and Racism in *The Land*

Throughout the story, Paul-Edward's feelings toward land evolve, and in each instance, the evolution signifies a deepened understanding of race and racism during the Reconstruction Era. The progression and complexity of Paul-Edward's racial awareness are encapsulated by the following thematic categories: (1) inspiration and adoration, (2) privilege and entitlement, and (3) freedom and security. In discussing the three themes, I rely on my previously described tenets of CRT to authenticate, describe, and explicate the protagonist's shifting views of land within the novel.

Inspiration and Adoration

Since Paul-Edward begins the novel by perceiving the land owned by his father as a source of inspiration and adoration, contemporary readers may be confronted with their own beliefs about recently enslaved individuals. How would this population feel about the land they had toiled under great duress? The feelings of inspiration and adoration experienced by Paul-Edward are those only he shares in the novel largely because of his mixed-raced heritage. For example, although enslaved, as the son of a White owner who aimed to treat his multiracial children as if their ethnicity did not matter, Paul-Edward Logan grew up in many ways estranged from other enslaved or sharecropping individuals living on his father's plantation. Unlike those who toiled the crop fields out of mandate or necessity, Paul-Edward was inspired by and admired the acreage owned by his father. The protagonist freely moved about and explored the beauties of what the land offered while others could not. Although Paul's appreciation of land's worth developed in the story, the affective connection held by the protagonist remained at his core throughout his manhood. Reflecting on the 400 acres he hoped to purchase after leaving the guardianship of his father, Paul thinks:

> I was awed by what I saw. All around me was emerald green, and above that, God's own bluest skies, blessed only with two or three perfect rolls of pillow-like clouds. And meadow lay all around me, and a forest of longleaf pine dotted with oak and hicory circled the meadow. Gazing from the slope where I sat beside the rock, I felt I was sitting where God Himself must have once sat and been pleased with Himself.
>
> *(Taylor, 2001, p. 159)*

Paul's initial encounter with the acreage he planned to own certainly represented something deeper and perhaps spiritual.

In contrast, Paul's best friend Mitchell, formally enslaved on Mr. Logan's plantation, explained that instead of wanting to settle down, he merely desired to be free of the land burden. When Paul asked Mitchell where he would go if he did not own anything, he replies, "Go where I can. One place 'bout the same as another t' me. 'Spect it don't matter, long as somebody's not whippin' on me" (Taylor, 2001, p. 119). Herein opposing views emerge between two individuals enslaved on the same plantation. Both characters articulate a convincing view. Together they constitute a counter-story since each account offers readers a view from the lived experiences of an exploited group, enslaved African Americans.

Despite what at first comes across as Paul-Edward's strictly aesthetic and agrarian views of a bountiful and adored land, Moss (1996) has written that in Taylor's novels she masterfully blends traditions of agrarian society often found in children's literature with "strategies of social realism" (p. 404). So, although Paul-Edward adored and received inspiration from land, as he grew older he became increasingly aware of its broader ideological meanings.

Entitlement and Privilege

Seeing ownership through his mixed-raced and somewhat privileged vantage point, Paul-Edward's decisions in the narrative partly derive from a strong belief in feeling entitled to owning acres of land. CRT points out that property ownership essentially in the hands of the White majority population has been a stable construct since the inception of the United States (C. Harris, 1993). Paul-Edward's situation in the novel provides some insight as to why this may have been the case.

In a number of ways the protagonist's desires differed from other recently emancipated African Americans who expected from their government a mere "40 acres and a mule," despite the decades of servitude they endured (Smith, 2003). Surely, some wanted (and a number of their descendants still argue for) what many now believe was within their legal rights to request. Others, like Paul-Edward and his African–Indian American mother, proudly dismissed any offer of acreage that derived from parceled land tilled on by enslaved men, women, and children. By instilling in her protagonist a desire to select and purchase his own 400 acres, Taylor conveys that freed African Americans from mixed-raced backgrounds may have experienced varying states of ideological entitlement and knowledge of the significance of property privileges and rights comparable to their White counterparts. Thus, as a form of CRT counter-narrative, this novel disputes unnuanced depictions of freed African Americans living during the Reconstruction Era and offers another perspective from which to read history.

Shedding some insight into feelings of entitlement, Paul-Edward could not comprehend that land possession might be a privilege unattainable even to him:

> I knew Miz Crenshow meant well, but I never told her what I truly wanted. That I told only to Mitchell. What I wanted was land. I wanted land like my daddy's. In a way, I suppose, I was driven by the thought of having land of my own. In my early years, before I truly realized my two worlds, I had figured that I'd always live on my daddy's land, that my daddy's land would be mine and I'd always be a part of it. When I discovered that wouldn't be, I created my own land in my mind I knew that land was what I had to have.
> *(Taylor, 2001, p. 142)*

This engrained sense of entitlement propelled the audaciousness in which the protagonist negotiated with White men. He eventually secured a deal in which he worked his first 40 acres and then purchased and arranged a payoff for the 200 acres (out of an intended 400) he subsequently obtained. Perhaps a metaphoric reference to the "40 acres and a mule" retribution African Americans believed they would receive during the Reconstruction Era, Taylor's protagonist viewed his 40 acres as an initial step toward eventually purchasing the acreage he dreamed about.

While contemporary legal disputes currently focus on whether the "40 acres and a mule" legislation was ever authorized, historians generally agree that African Americans expected some compensation for their servitude (Smith, 2003). In *The Land* and in history, the 40 acres were not allotted to Paul-Edward even though he maintained his part of the contract. Just like countless others, he worked and received nothing tangible in return. Again closely resembling history, Paul-Edward never receives his share. But he is offered, under false pretense, a chance to sharecrop for Mr. Granger, who explains, "Now you can stay on and sharecrop, if you want. I'm being as fair as I can be with you, considering what you gone and done" (Taylor, 2001, p. 343). Mr. Granger and others living during the Reconstruction period certainly understood how property ownership ensured a modicum of family security, earnings, and even political rights as current CRT scholars point out (C. Harris, 1993). Although this idea was in its infancy, these certainties may have been realized by Paul-Edward as well. Along with feeling inspired by and entitled to land, an augmenting view in the story suggests that a title to land represented true freedom to counter the grips of institutionalized racism.

Freedom and Security

The protagonist's steadfast determination to purchase Hollenbeck's 200 acres provides an illustrative example of how the ending of slavery did not necessarily guarantee African American freedom and security, so to speak. In fact, after Emancipation, racism perpetuated itself not necessarily on legal grounds but on so-called moral ones as advanced by CRT scholars (Lynn & Adams, 2002). Below, a banker explains why his ethics prevent him from giving Paul-Edward a loan:

> "You have no financial record here. You have no farming background here. That four hundred acres is good land, all right, but it's a white man's kind of land, too expensive for you. Why it wasn't so long ago it was against the law for a negra, I don't care how white looking to even own farmland in the state of Mississippi, and here you are talking about buying Hollenbeck land?"
>
> *(Taylor, 2001, p. 298)*

Throughout Taylor's body of work, the persistence of racism across generations and the degree to which the prevention of land ownership perpetuates varied injustices remains central. In *Roll of Thunder Hear My Cry* (Taylor, 1976) much of the plot revolves around aggressive and blatant efforts to take back the acreage

Paul-Edward eventually purchases. Toward the concluding chapters in *The Land*, Paul receives a number of opportunities to give back his freedom and security. Reflecting on Charles Jamison's extended hand of friendship, Paul recalls, "I thanked Charles Jamison for his offer, but I didn't figure to ask his help on anything. I liked him and I liked his son, but I didn't intend to be beholden to any white man. Not again" (Taylor, 2001, p. 268). Early in the novel, a foreshadowing of the freedom and security the protagonist desires comes from his mother who says:

> "Paul, you still got your deciding what you want. There's time enough. But whatever you decide on, I want you to have something of your own. That's important. You gotta have something of your own."
>
> *(p. 69)*

Later, readers find out that Paul-Edward's mother wanted this dream for herself as well. She saved money over the years to purchase the small plot she lived on and bequeathed to Cassie and Paul-Edward. However, she hoped Paul would use the gift not to settle on, but to make a better life for himself somewhere else. As if this desire represented what many free women of color wanted for their offspring during Reconstruction, Taylor chooses to reiterate the memorable idiom in the novel's final pages. Through the speech of Caroline's (Paul's fiancé) mother Rachel Perry, the enduring hope is conveyed to her eventual son-in-law, "Paul Logan, I gots my worries 'bout Caroline stayin' on here, but I ain't been tryin' t' get her t' leave. . . . This here's her place now. She needs t' keep it. She needs t' work it. She needs t' be on it. I wants her t' have somethin' of her own" (Taylor, 2001, p. 323). In the end, Paul-Edward and his wife, Caroline, deeply appreciate the significance of having something of their own. They grow to perceive land ownership as something tangible to secure their family and vital to freeing themselves from the grips of oppression.

Discussion and Conclusion

Standing in opposition to slavery, sharecropping, and, thus, institutionalized racism, Paul-Edward Logan's desire to acquire 400 acres represents both a counter-story and a rhetorical move against the historical White-male normativity of property ownership and endemic racism explicated in CRT. The ownership of land has always symbolized citizenship in America. It was the device used by "our founding fathers" to decide who voted and who did not; who had a voice and who went silent. Land defined the "haves" and the "have-nots" in American history. As a result, symbolically land acted as a mythical divide along racial lines. Black people were not supposed to own land or property (along with humanity and dignity), they were supposed to be property and on paper synonymous with the land itself. The character Paul-Edward Logan disrupts this American mythology and asks readers to reconsider the ambiguity of racial and geographical divides.

Throughout this chapter, I have demonstrated how applying CRT as a tool for critical content analysis enables a foregrounding of racial issues applicable to a wide range of young adult historical fiction. Since studies of reader response to literature reveal how youth can construct sophisticated understandings of narratives that situate characters as participants in a highly racialized society (Brooks & McNair, 2009), coupling historical fiction like *The Land* to a theoretical frame such as CRT appears significant for a least three essential reasons.

First, the CRT lens enables researchers, teachers, and teacher-educators as well as youth to systematically understand some of racism's enduring influence from the perspective of those exploited. Counter-stories acknowledge the ways in which experiential knowledge performs as a valid methodological source for conveying and authenticating one's life circumstances. When viewing the novel as a whole, Taylor evokes this authentication through the counter-narrative of the protagonist Paul-Edward Logan. By chronicling the life of an African/Indian/European adolescent, enduring and living beyond the years of slavery, this novel portrays the complexities of race and race relations in the United States. For a number of reasons, these complexities are still overlooked in many of the texts read in today's schools. The grand narrative of Black life in America is further complicated and nuanced by Paul-Edward's story.

Second, through the tenet addressing property ownership and its relationship to Whiteness, a reader or a teacher facilitating a reading or literature discussions can tangibly grapple with one of racism's antecedents. Undoubtedly, CRT focuses close reads of historical fiction in such a way that racism becomes the center of the analysis. This is not to suggest that historical fiction must only be read through such a racialized viewpoint. It does mean, however, that when warranted a tenet focusing on property ownership provides an illustrative example through which to address the vast and sometimes elusive concept of racism.

Third, because CRT represents a contemporary rather than a historical theoretical frame, connections between the past and present are evoked for readers. It remains important not to disproportionately situate injustices in the past. CRT points out that institutionalized racism in the form of property ownership still maintains a pervasive hold in our society. Indeed cultural critics have argued that a lack of home ownership in poor communities of color disproportionately affects the quality of education children receive because of a diminished tax base. Home ownership and residential segregation likewise play a role in reinscribing the racial and class-based stratification present in parts of today's urban and suburban areas (Lynn & Adams, 2002). To illustrate such a claim for young readers, I suggest using an approach that highlights past–present racial linkages between texts. For instance, when discussing *The Land* and other novels of historical fiction a pedagogical decision might be to read this genre with a companion text. An example of a historical–contemporary pairing that could be analyzed and read through a CRT lens includes: *The Land* paired with Andrea Pinkney's (1995) *Hold Fast to Dreams* (a book about a Black family moving to a home in an all-White community) or *The Land* paired with Jaime Adoff's (2005) *Jimi & Me* (a book about a mixed-raced teenager who defies typical representations of an African American young male). Both of these pairings would set the context for discussions of racism as manifested in the past as well as within the milieu of today's society. *The Land*, the story of Paul-Edward Logan's steadfast quest to feel inspired by, entitled to, and then fully freed through land ownership, represents the one story Mildred Taylor felt deeply compelled to write (Brown, 2001). Taylor's narrative suggests a relationship between land and racial identity that is pervasive throughout American history. Taylor's fictionalized Logan family struggled across generations to both endure and stand up against racism and to ultimately acquire land as "something of their own." When considered through a CRT lens, this novel authenticates the lives of many and provides a great deal of insight regarding issues of race and racism in the past and present.

Note

1 With kind permission from Springer Science+Business Media: *Children's Literature in Education: An International Quarterly*, An author as a counter-storyteller: Applying critical race theory to a Coretta Scott King Award book 40(1), 2009, 33–43, Wanda Brooks.

References

Bader, B. (2002). How the little house gave ground: The beginnings of multiculturalism in a new, Black children's literature. *The Horn Book Magazine*, November/December, 657–673.

Bell, D. (1995). Who's afraid of critical race theory? *University of Illinois Law Review, 95*, 893–910.

Bishop, R. (2007). *Free within ourselves: The development of African American children's literature.* Westport, CT: Greenwood Press.

Brooks, W. & McNair, J. (2009). "But this story of mine is not unique": A review of research on African Americans in children's literature. *Review of Educational Research, 79*(1), 125–162.

Brown, J. (2001). Stories behind the book: The land. *Publishers Weekly*, October, 24–27.

Davis-Undiano, R. (2004). Mildred D. Taylor and the art of making a difference. *World Literature Today*, May–August, 11–13.

Delgado, R. & Stafacic, J. (Eds.). (2013). *Critical race theory: The cutting edge.* Philadelphia: Temple University Press.

Franzak, J. (2003). Hopelessness and healing: Racial identity in young adult literature. *The New Advocate, 16*, 43–56.

Glesne, C. (1999). *Becoming qualitative researchers: An introduction.* New York: Longman.

Harris, C. (1993). Whiteness as property. *Harvard Law Review, 106*, 1707–1791.

Harris, V. (1990). African American children's literature: The first one hundred years. *Journal of Negro Education, 59*, 540–555.

Harris, V. (1997). Children's literature depicting blacks. In V. Harris (Ed.), *Using multiethnic literature in the K-8 classroom* (pp. 21–54). Norwood, MA: Christopher-Gordon.

Johnson, D. (2004). A tribute to Mildred Taylor. *World Literature Today*, May–August, 4.

Ladson-Billings, G. & Tate, W. (1995). Towards a critical race theory of education. *Teachers College Record, 97,* 47–69.

Lynn, M. (2006). Race, culture and the education of African Americans. *Educational Theory, 56*(1), 107–119.

Lynn, M. & Adams, M. (2002). Introductory overview to the special issue on critical race theory and education: Recent developments in the field. *Equity & Excellence in Education, 35,* 87–92.

Martin, M. (1998). Exploring the works of Mildred Taylor: An approach to teaching the Logan family novels. *Teaching and Learning Literature,* January–February, 5–13.

McNair, J. C. (2008). A comparative analysis of *The Brownies' Book* and contemporary African American children's literature written by Patricia C. McKissack. In W. M. Brooks & J. C. McNair (Eds.), *Embracing, evaluating, and examining African American children's and young adult literature* (pp. 3–29). Lanham, MD: Scarecrow.

Moss, A. (1996). Mildred D. Taylor. In M. Kutzer (Ed.), *Writers of multicultural fiction for young adults* (pp. 401–413). Westport, CT: Greenwood Press.

Patton, M. (1990). *Qualitative evaluation and research methods.* Newbury Park, CA: Sage.

School Library Journal. (2004). Censorship roundup, March, 22.

Smith, J. (2003, February 21). The enduring myth of forty acres and a mule. *The Chronicle of Higher Education, 39,* pp. B11 & F24.

Strauss, A. (1999). *Qualitative analysis for social scientists.* Cambridge: Cambridge University Press.

Taylor, M. (1977). Newbery award acceptance. *The Horn Book,* August, 401–409.

Taylor, M. (1998). Acceptance speech for the 1997 Alan Award. *The ALAN Review.* 8 pars. Retrieved August 29, 2007 from http://scholar.lib.vt.edu/ejournals/ALAN/spring98/

Children's Literature References

Adoff, J. (2005). *Jimi & me.* New York: Hyperion.

Curtis, C. P. (1995). *The Watsons go to Birmingham—1963.* New York: Delacorte.

Curtis, C. P. (2007). *Elijah of Buxton.* New York: Scholastic.

Draper, S. (1994). *Tears of a tiger.* New York: Simon and Schuster.

Draper, S. (2006). *Copper sun.* New York: Simon and Schuster.

Hamilton, V. (1988). *Anthony Burns: The defeat and triumph of a fugitive slave.* New York: Knopf.

Lester, J. (2005). *Day of tears: A novel in dialogue.* New York: Hyperion.

Myers, W. D. (1988). *Fallen angels.* New York: Scholastic.

Myers, W. D. (1994). *The glory field.* New York: Scholastic.

Pinkney, A. (1995). *Hold fast to dreams.* New York: Morrow.

Taylor, M. (1976). *Roll of thunder hear my cry.* New York: Puffin.

Taylor, M. (1987). *The friendship.* New York: Puffin.

Taylor, M. (2001). *The land.* New York: Penguin.

Williams-Garcia, R. (2010). *One crazy summer.* New York: HarperCollins.

7

REPRESENTATIONS OF SAME SEX MARRIAGE IN CHILDREN'S PICTURE STORYBOOKS

Janine M. Schall

> Mom was dancing around the living room. In the afternoon. On a school day!
>
> "What're you doing?"
>
> Mom picked me up and started dancing again. "Rosie, I'm so happy, I'm almost as happy as the day you were born. . . . Mum and I are getting married!"
>
> (Setterington, 2004)

It's an exciting day when Mom and Mum decide to marry, second only to the day of Rosie's birth. *Mom and Mum Are Getting Married* (Setterington, 2004) begins with this happy scene. This book, originally published in Canada, appeared during a time of change, after court decisions had legalized same sex marriage in 8 of 10 Canadian provinces, but before the Civil Marriage Act of 2005 provided a gender-neutral definition of marriage. The United States has recently undergone its own state of change as a patchwork of states individually legalized or banned same sex marriage before a Supreme Court decision in June 2015 finally legalized it across the United States.

Marriage equality advocates have argued that marriage is a right, not a privilege in the United States. However, the fight for marriage equality was a difficult process, with multiple roadblocks and setbacks. Despite the Supreme Court decision, the fight continues in other forms as some states and localities introduce legislation that allows government officials and commercial vendors who oppose same sex marriage to opt out of providing services. However, same sex marriage is now legal in the United States, and social acceptance is growing as new kinds of family structures are legitimated by social custom and legal recognition. While stable and lasting same sex relationships have existed for many years and were increasingly accepted in many parts of the country even before the Supreme Court decision, legal recognition opens the door to a variety of legal and economic benefits.

Although there continues to be resistance to same sex marriages by certain cultural, political, and religious groups, acceptance is increasingly evident. Today's children will experience these expanded family structures as both normal and equal to traditional heterosexual relationships. One way that children can learn about these expanded possibilities is through children's books. Books that depict same sex marriages in authentic, positive ways are important for children who have same sex parents and for children who are themselves lesbian or gay. In addition, these books provide a resource for all children who are learning about the many ways of being in this world. However, books can also reinforce negative or limited perspectives and perpetuate the status quo. Children's book publishing has struggled with issues of diversity and representation of all kinds (Horning, 2014), with increasing numbers of people wondering why certain groups are privileged with abundant representation while others are all but invisible. In this chapter I explore how these issues play out in children's picture storybooks featuring same sex marriage.

Theoretical Frame

Intersectionality and privilege theories are theoretical frames that are useful in examining picture storybooks where same sex marriage is a central part of the plotline. Intersectionality arose from black feminist theory out of a recognition that feminist thinking of the time often privileged the issues and experiences of white, middle-class women, while ignoring or negating the experiences of women of color (Berger & Guidroz, 2009). Kimberlé Crenshaw, a legal scholar working with black feminist issues, is often credited with coining the term 'intersectional' as a label for an approach to thinking that recognizes the limitations inherent in a examinations of single aspects of identity (Grzanka, 2014a).

Intersectionality is the examination of how various aspects of identity intersect within systems of social, cultural, and political power structures and beliefs to produce the lived experiences of people (Berger & Guidroz, 2009; May, 2015). Key tenets of intersectionality include:

- Lived identities exist within a dynamic matrix of different group memberships, power structures, and sites of oppression and resistance. Identit(ies) are not cumulative or additive.
- Any examination of identit(ies) must include an analysis of systems of power and inequality, in which privilege and oppression are enmeshed.
- The analysis itself is a form of social justice and a call for social action. Rather than being neutral research, its overt goal is meaningful change.

Although many examinations of identity focus on one dimension such as race or sexual orientation at a time, intersectionality understands that "individuals are simultaneously members of many groups that are distinct yet interact to impact their lives simultaneously" (Ferber & Herrera, 2013, p. 97). Intersectionality rejects binary thinking, such as the idea that a black lesbian can choose to be or will be treated as only black or only a lesbian in different contexts. It also rejects an additive approach to identity: a black lesbian is not black + female + homosexual, with each identity being added to the others. Instead, all the aspects of a person's identity influence and interact with each other, forming a new way of being. This matrix thinking explores the multiplicities of identity and how they are formed by, exist within, and perpetuate or resist systems of power, oppression, marginalization, and privilege. This does not mean, however, that every aspect of identity carries equal weight in the eyes of the individual or in the eyes of society. By treating every aspect of identity as equally important, it becomes easy to deemphasize aspects such as race, which can be difficult and uncomfortable to confront. While an intersectional approach must consider all the intertwined and simultaneous aspects of identity, a "flattening of difference" that equalizes the weight of the different aspects tends to lose a focus on race, as privileged white people shift the discussion, often unconsciously, to other aspects they may find easier to discuss (Luft, 2009).

Intersectionality recognizes that people live within systems and structures of power, which produce and sustain both privilege and oppression. Various systems of inequality intersect and work together to produce discriminatory and oppressive practices and the way people live their lives can't be examined without an explicit analysis of these systems (May, 2015). For example, in the United States the fight for marriage equality took place within a political and economic system that rewards marriage with multiple legal and financial benefits that are not available to the unmarried, even those in long-term, committed relationships. By being excluded from legal marriage, LGBT people were defined, at least in part, as lesser by these systems.

Grzanka (2014a) notes, "Intersectionality is foremost about studying multiple dimensions of inequality and developing ways to resist and challenge these various forms of oppression" (p. xv). This approach examines hidden forms of collusion between resistance and oppression and oppressive practices which are often hidden in plain view. For example, a school may try to promote girls' interest in science by holding a "Mom and Me" science night where girls and their mothers do fun science experiments. The school is doing positive work confronting gender stereotypes and inequalities even as it excludes girls who have a family structure that does not include a mother or girls in families where the mother works at night. As such, intersectionality is a form of social justice, bringing to light inequalities. Intersectionality has "been forged in the context of struggles for social justice as a means to challenge dominance, foster critical imaginaries, and craft collective models of change" (May, 2015, p. xi).

Privilege theory is closely related to intersectionality. A key tenet of privilege theory is that unearned privilege is the flip side of oppression (Case, 2013). In order to examine the world as it is, privilege must be examined along with oppression. Privilege theory arose from McIntosh's (1988) early work and reflections on the "invisible backpack" of white privilege. It examines the unearned advantages provided by perceived membership in dominant social groups and is inextricably intertwined with oppression and inequality (Case, 2013). Everyone has a mix of privileged and oppressed identities that contribute to the lived experiences of a person; a person can be both privileged and oppressed at the same time. For example, a white gay man carries gender and race privilege while at the same time dealing with oppressive aspects of social and institutional homophobia.

People can be privileged along many aspects of identity—and doubly privileged when two or more privileged identities intersect. For example, heterosexual privilege defines the sexual orientation norm and includes unearned benefits afforded to those with a heterosexual orientation (Griffin, D'Errico, Harro, & Schiff, 2007). One example of this benefit is the ability to find positive representations of people like one's self in books. Rios and Stewart (2013) ask, "Why are lesbian, gay, bisexual and queer persons denied the privilege of positive representations and information about themselves in mainstream educational curricula? And, finally, do heterosexual students earn the privilege of seeing exemplars with whom they identify each day they attend school?" (p. 122).

Membership in a privileged group obviously provides benefits for a few, while excluding many others from those same benefits, but less acknowledged is that privilege has costs as well as benefits (Wise & Case, 2013), because group members must conform to group norms which can be restrictive and damaging. Questioning and dismantling privilege ultimately benefits both the non-privileged and the privileged.

A few recent studies have applied intersectionality theory to children's literature. Lester (2014) examined 68 LGBT-themed children's books through an intersectional frame and discusses how the books reinforced heteronormativity at the expense of diverse queer identities. Blackburn and Smith (2010) share how they examined the limitations of their attempts to use LGBT-themed texts to combat homophobia within a deeply heteronormative context. They suggest an intersectional approach as a way to help adolescent readers think more deeply about such texts.

Methodology

Several years ago I began examining picturebooks with LGBT characters through a content analysis that focused on the authenticity and representations of the LGBT characters. As part of this work, I compiled a list of all the picturebooks I could find that had at least one LGBT character, were available for purchase in the United States, and were either traditionally published or, if self-published, had been reviewed by a respected source. Over the years I have added to the list and examined each book for the sexual orientation, race/ethnicity, social class, gender representations, and family role, among other things, of each LGBT character.

Among the books on the list are a small number of picture storybooks that feature a same sex wedding as part of the plot.

I began this critical content analysis by asking, *How are same sex marriages depicted in children's picture storybooks?* For this question I looked at the picture storybooks with LGBT characters in my broader collection and gathered together the books that had a same sex marriage as the central plotline. It should be noted that there are several self-published picture storybooks featuring same sex marriage such as *My Uncle's Wedding* by Eric Ross (2011), which I did not include. I examined the following six books in this specific order, reflecting the dates and social context in which the books were published.

- *Daddy's Wedding* by Michael Willhoite (1996) is a sequel to Willhoite's *Daddy's Roommate* (1990), the first picture storybook that featured gay parents. In *Daddy's Wedding* 10-year-old Nick's father and his roommate Frank have decided to get married. When Nick questions whether two men can get married, they explain that they'll have a commitment ceremony. Nick, his mother, and his stepfather are all invited to the festive backyard wedding, with Nick serving as best man.
- *King & King* in 2000 by Linda de Haan and Stern Nijland is a fairy tale import from the Netherlands. The Queen decrees that her son must find a bride and marry. Although he's unenthusiastic about the task, potential brides soon arrive at the palace from all over the world. None meets with his approval, until the last princess arrives accompanied by her brother. It's love at first sight, and the two princes marry with the Queen's blessing.
- *Mom and Mum Are Getting Married* written by Ken Setterington and illustrated by Alice Priestley in 2004 is the first picture storybook with a lesbian couple getting married. Rosie works hard to convince her moms that they really need a flower girl at their wedding. Although they decide that Rosie and her brother Jack can carry the rings—and Rosie can also scatter some flower petals while she serves as ring bearer—on the day of the wedding Mom and Mum worry that the children won't be able to handle their responsibilities. Rosie comes up with the perfect plan and the wedding goes smoothly.
- The next book to appear, *Uncle Bobby's Wedding* by Sarah Brannen (2008), features a gay couple, this time pictured in the illustrations as anthropomorphized guinea pigs. Chloe's Uncle Bobby and his friend Jamie have decided to get married. Chloe is dubious, afraid that she'll lose her favorite uncle. He reassures her that their relationship won't change, and after having several fun experiences with both Bobby and Jamie, Chloe becomes happy to participate in the wedding as flower girl.
- *Operation Marriage* written by Cynthia Chin-Lee and illustrated by Lea Lyon is one of two books with lesbian couples getting married published in 2011. The book is set during the time period when California was getting ready to vote on Proposition 8, which would, if passed, prohibit same sex marriage. Alex loses her best friend Zach when he tells her that her parents aren't

married because two women can't get married. Alex's mothers reassure her that they've had a commitment ceremony, but Alex and her brother decide that they want their moms to get married instead. After a successful campaign by the children, Mama Lee and Mama Kathy marry surrounded by family and friends.

• *Donovan's Big Day* written by Lesléa Newman and illustrated by Mike Dutton was also published in 2011. The book follows Donovan from the time he wakes up through a day of activities, tracking all the things he has to do to get ready for and to participate in his mothers' wedding.

My goal with this study is not to decide whether these six books are good or bad, but rather to "connect them to larger cultural constructs and social forces that may simultaneously reflect or subvert structural inequalities" (Grzanka, 2014b, p. 135). While I was familiar with all of these books and had examined them in terms of identity categories (race, ethnicity, socioeconomic status, family role, etc.), in some cases it had been several years since I read the books. I began this study by rereading each to refamiliarize myself with the plot and characters. As I read, I made notes about my response to the books and my thinking about their depictions of same sex marriage.

Next, I turned to the professional literature. I explored critical multicultural theory and postcolonial theory, which led me to intersectionality. From my initial forays into intersectional theory, I felt it had the theoretical complexity to shed light on some of the contradictions I'd seen and frustrations I'd had with this collection of books. I continued reading as much as possible about intersectionality, eventually expanding into privilege theory as well, taking notes as I read to keep track of my thinking.

When I felt I had a good understanding of both theories, I developed a short list of questions to frame my analysis and returned to the picture storybooks. As I carefully reread each book and examined the illustrations, I asked, *Where are the sites of oppression and privilege? How is power and privilege operating in these books across different levels? Where are the intersections between aspects of identity and social structures, between identity and power, etc.?* As I read, I kept track of my thinking by writing memos to myself for each book.

After this initial analysis, I revisited the theory and did a second close reading of the picture storybooks. This time I paid particular attention to the representations of lesbian or gay characters, their relationships with others, and the textual and visual depiction of the wedding ceremony and celebration. Again, I wrote memos to keep track of my thinking. As I concluded my analysis I examined my research memos to see what themes and patterns appeared repeatedly.

Findings and Discussion

The findings are organized around several interrelated themes that emerged from my analysis of the books.

Lesbians and Gays Are Depicted in Ways that Promote Invisibility of LGBT People of Color and Other Large Segments of the LGBT Community

Lesbians and gays are incredibly diverse, coming from every racial, ethnic, and religious group and ranging from destitute to wealthy. Yet their depictions in these books are narrow, with no evidence of diversity. All the major lesbian or gay characters are white, middle-class, English-speaking adults in stable relationships who are pursuing marriage. All are able-bodied and gender-conforming. While these books normalize same sex marriage, they do so by perpetuating the myth that lesbians and gays are middle-class white people. As Bérubé (2001) notes, "In the United States today, the dominant image of the typical gay man is a white man who is financially better off than most everyone else" (p. 234).

The fact that gay men—and by extension, lesbians—equals white in many people's eyes and in the depictions in these books is no accident. Bérubé (2001) describes social and political whitening practices that support "a web of unquestioned beliefs—that gay whiteness is unmarked and unremarkable, universal and representative, powerful and protective, a cohesive bond" (p. 237). The equal status of gay marriage is established through reliance on the dominant norm. Books such as these, where lesbian and gay characters of color are nonexistent, result from and perpetuate such beliefs, thus fitting neatly into dominant cultural, political, and economic systems. The result is the continuation of oppressive practices such as higher rates of employment issues for LGBT people of color than for LGBT people who are white (Stachelberg & Burns, 2013).

In addition, the books portray all lesbian or gay couples as wanting to be married, in large part, because they are raising or want to raise children. Each book, with the exception of *King & King*, is centered around a child. In the books with lesbian characters, this child is the son or daughter of the couple getting married and the story is told from the young child's viewpoint. Because all of the lesbian couples already have children it is clear that marriage is not necessary to produce children. However, having children within a legally recognized relationship—a marriage—is highly valued and expected in the United States. As the lesbian couples marry, this regularizes their union and provides a better home environment for children in the eyes of many. Of course, marriage also provides explicit protections to children and their parents, as *Operation Marriage* alludes to in this conversation between Mama Kathy and her two children:

"We had a commitment ceremony, but we couldn't get a marriage license back then."

"So you're not really married?" I asked.

"Well, no, but we've done everything possible to have the same rights as married people. You know that I've adopted both of you."

(Chin-Lee, 2011, unpaged)

The books with gay characters are also, for the most part, child-focused. In *Daddy's Wedding*, Nick is the son of one of the men getting married. In *Uncle Bobby's Wedding*, the story centers around niece Chloe, who is comforted by the idea that her beloved uncle is getting married so he can have a child just like Chloe. It should be noted that the one exception to the child-centered focus, *King & King*, has a sequel, *King & King & Family* (de Haan & Nijland, 2004), which is about the princes adopting a child. There are no books with any major lesbian or gay characters who are single, or who choose not to marry.

These books portray a very small selection of the lived realities of lesbian and gays, leaving everyone else overlooked and invisible. One privilege carried by the white middle class is that their lives are regularly depicted in books for children. In these six books—the only children's storybooks featuring same sex marriage available from traditional publishers in the United States that I am aware of—the white, middle-class characters extend the privilege of representation in children's literature to a narrow, previously excluded group: white, middle-class lesbian and gay characters who are pursuing marriage. Yet the greater proportion of lesbians and gays remain unrepresented. Their invisibility reinforces the idea that lesbians and gays are white. In this set of books, African American or Latino lesbians and gays are invisible (Fryberg & Townsend, 2008) with no representation at all available through the major characters or even in the few same sex couples depicted in the background illustrations. These groups are invisible at the intersections of race, ethnicity, and sexual orientation (Purdie-Vaughns & Eibach, 2008), which means that these books "promote positive possible selves for privileged students . . . while rendering invisible other information that might inform positive possible selves for marginalized students" (Rios & Stewart, 2013, pp. 117–118).

The Books Exist Within, Are Written Out Of, and Perpetuate Various Social and Political Contexts

These books are a product of specific historical and political contexts and also help produce future historical and political contexts. *Daddy's Wedding* appeared at a time when legal same sex marriage seemed like an impossible dream to most LGBT people—and to many a political issue so far from achievable that few wanted to spend time advocating for it. In the book, Daddy carefully explains that by 'wedding' he means 'commitment ceremony.' This book appeared four years before Vermont became the first U.S. state to legalize same sex commitment ceremonies, so the event in *Daddy's Wedding* celebrates a personal bond that is not sanctioned by the state. However, *Daddy's Wedding* was no doubt an important book for gay parents and may have played a role in the slow movement toward marriage equality.

Mom and Mum Are Getting Married, originally published in Canada, appeared in 2004. At this point in Canadian history, court decisions had legalized same sex marriage in 8 of 10 provinces and for the 90% of Canada's citizens who lived in these areas. In 2005 the Civil Marriage Act provided a gender-neutral defini-tion of marriage, thus legalizing it across the nation. *King & King* appeared in the Netherlands one year before that country became the first country in the world to legalize same sex marriage. *Uncle Bobby's Wedding* and *Donovan's Big Day* both appeared during the rapidly expanding political push for marriage equality. These books reflect the political and social contexts of the time in which they are writ-ten but also help solidify the gains of the fight for marriage equality and normal-ize the strongly contested event of same sex marriage.

Operation Marriage is the only book that explicitly discusses politics, referencing the campaign for Proposition 8, a California ballot proposition and state consti-tutional amendment which banned same sex marriage after being passed by the voters in 2008:

> Our parents looked worried. "Sounds like Prop 8 might pass. If it does, we won't be able to marry," Mama Kathy told us.
> Soon, signs popped up in our neighborhood. Mama Lee hammered one into our lawn.
> Let's Keep California Great. Vote No On Prop 8.
> *(Chin-Lee, 2011, unpaged)*

Operation Marriage describes the brief period of time between same sex marriage being legal and being banned in California and the effects on one family. As such, this book realistically documents a time of turmoil and conflict and places the decision to marry within this political context.

Marriage has meant different things to different people across history (Monsma, 2014). At various times and in certain cultures it meant polygamy. In others, it meant the union of one man and one woman. In some times it relegated the wife to be the property of the husband. And sometimes marriage has been limited to particular groups. One good example of how marriage has changed in the United States is shown in *The Case for Loving: The Fight for Interracial Marriage* by Selina Alko (2015), who draws parallels between the fight for interracial marriage and the fight for same sex marriage in her author's note. However marriage has changed over the years, it has always been bound by civic and religious rules, accompanied by social customs that have defined what marriage is, who has access to it, what it should look like, and what marriage means in terms of legal rights. Today, marriage in the United States brings with it multiple legal and financial benefits, most of which are inaccessible to unmarried couples. Then, too, mar-riage plays a strong ideological role in the conception of what relationships are valued and how family life should be organized. This can be seen in the rallying cry of the need for strong family values, heard across the political spectrum, which almost always holds married couples with children as the valued standard.

Many lesbians and gays want both the legal protections and the societal rec-ognition that marriage implies. Each of these books highlights the social approval given to marriage, with each happy couple surrounded by approving family and friends at the wedding ceremony. In two books the child at the center of the story is briefly doubtful about the need for marriage—"Married, like a wedding? How come? Why can't we stay the way we are? I like us like this" says Rosie in *Mom and Mum Are Getting Married*—but both she and Chloe in *Uncle Bobby's Wedding* are easily enticed into supporting the marriage through the promise of a role in the ceremony. In *King & King*, the prince is unenthusiastic about getting married and taking the throne, until he meets the right person and joins the wedding excitement. *Operation Marriage* is the only book that mentions legal reasons for marriage, acknowledging that marriage provides rights that unmarried couples don't have access to as Mama Kathy states, "We've done everything possible to have the same rights as married people." *Daddy's Wedding*, published in 1996, seven years before any state in the United States recognized legal same sex marriages, acknowledged that "We call it a commitment ceremony, Nick," said Frank. "That's like a wedding."

While the desire to gain access to marriage is understandable given the multiple benefits, marriage is portrayed in narrow, traditional ways in these books. Boyd (2014) notes how same sex marriage has consumer value, saying, "The commodification of gay marriage via marketplace activity produces a new kind of queer citizen, one that participates in civic life via the social rituals of marriage and the commercial rituals of conspicuous consumption" (p. 122). Both *King & King* and *Donovan's Big Day* feature elaborate church weddings. While the wedding ceremonies in the other books are smaller and less formal, even the simplest backyard ceremony, such as in *Daddy's Wedding*, has a tiered wedding cake and grooms wearing tuxedos. Marriage in these books is not only a matter of two people who love each other but a consumer act that exists along very traditional lines. These lesbian and gay couples are not planning innovative ceremonies that make the act of marriage their own or advocating for a new and different kind of marriage; rather, they are eagerly participating in the same narrow, traditional customs of heterosexual couples. Of course, there's nothing necessarily wrong with these customs, but adopting them so rapidly and unquestioningly is a lost opportunity to expand the conception of marriage for everyone.

In addition, these books are simultaneously typical, pleasant examples of children's literature while also serving as an act of resistance that challenges dominant religious, cultural, and political systems of power. Although acceptance of LGBT people and same sex marriage has been increasing, there remain a number of dominant religious, cultural, and political groups who disapprove of, and in some cases actively work against, LGBT interests. While these six books are, for the most part, blandly enjoyable with minor, easily solved conflicts, to these groups the very existence of picture storybooks that feature same sex marriage is an offense and an affront, threatening their worldview and serving as a direct challenge to the systems of power that seek to perpetuate traditional views of marriage.

Any children's book with an LGBT character is subjected to scrutiny and probable disapproval by these groups, as can be seen by frequent attempts to challenge and/or censor books with LGBT content. For example, *And Tango Makes Three* (Richardson & Parnell, 2005), a story of two male penguins who raise a baby together is fourth on the American Library Association Top 100 Banned/ Challenged Books: 2000–2009, while *King & King* is 20th on the list. Making these books accessible in schools can also be difficult. Most recently, a teacher in North Carolina became mired in controversy after reading aloud *King & King* to a group of elementary students (Murdock, 2015). For some groups, books featuring same sex marriage are highly fraught, as they challenge ideas of what marriage is, who should have access to it, and what role LGBT people have in our society.

Others may be more supportive of LGBT rights but still see these books as a source of discomfort either because of unconscious, unexamined homophobia or because books featuring same sex marriage simply don't fit their schema for children's books. In these cases, the existence of these books is likely less fraught, but exposure to them still provides a useful space where people can begin to challenge their preconceptions and examine hidden biases.

As the number of states that allowed same sex marriage increased over the past 10 years, eventually culminating in the Supreme Court decision that legalized it across the United States, those opposed to same sex marriage have turned to other avenues in order to protect their privilege and perpetuate discrimination against the LGBT community. Many states and localities are now proposing laws that allow businesses, public officials, and religious leaders to refuse participation in same sex weddings (Fausset & Blinder, 2015). While, understandably, these laws are denounced by LGBT groups, they are also often opposed by business leaders who generally are against any law that would be perceived as discriminatory toward LGBT people. In some cases, this likely arises from moral and ethical considerations. An even stronger impetus, though, is consumerism: these laws would be bad for business. Bérubé (2001) writes,

> To gain recognition and credibility, some gay organizations and media began to aggressively promote the so-called positive image of a generic gay community that is an upscale, mostly male, and mostly white consumer market with mainstream, even traditional, values. Such a strategy derives its power from an unexamined investment in whiteness and middle-class identification.
>
> *(p. 235)*

The Complex Realities of Day-to-day Life as an LGBT Person Are Minimized and Decontextualized

It's clear that many segments of the LGBT community are invisible in these books. However, even those who are depicted have representations that minimize the complexities of life as a lesbian or gay person in a world of oppressive cultural, political, and religious systems of power. Lesbians and gays contend with a mixture of privilege and oppression. This is true even of white, middle-class lesbians and gays such as those depicted in these books who carry privilege from their race or socioeconomic status but still may face difficulties related to their sexual orientation. The day-to-day lives of LGBT people are impacted by cultural values, social customs, political systems, and legal systems, which shape who they are and how they live their lives. However, in these books, the lived realities of lesbians and gays is oversimplified and decontextualized.

Although acceptance of LGBT people and issues is increasing (see http://www.gallup.com/poll/1651/gay-lesbian-rights.aspx for the results of polls over time), many lesbians and gays still struggle with familial and societal acceptance. Tensions between some or all family members are common, and may be more likely in particular racial or religious groups. For example, an African American lesbian may experience greater family tension than a white lesbian, because the African American community as a whole has been slower to acknowledge and accept LGBT people from their own community (Sherket, de Vries, & Creek, 2010). Yet, in each book the same sex couples are surrounded by happy and supportive families and friends. There is no evidence of tension or strained family relationships.

Then too, social acceptance varies widely across the United States, with some areas, for example, providing legal protections against job discrimination and hate crimes while other places don't. Because life can be precarious for LGBT people, at least in certain contexts, many have developed strong, supportive networks of friends and community organizations (Easterbrook, Carpiano, Kelly, & Parsons, 2014; Meyers, 2003). Little of this appears in any of the books featuring same sex marriage. *Daddy's Wedding* and *Donovan's Big Day* each have a same sex couple as guests at the wedding, showing at least that LGBT people other than the main characters exist in book worlds. Also, in *Mom and Mum Are Getting Married*, Uncle Peter and Mike, who own a flower shop together and are clearly meant to be read as gay, play a small role in the plot. Otherwise, there is no indication of any sort of LGBT community in any of the books thus erasing its existence and potential power as a political, economic, and cultural force.

Finally, there's no worry or tension surrounding the act of getting married. No character is worried about getting denied a marriage license or running into a vendor who won't work with same sex couples. There's no difficulty with finding someone to conduct their ceremony. Five of the six books show some sort of officiant. In *Operation Marriage* it's Pastor Bob and in *Daddy's Wedding* it's Reverend Powell. The other three officiants appear to be religious figures, but are not explicitly so.

Conclusion

These six picture storybooks provide positive, if limited, depictions of same sex marriage. If one aspect of privilege is the ability to see positive representations of your life depicted in books, media, and school curricula (McIntosh, 2007) then these books succeed—at least for that narrow segment of lesbians and gays who are white, middle class, gender-conforming, and child-focused. Yet at the same time that they provide representation in books for a small group of people, they fail at exploring the complex, lived experiences of a wide variety of lesbians and gays and an expanded conception of marriage. Of course, these are 32-page picture-books, but there are hundreds of children's picture storybooks that have storylines that acknowledge the complexities of life. While they vary in literary quality, each of these books would be appropriate to have in a home, public, or school library or to use in a classroom with children. Although I have argued that these books have narrow depictions of lesbians and gays, the fact that they are, for the most part, bland, idealized, and whitewashed may actually make it easier to bring them into the classroom than more complex, realistic books. However, now that same sex marriage is legal across the United States, it is possible that it will be easier for publishers to produce and market additional books on this topic. If so, it is to be hoped that new picture storybooks about same sex marriage will reflect the diverse realities of LGBT people.

References

Berger, M. & Guidroz, K. (2009). Introduction. In M. Berger & K. Guidroz (Eds.), *The intersectional approach: Transforming the academy through race, class and gender* (pp. 1–22). Durham: University of North Carolina Press.

Bérubé, A. (2001). How gay stays white and what kind of white it stays. In B. Rasmussen, E. Klinenberg, I. Nexica, & M. Wray (Eds.), *The making and unmaking of whiteness* (pp. 234–265). Durham, NC: Duke University Press.

Blackburn, M. & Smith, J. (2010). Moving beyond the inclusion of LGBT-themed literature in English language arts classrooms: Interrogating heteronormativity and exploring intersectionality. *Journal of Adolescent & Adult Literacy, 53*(8), 625–634.

Boyd, N. (2014). Sex and tourism. In P. Grzanka (Ed.), *Intersectionality: A foundations and frontiers reader* (pp. 119–125). Philadelphia, PA: Westview Press.

Case, K. (2013). Beyond diversity and whiteness. In K. Case (Ed.), *Deconstructing privilege: Teaching and learning as allies in the classroom* (pp. 1–14). New York: Routledge.

Easterbrook, A., Carpiano, R., Kelly, B., & Parsons, J. (2014). The personal experience of community among urban gay men, lesbians, and bisexuals: Melting pot or mosaic? *Social Science Quarterly, 95*(3), 682–700.

Fausset, R. & Blinder, A. (2015, March 5). States weigh legislation to let businesses refuse to serve gay couples. *New York Times.* Retrieved from http://www.nytimes.com

Ferber, A. & Herrera, A. (2013). Teaching privilege through an intersectional lens. In K. Case (Ed.), *Deconstructing privilege: Teaching and learning as allies in the classroom* (pp. 83–101). New York: Routledge.

Fryberg, S. A. & Townsend, S. S. M. (2008). The psychology of invisibility. In G. Adams, M. Biernat, F. Branscsombe, C. S. Crandall, & L. S. Wrightsman (Eds.), *Commemorating Brown: The social psychology of racism and discrimination* (pp. 173–193). Washington, DC: American Psychological Association.

Griffin, P., D'Errico, K. H., Harro, B., & Schiff, T. (2007). Heterosexism curriculum design. In M. Adams, L. A. Bell, & P. Griffin (Eds.), *Teaching for diversity and social justice: A sourcebook* (2nd ed., pp. 195–218). New York: Routledge.

Grzanka, P. (2014a). Introduction: Intersectional objectivity. In P. Grzanka (Ed.), *Intersectionality: A foundations and frontiers reader* (pp. xi–xxvii). Philadelphia, PA: Westview Press.

Grzanka, P. (2014b). Media as sites/sights of justice. In P. Grzanka (Ed.), *Intersectionality: A foundations and frontiers reader* (pp. 131–137). Philadelphia, PA: Westview Press.

Horning, K. (2014). Children's books: Still an all-white world? *School Library Journal, 60*(5), 18.

Lester, J. (2014). Homonormativity in children's literature: An intersectional analysis of queer-themed picture books. *Journal of LGBT Youth, 11*(3), 244–275.

Luft, R. E. (2009). Intersectionality and the risk of flattening difference: Gender and race logics, and the strategies use of antiracist singularity. In M. Berger & K. Guidroz (Eds.), *The intersectional approach: Transforming the academy through race, class and gender* (pp. 100–117). Durham: University of North Carolina Press.

May, V. (2015). *Pursuing intersectionality, unsettling dominant imaginaries.* New York: Routledge.

McIntosh, L. (2007). Does anyone have a band-aid? Anti-homophobia discourses and pedagogical impossibilities. *Educational Studies, 41*(1), 33–43. doi:10.1080/00131940701308874

McIntosh, P. (1988). *White privilege and male privilege: A personal account of coming to see correspondences through work in women's studies.* Wellesley, MA: Wellesley College Center for Research on Women.

Meyers, I. H. (2003). Prejudice, social stress, and mental health in lesbian, gay, and bisexual populations: Conceptual issues and research evidence. *Psychological Bulletin, 129*, 674–697.

Monsma, S. (2014). (Re)defining marriage: Changes and challenges. *Journal for the Sociological Integration of Religion & Society, 4*(1), 23–32.

Murdock, S. (2015, May 18). *North Carolina teacher Omar Currie reads his class gay fable after third-grader is bullied.* Retrieved from http://www.huffingtonpost.com

Purdie-Vaughns, V. & Eibach, R. P. (2008). Intersectional invisibility: The distinctive advantages and disadvantages of multiple subordinate-group identities. *Sex Roles, 59*(5–6), 377–391. doi:10.1007/s11199-008-9424-4

Rios, D. & Stewart, A. (2013). Recognizing privilege by reducing invisibility: The Global Feminisms Project as a pedagogical tool. In K. Case (Ed.), *Deconstructing privilege: Teaching and learning as allies in the classroom* (pp. 115–131). New York: Routledge.

Sherket, D., de Vries, K., & Creek, S. (2010). Race, religion, and opposition to same-sex marriage. *Social Science Quarterly, 91*(1), 80–98.

Stachelberg, W. & Burns, C. (2013, April 24). *10 things to know about the employment non-discrimination act.* Retrieved from https://www.americanprogress.org/

Wise, T. & Case, K. (2013). Pedagogy for the privileged: Addressing inequality and injustice without shame or blame. In K. Case (Ed.), *Deconstructing privilege: Teaching and learning as allies in the classroom* (pp. 77–33). New York: Routledge.

Children's Literature References

Alko, S. (2015). *The case for loving: The fight for interracial marriage.* New York: Arthur A. Levine Books.

Brannen, S. (2008). *Uncle Bobby's wedding.* New York: Putnam's.

Chin-Lee, C. (2011). *Operation marriage.* Illus. by Lea Lyon. Oakland, CA: PM Press.

de Haan, L. & Nijland, S. (2000). *King & King.* Berkeley, CA: Tricycle Press.

de Haan, L. & Nijland, S. (2004). *King & King & Family.* Berkeley, CA: Tricycle Press.

Newman, L. (2011). *Donovan's big day.* Illus. by Mike Dutton. Berkeley, CA: Tricycle Press.

Richardson, J. & Parnell, P. (2005). *And Tango makes three.* New York: Simon & Schuster.

Ross, E. (2011). *My uncle's wedding.* Illus. by Tracy Greene. Self-Published.

Setterington, K. (2004). *Mom and Mum are getting married.* Illus. by Alice Priestley. Toronto, CA: Second Story Press.

Willhoite, M. (1990). *Daddy's roommate.* Los Angeles, CA: Alyson Wonderland.

Willhoite, M. (1996). *Daddy's wedding.* Los Angeles, CA: Alyson Wonderland.

8

RE-IMAGINING AN ALTERNATIVE LIFE AFTER THE DARFUR WAR

Writing as Emancipatory Practice

Vivian Yenika-Agbaw

Conflict whether in Africa or anywhere else across the globe disrupts the lives of children, often displacing them from stability. Portrayed in the media, such children are regarded as desperate and "lost" as they hover around relief workers at refugee camps, hoping to be relocated to more stable environments. Many in the West see these events through the mesh of their national and local media, and so images of destitution, homelessness, and hopelessness are engrained in their minds, reducing child refugees to objects of pity. As one whose heritage and beginnings lie in Africa, I am sensitive to this negative portrayal of African children to the broader global community.

The media is not the only source of these images. Publishers of children's and adolescent books circulate images of conflicts too. One image of Africa that has recently dominated the literary scene is Child Soldiering, appearing in historical accounts in fictionalized narratives, but more often as memoirs. Khorana (2014), an esteemed scholar of children's literature, posits that memoirs can be problematic because while they are "assumed to be true accounts," they are based on the memory of what authors recall "about traumatic experiences" (p. 106).

Stories about conflicts have also appeared in various formats and genres including the graphic novel and narrative verse. While McKay and Lafrance's (2013) graphic novel, *War Brothers*, continues the trend of children surviving conflicts through forceful enlisting as child soldiers, Andrea Davis Pinkney's (2014) narrative verse, *The Red Pencil*, with illustrations by Shane W. Evans offers an alternative view; one of a protagonist using art (drawings and writing) to transcend the immediate trauma of war. This view affords readers an opportunity to further understand the tenacity of the human spirit in the face of adversity, and to recognize the role that art can play in transforming lives. The stereotypical image of children in war-torn countries in Africa only as child soldiers is deconstructed, allowing readers to ponder the fate of those who refuse to be coerced and the strategies they employ to survive the trauma of war. This chapter focuses on *The Red Pencil* as an example of one girl's tenacity during the Darfur war and examines how she, a Survivor, uses writing to transform her life.

An inquiry into literature as an outlet for children undergoing traumatic experiences affords an opportunity to enable children to articulate their fears and concerns about trauma and to name their pain and aspirations through writing. Literature provides a model on which writing pedagogy can be based, with its genre variations serving as exemplars for young writers (Yenika-Agbaw & Sychterz, 2015). This chapter is informed by interpretive strategies of critical content analysis to locate instances of social injustice in texts and educational practices within specific cultural contexts through the use of third world feminist theories on discourses of gender as practiced within global communities. By reflecting on the curriculum decisions we make daily and the literary texts we select for literacy programs, this basic critical process can reveal whether a teacher's pedagogical practices considers children's divergent experiences.

Grounded in these theories to investigate how gender is shaped by cultural context, this study also considers critical content analysis as a research method to understand the emancipatory power of art in a pre-teen's life. Amira is constructed not just as any other pre-teen, but as a female child and refugee with the capacity to imagine a better life in order to survive and transcend the trauma of war.

Pinkney's award-winning novel for adolescents recounts 12-year-old Amira's story before and after the 2003 Darfur war. Although fictionalized, it is inspired by accounts that Pinkney read about "children growing up inside an unthinkable reality" (Author's note, unpaged). It is written in free verse accompanied by pencil drawings. In this form, Pinkney professes that, "the story celebrates the power of creativity, and the way that art can help us heal" (unpaged). In its poetic form, *The Red Pencil* offers adolescent readers new insights about art and healing, and new avenues through which they can delve into difficult topics such as the devastating effects of war. This fictional narrative on the Darfur war between 2003 and 2004 captures just one moment of the complicated histories of the people of Fur and Sudan, placing their humanity at the center to remind readers of our connectivity as human beings. This type of story compels readers to rethink their perhaps "naïve" perspectives on wars and civil strife in Africa and instead contemplate the historical origins of these crises, and the larger ramifications of violence in society. They beg the question of how we address our differences and resolve conflicts.

Historical Context and Third World Feminisms

Conflicts in modern Sudan date back to the early nineteenth century in the defeat of Sudan by Turkey and Egypt (Sudan Profile, 2015). Since then a series of wars has occurred as Sudan struggles to emancipate itself from British and Egyptian colonial rule and from a series of oppressive governmental regimes whose ideological differences stifled progress and liberation of the Sudanese (South Sudan Profile, BBC). Some of the key issues in these endless conflicts relate to oil, ethnicity, and religious laws. The conflicts in Sudan have generated a lot of interest within the international community with lots of books for adults and children published consistently on Sudan and Darfur.

Alexander de Waal (2007), an authority on Sudan, notes that, "Darfur's historic identity has been both 'African' and 'Arab' with no sense of contradiction between the two" (p. 2). This book focuses on the tensions that have resulted in endless conflicts and the ongoing peace negotiations. From de Waal's (2007) perspective negotiating peace has been equally as taxing as the wars on all involved. The 2015 Human Rights Watch report, which keeps counts of the instances of violence in the region, confirms this. The Darfur conflicts seem thus, in every aspect, complex and beyond the scope of this chapter. Any attempt to try to unpack the nuanced and historical nature of the conflicts would divert the chapter from its focus on one instance of the conflict and the role that writing plays in a Survivor's life.

Third world feminisms frame this inquiry. Often associated with Chandra Mohanty (2003), these theories emphasize the intersectionality of oppression in relation to the experiences of women of color, including gender inequality. Their struggles for equality are couched within their specific histories and cultures. In the case of women from Africa, their colonial histories are compounded with their national, religious, ethnic, traditional, and family histories. These intersect to form a complex system of oppression that resonates with Kimberlie Crenshaw's (1991) theory of intersectionality. Mohanty (2003) and Patricia Hills Collins (2009) also embrace the idea of women of color located at crossroads of oppression both at the global level and within the United States. Further, Smith (2013/2014) notes that intersectionality is indeed "a description of the way multiple oppressions are experienced" (unpaged).

Crenshaw (1991) reiterates the importance of intersectionality for women of color, arguing that there is the "need to account for multiple grounds of identity when considering how the social world is constructed" (p. 1245). Although her focus is violence and women of color in the United States, her concepts apply to African women whose social reality includes ethnic, religious, and colonial histories. She explains how the notion of intersectionality can serve communities through what she refers to as "coalition" building (p. 1299). In this way, an African female in Sudan may be able to connect with the males in her community through colonial histories, ethnicity, class, and religious affiliation, connect with other women through gender, and others through commonly held aspirations. Crenshaw adds that, "With identity thus reconceptualized, it may be easier to understand the need for and to summon the courage to challenge groups that are after all, in one sense, 'home' to us, in the name of the parts of us that are not made at home" (p. 1299).

A third world feminist lens frames my beliefs about writing as an emancipatory practice by arguing for the need to make visible aspects of our identities that position us as Other within dominant spheres of practices. In this way, room for women is made available at the margin—so that the subaltern speak their reality in their own voices (Spivak, 2006) through an artistic mode, rather than depend on a representative to speak for them, as suggested by Linda Alcoff (1998) in extreme cases. This lens acknowledges the histories of women within their present and past cultural spaces that have contributed in shaping their ongoing understandings of who they may think they are, have been, or would like to become. These women are not trapped in notions of "genderism," a concept Oyeronke Oyewumi (2011) equates with the "universal and timeless" nature of "male dominance in human affairs" (p. 30). Rather, she reiterates that women are shaped by their unique histories and cultures as their lives unfold at any given time.

Key tenets of third world feminisms that frame this study include:

- the diverse nature of the struggles of women from regions in the developing economy;
- the specific histories that shape their different struggles; and
- the intersectionality of their experiences that predispose them to different forms of exclusionary practices.

In *The Red Pencil*, this intersectionality considers Amira's reality as a female child growing up in an agrarian society within a traditional family unit. Her sociocultural reality changes within a year, rendering her homeless and fatherless, and according her a refugee status that further fuels her desire to go to school. "If we say that women's oppression just not only depends on their sexuality, but also depends on their race, class, the ways they practice gender, history, and contexts, then we are applying the theory of intersectionality to analyze the issue of women's oppression" (Asian University for Women, 2013). In Amira's case, this intersectionality also includes ethnicity and religion.

Third world feminisms guide this inquiry as they afford significance to how female characters in literary texts practice and interpret gender within their cultural spaces albeit in fictionalized settings. The use of narrative verse and pencil drawings that translate private thoughts into written and visual texts allows adolescent readers to piece together Amira's personal and public struggles, which in turn may augment these readers' chances of understanding the sociocultural dynamics at play in the novel. It may also increase their chances to empathize with the 12-year-old, as they put themselves in her shoes figuratively to accompany her on the journey to self-actualization, though from the safe comforts of their homes and/or classrooms. They are afforded opportunities to learn about children located in different geographical spaces in Africa, whose lives might have been shaped to some degree by historical encounters with the West.

This new knowledge allows readers to forge links based on common experiences as youth in their quest for freedom from the yoke of adult expectations and colonialism. At this universal level their collective humanity may take precedence, even as they ponder the cultural differences that may make Amira and her people's experience unique, alien, and perhaps a bit unsettling in their Western eyes and consciousness. However, the ability to empathize with the main character and to navigate the mode through which she expresses her frustrations, pain, and aspirations while appreciating the mode of expression has the potential for transforming adolescent readers into creative thinkers and writers.

Related Studies

Few studies exist on this topic in children's literature with Jane Gangi's (2014) *Genocide in Contemporary Children's and Young Adult Literature: Cambodia to Darfur* as the most recent. Gangi examines titles that perpetuate stereotypes and those that construct war authentically. Books set in Africa are just a few Gangi analyzes among others set elsewhere across the globe. Other studies tend to be topical. For instance, Khorana (2014) deconstructed the bestselling memoirs of African child soldiers. She interrogates the narrative voices of the protagonists as does Allison Mackey (2013), who looks at relationality in African child soldier narratives. At the core of these studies is the examination of how conflicts in books for children set in Africa are represented, but none of the existing research approaches the topic from an emancipatory perspective.

Two studies from Canada seek to explain aspects of the conflicts in certain regions of Africa, as constructed in literature in the West. Kate O'Neill's (2012) dissertation is framed within postcolonial and trauma theories to analyze the Rwandan genocide as a way to re-educate Western readers on the humanity of Rwandans. As an extension, Julie Cairnie (2011) presents readers with representations of war in Africa and the strategies female characters adopt to survive. The primary goal seems to be one of getting Canadian girls to empathize with the fate of the African girls in conflict zones.

Research Methodology

The Red Pencil is divided into two parts: before the Darfur war and at Kalma camp. My approach to analysis reflects a critical consciousness. Willis et al. (2008) assert that one of the greatest challenges to critically conscious research is the issue of subjectivity. They also claim that, "What makes a person critically conscious is challenging the underlying assumptions that work in the internal and external worlds to privilege some while dispriviliging others" (p. 5). In this inquiry, I examine Amira's "internal and external worlds" as conveyed through the different poems, noting the shifts between the poetic forms and messages in parts 1 and 2 to understand how she, the focalizer, uses art. In particular, I examine how her use of art to record her daily experiences discloses her intersectionalities first as a daughter, female, villager, friend, and an aspiring writer, and later as a displaced person, fatherless child, refugee, survivor, and an aspiring educator. This analysis gives readers a glimpse of the struggles she faces and the strategies she adopts to stay physically, psychologically, emotionally, and spiritually centered as she works to forge a new self.

A third world feminist lens guides the analysis shedding light on how ideas and meanings are constructed through *words, phrases, sentences, artistic forms,* and *visual images.* Therefore, words and/or phrases that reflect the sociocultural contexts of gender, the sociopolitical dynamics of the cultural space, the poetic forms, and the author/illustrator perceptions formed coding units that reveal thematic patterns, which in turn serve as analytical categories. This practice is consistent with Yan Zhang and Barbara M. Wildemuth's (2009) view that qualitative content analysis "uncovers patterns, themes, and categories important to social reality" (p. 5).

Like most critically conscious scholars who engage in qualitative content analysis, I believe that ideas matter; and like Gramsci, I have come to understand that it is all about "the struggle for meaning" and who defines "ideas or reality/ies" (Willis et al., 2008, p. 20). In the context of *The Red Pencil* whoever is constructing meaning has the power. Is it the "ruling class" as Gramsci theorizes about meaning-making in society, which in this case would be the elders of the fictional society? Is it Amira, the child protagonist who may be regarded as an underdog; or is it both the elders and Amira? If both, how do the author and illustrator enable this type of collaborative meaning construction through their art? My analysis delves into these questions.

With the understanding that qualitative content analysis grounds "the examination of topics and themes, as well as the inferences drawn from them, in the data" (Zhang and Wildemuth, 2009, p. 1), this inquiry regards the novel as a cultural product that stems out of a social context, and thus poses the following research questions:

- How do the author and illustrator utilize art (drawing and writing) to emancipate Amira, a survivor of the 2003 Darfur war from her multiple realities as a child, Sudanese female, and refugee?
- How do the author and illustrator consider cultural authenticity in their *re*constructions of gender relationships prior to and after the 2003 Darfur war?

The sites from which I conduct inquiry as always reflect my intersectional backgrounds as a scholar of children's literature, a literacy educator with a passion for social justice, and a woman of color.

Book Selection Criteria

To select a book for this study, I perused a list of Children's Africana Book Award (CABA) winning titles published since 2010 (http://africaaccessreview.org/africana-awards/). The year 2010 was only as important in that the book that would be studied had to be recent, as such would fall within a five-year-period. Because

of my background as a former high school teacher of English, I was more interested in novels that targeted students in the middle grades and up. Three titles
stood out: Pinkney's *The Red Pencil* (2015 CABA winner), Roberts' *Far from Home*
(2013 CABA winner), and Kent's *Stones for My Father* (2012 CABA winner).
Though all had conflicts and displacements for themes, I decided on *The Red
Pencil* because unlike the others race/ethnicity was not a central focus, although it
was implied. I was also drawn to the book for its creative format.

Features of the Book

The background color of the front jacket cover is red with an image of a girl
dressed in a blue *toob*, the traditional outfit often identified with cultural groups
from that region. In her hands is a red pencil. The book title is inscribed in yellow on the black girl's frame. The colors of the back jacket cover are yellow, red,
blue, and yellow in that order with two red pencils saddled above the lining of
the first red section and the blue that follows. There are inscriptions on the cover
that celebrate the novel; but the first one that appears in the yellow shaded space
is a direct quote from one of the verses in the book: "'**Amira**, look at me,' Muma
insists. She collects both my hands in hers. 'The Janjaweed attack without warn-
ing. If ever they come—**run**'." One could infer that this quote is important as it
draws attention to the men behind the historic conflict.

The front matter contains a map of the region with pencil illustrations of people walking in a straight line underneath it. The double-page spread illustration
that follows is of the farm where Amira spent the first 12 years of her life. The
pastoral setting seems peaceful.

There are 97 poems in part one. Each revolves around life on this farm, in
South Darfur between September 2003 and March 2004, a place Amira considers home. The 51 poems in part two focus on life at the refugee camp, Kalma,
between April and June 2004. "Wheat," the first poem, introduces readers to
the12-year-old narrator, the focalizer, and sets the tension around gender. "Flight,"
the last poem, closes with Amira's resolve to seek out "*What else is possible?*" one of
her father's catch phrases. The verses in between chronicle her physical, emotional,
psychological, and spiritual journeys in this quest for self-actualization, addressing
different facets of the conflicts she encounters. The novel concludes with back
matter that provides background information on the story's origin, including an
author's note, acknowledgment, glossary of words, and terms. Because the illustrations mostly confirm the verses, both texts (poems and drawings) imbibe tenets of
third world feminisms such as the diverse sources of conflicts, the complex nature
of female oppression, and the intricacies and intersectionalities of these struggles.

My analytical process entailed describing the novel format and comparing
the poems in parts one (South Darfur, September 2003–March 2004) and two
(Kalma, April 2004–June 2004). Each poem/illustration was examined to comprehend how meaning is constructed within the sociocultural context. First,

I read the entire poem/illustration to be familiar with the artistic styles; next, I read all the poems/illustrations. I reread each poem/illustration focusing initially on stanzas (and sets of images) as coding units. These varied with poems that alternated between multiple-lined and one-lined stanzas or images that appeared as double-page/single-page spreads or as isolated illustrations. In subsequent readings I concentrated on words, phrases, and sentences, and the corresponding visuals to form coding units. These were arranged on coding sheets, which made visible the ensuing patterns that emerged in order to create analytical categories. An example of this analytical procedure focusing on the first three poems: "Wheat," "Dando's Delight," and "Lost Tooth" (pp. 2–7) follows.

Sample Analysis

"Wheat" reminds readers of Amira's gender and her domestic chores and announces the significance of her birthday. She is 12 years old and will "make flour,/loaves,/golden cakes" (p. 3) from wheat. Her mother reminds her of this village tradition. The poem tackles Amira's intersectionalities as a young female on a farm. "Dando's Delight" offers an alternative view. Amira can fly like a sparrow; she is "precious" and "Bright" (p. 5). Readers encounter contradictory messages within her family, which echo tenets of third world feminisms in the diverse struggles of women from developing economies and their intersectionalities. "Lost Tooth" (p. 6) introduces "Halima, my so-close friend" (p. 6) who is heading to school and *problematizes* gender expectations that are *confirmed* in "Wheat," and *ignored* in "Dando's Delight." In "Lost Tooth" both girls agree that while pulling Halima's tooth might have "hurt," she is "free" (p. 7). These poems frame the gender conversation around Amira, the girl/daughter at cultural crossroads, whose mother expects her to follow tradition, whose father expects her to aspire, and whose best friend shows her opportunities.

The tension introduced in "Wheat" that ushers in a new year for Amira is developed throughout the book, often taking various forms depending on the physical, psychological, emotional, sociocultural, and spiritual spaces within which Amira finds herself as a child, girl, village farmer, and refugee. Examples of words/phrases from these poems that form coding units through the third world feminist frame include:

- "I am twelve./Old enough to wear a *toob*"; "farm chores" (p. 3).
- "make/flour/loaves/golden cake/ ... Our village ... /greets me ..." (pp. 2–3).
- " Come, girl child, fly!/ ... Amira Bright ... /Girl child, rising./ ..." (pp. 4–5).
- "That tooth was stubborn/ ... I pinched the tooth/ ... Halima's tooth flew ..." (pp. 6–7).

From a critical stance, the selected words/phrases from these sample poems, and others embedded in the collection, enable me to ponder "the underlying assumptions that work in the internal and external worlds" (Willis et al., 2008, p. 5) to "privilege" and at once "disprivilege" Amira in this fictional setting.

Being critically conscious and using third world feminisms to guide my analysis process, I noticed the diverse forms Amira's struggles take and how her intersectionality complicates, frustrates, and liberates her from an otherwise gendered identity imposed by her environment and sociocultural history. Further, on closer look at the words/phrases to code the emerging pattern of themes and examine the repetitive nature of some of the verses in form/content/style, I re-examined Amira's internal and external worlds to understand what may be privileging and/or disprivileging her. This further enabled me to create analytical categories.

How Amira's Internal and External Worlds Privilege Her

From the first through the last poem, family, tradition, friendship, and community work to privilege Amira. She is a cherished child in Goz ("Family Pictures," p. 78) and Kalma ("New Family Pictures," p. 250). Her biological family celebrates her: "When Dando tells of my birth,/he smiles as wide as a moon's crescent" (p. 26). Her "Birth Story" is unique. The pencil illustration of her pregnant mother that accompanies the poem reinforces her specialness. Key figures in her village like Old Anwar and at the camp like Miss Sabine, the relief worker, take note.

Tradition ("Tradition Hut," p. 48), whether positive or negative, roots her within the village and affords her an identity of a Sudanese female from that part of Darfur. She understands that tradition exists for a purpose, even if she does not agree with some of the rules, especially as they pertain to females. Nonetheless, she can ask questions. She may not necessarily get the responses she envisages but community members grant her audience.

Third, she is loved and accommodated by friends, and parental figures. Halima inspires. Parental figures teach her about their region enabling her to understand their histories of turbulence. In time she recognizes the difference between Janjaweed (pp. 58, 61, 110), war, and haboob, the "dust storm" (p. 89). These privileges, if nothing else, allow her to put things into perspective.

How Amira's Internal and External Worlds Disprivilege Her

Ironically, her sources of strength and support such as family, tradition, friends, and community often work to disprivilege Amira too. Muma, her mother who loves her dearly, suffocates her with tradition. She does not encourage formal schooling for girls; Dando is taciturn on the subject but offers Amira "a sturdy twig/ . . . 'For making your sand pictures, Amira Bright'" (p. 32). Consistent with some tenets of third world feminisms, Amira is comfortable and uncomfortable at "home."

The conflicting views held by Muma and Halima's mother on gender also confuse Amira and serve to disprivilege her internal and external worlds. So do the actions of the Sudanese female relief worker and Old Anwar at Kalma where gender expectations seem equally ambiguous. Halima's parents are "not stifled by tradition" (p. 12); however, her mother, Muma, is "locked in a hut of tradition./ . . . /A closed-off place/with no windows for letting in fresh ideas" (p. 13).What also works to disprivilege her are the Janjaweed's quest for violence.

From this brief discussion, readers can recognize the basic tenets of third world feminisms at play: the diverse struggles Amira's character faces, the histories of violence perpetuated by the Janjaweed, and how her intersectionality predisposes her to further marginalization—a child controlled by adults, a female bound by gendered traditions, a farmer at the mercy of the elements, an artist in need of tools, and a dreamer seeking to escape the familiar cultural spaces that stifle her.The idea then of women from the third world "as a homogenous 'powerless' group often located as implicit victims of particular socioeconomic systems" becomes mute (Mohanty, 2003, p. 23).

Third World Feminisms: Thematic Analysis

After analyzing these poems, four themes emerged that consider the sociocultural contexts of the activities in which the survivor engages. Mohanty (2003) remarks, "The distinction between the act of mothering and the status attached to it is a very important one—one that needs to be stated and analyzed contextually" (p. 26). Although her reference point is mothering, the concept is applicable in this study. Thus, the meaning of Amira's drawings/writing is of great significance given the circumstances under which these acts occur and the rationale. As I proceed, I must make clear that I am unable to cite extensively from the poems, because of fair use regulations. Depending on the point being made, I reference titles or provide summaries.

Using Art to Record the History and Cultural Practices of Darfur People Prior to and after Displacement

This theme explores the question: How do the author and illustrator record these histories and cultures through art? One of the tenets in third world feminisms is the role cultural histories play in the unique struggles of females of color. Artists utilize various modes within their verbal/visual narratives through which Amira is able to learn about her people, reflect on their practices, rethink the fairness of certain practices in regard to gender and the origin of conflicts, share her feelings, and make decisions based on her unique circumstances. Embedded in these poems are intimate conversations about Darfur's past and tradition. For instance, in "War" (p. 20), Pinkney presents a conversation between Amira and Dando on conflicts: "My father tries to explain something/that is more twisted . . . / He is telling./I listen./ . . . 'There has been fighting for land'/ . . . /'It's senseless/to fight over something/Allah has made for everyone'" (pp. 20–21). Amira's feelings about war in the last stanza are concretized so the words represent the "twisted" nature of war.

This style deviates from the linear pattern Pinkney adopts to construct a similar conversation between Muma and Amira in "The Janjaweed" (p. 58) and on gender in "Tradition Hut" (p. 48). ". . . I must endure/today's lesson from Muma/about something called the Janjaweed . . . / 'The Janjaweed are bad people' . . ." (p. 58).

Poems such as "Possibilities" (p. 62) take the form of a "game," focus on how Amira's father teaches her not to be a victim: "'If you wake to find your sandals gone, do you worry?'/ . . . /Better to ask, 'What else is possible?'" (p. 62). The accompanying illustrations present daughter and father performing the game.

Other poems explain who the Darfur people are through verses that integrate refrains ("Goz," p. 52), rhetorical questions ("Happenings," p. 110; "Scraps," p. 142; "Crowded Kalma," p. 153), and reference traditional beliefs ("Unwelcome," p. 173; "Talking to Sayidda Moon," p. 272). Readers learn along with Amira, following her doodling and writing, projected through the voices of the author, illustrator, and Amira, the artist.

Using Art to Assist Amira to Reflect on Darfur People's Perceptions on Gender

This theme responds to the question: How do the author and illustrator use art to assist Amira in her quest for gender equality? A major tenet of the third world feminisms is the diverse nature of the struggles of females of color. To assist Amira in navigating the systems of practice within Goz and Kalma, Pinkney and Evans present models of gendered lives by comparing and contrasting important figures in Amira's life and how each navigates the traditional systems. They also equip her with tools to re-imagine her world: "Twig" (p. 32) and "The Red Pencil" (p. 184), writing tools that enable her to visualize/verbalize her possibilities. Patricia Kuntz, a judge of the Children Africana Book Awards (CABA) observes:

> The symbol of this instrument [the red pencil] is subtle; however, North Americans know the difference between the #2-yellow painted pencil and the red pencil. Only teachers use red pencils to show errors . . . This distinction is clearly key for the remainder of the story. Amira stands out for her leadership and critical thinking skills.
>
> *(Kuntz, 2015)*

While gender is at the core of the collection, it is addressed more directly in some poems than others. Amira compares her mother's views with other females' in "School" (p. 11), "Traditional Hut" (p. 48), "Chasing the Wind" (p. 50), "Miss Sabine" (p. 179), "Parting Glance" (p. 187), "Wife" (p. 192), and "Tug-O-War" (p. 266). Muma does not believe in formal education for females—marriage is their goal. Her perspective on tradition persists until near the end ("Muma Blooming," p. 269) when she expresses interest in Amira's drawings. Amira also considers the views of her peers comparing Halima's schooling ambition with the young girl's choice of "a rude husband" in "Wife" (p. 192).

Models of patriarchy are compared with Dando, Old Anwar, and Halima's Dad, men who are privileged by tradition but who empathize with their daughters' desire for more. Their perspectives are contrasted with those of the Janjaweed soldiers ("The Janjaweed," p. 58), the husband in "Wife," and the Kalma guards in "Stuck" (p. 164).

Using Art to Emancipate the Self from Oppressive Cultural Realities

This theme emerged from the question: How do the author and illustrator use art to enable Amira to act on the desire to liberate herself from the shackles of tradition and the misery of life at Kalma? Central to the tenets of third world feminisms is the idea of liberation. Pinkney recognizes this theme of emancipation as vital to human existence. She writes, "Part novel, part sketchbook, this story celebrates the power of creativity, and the way that art can help us heal" (unpaged). By integrating flight and voice motifs throughout the novel beginning with the sparrow readers encounter in "Dando's Delight" (p. 4), the sparrow that assists Amira to draw in "Hand, Twig, Sparrow" (p. 56), the sparrow in "Fence" (p. 206) whose "spirit-wings that soar/when I draw,/are trapped . . ." (p. 206), and the sparrow Amira imagines herself becoming in "Flight" (p. 308) where she, a "*sparrow* child" rises "high,/wings/spread" escapes in search of "*What else is possible?*," the author and illustrator involve readers in Amira's emancipatory process. Recognizing the power of creativity and art, the artists position Amira as a girl-child, learner, and refugee in the company of enabling adults such as Dando, Old Anwar, and Miss Sabine, who provide her with the tools and mindset that foster creativity. Pinkney also positions Amira in situations where she must listen to understand her cultural reality before becoming the "sparrow child" that flies out!

The twig and red pencil can be interpreted as metaphors for liberation through which Amira can dare to aspire. In "I am" (p. 279) she becomes "*the red pencil!/ . . . the line./ . . . the swirl/* The girl with the *sparrow/* who knows/how to draw,/how to write" (p. 279). These last series of poems celebrate her newfound confidence. She is no longer one of the Sudanese flowers at Kalma; she "want[s] to erase" (p. 287) this. And so she escapes from that physical space; from the psychological trauma of war and multiple losses; and the limitations these realities impose on her. To accomplish this feat, the author accords her the memory of her father's inspirational words, "What else is possible?" Creativity and art work together to liberate the human spirit: Amira's!

Telling the Story "Authentically" by Fusing Minds and Hearts with Exemplary Craftsmanship

This theme demonstrates how the cultural voices of the "artist" character and real-life artists converge by exploring the question, How does Amira's artistic voice converge with the verbal and visual narrative voices of the author and illustrator to reconstruct a segment of the "Darfur War" in a culturally authentic way?

One of the most successful artistic features in *The Red Pencil* is the author's designation of Amira as the focalizer and narrator, through whose lens readers see events and follow the plot. She narrates the story through a poetic mode, which adds to the aesthetic appeal. Pinkney admits in the author's note that, the choice of this mode was "deliberate" as "verse could be a means of insulating young readers from the tragic realities of genocide and could offer a way to make the horrors of war easier to comprehend" (unpaged). In this way, Amira is constructed as a young character learning to understand the culture of the Darfur people—her people in the same way that the author's research on the culture positions her as a learner. She is also constructed as an artist, which Evans represents through his childlike illustrations. Thus, the three voices converge at the artistic level to skillfully create a story that is culturally authentic.

Amira is the focalizer, as the story is told from her point of view, and a vehicle through which ideas are imagined and encoded. Readers hear her voice in the poems, see her childlike drawings evolve into creative art ("Funny Bugs," p. 230), experience her joys and fears ("Double Joy," p. 42; "Happenings," p. 110), share her pain ("Shock," p. 84), and fly with her ("Flight," p. 308).

As the focalizer, Amira does not only comment on gender relationships in Darfur and the sociocultural/political nature of conflicts and the aftereffects, but also communicates her frustrations and ambivalence to the reader through the poetic expressions. This echoes the tenet of intersectionality acknowledged by third world feminists as a reality for women of color. Titles of the poems give readers a clue to Amira's concerns and anxieties ranging from the first poem that establishes their connection to the farm through "School" (p. 8) that draws attention to her desire to be educated, "Shock" (p. 84) that expresses the trauma she feels at losing loved ones, and "Flight" (p. 308) that celebrates her escape.

The author also adds credibility by integrating local names or terms of endearment for the characters (Amira, Muma, Dando, Halima, Old Anwar), and modified forms of names of institutions identified with that region (Gad Primary School). She references real refugee camps (Kalma), and taps into the tribal beliefs of calling the moon in the poems, "Glowing Sayidda" (p. 36) and "Unwelcome" (p. 172). In the back matter, Pinkney discusses her research process and outlines a brief history of Darfur. She provides key statistics noting that, "Since 2003, at least 300,000 people have been killed and more than 2.5 millions have been displaced" (unpaged). She positions herself as an outsider with a mind and heart who longs to tell the story in a skillful and engaging manner: "I wrote this novel with a weeping heart" (unpaged). By acknowledging her subjectivity vis à vis the story she tells through Amira, an insider persona of her creation, she adds a layer of authenticity. To accomplish this feat Pinkney says she "spent countless hours interviewing individuals who have lived through the Darfur conflict" (unpaged). And so I conclude that the outside voices of the author and illustrator, through research and imagination, reconstruct an "authentic" voice of the focalizer that reiterates the power of art as one form of emancipatory pedagogy.

Discussion and Conclusion

In this last section, I discuss the findings of the study and their significance within the fields of children's literature and literacy. My purpose was to understand how art is used in *The Red Pencil* to liberate a female survivor of the 2003 Darfur war, as well as to ascertain how the author and illustrator ensure the cultural authenticity of the story. My findings indicate that they accomplish this in various ways:

* constructing a narrator who is not only the focalizer but also a cultural insider;
* having her participate in the daily life of her people, and providing her with age-appropriate tools to record their cultural histories as related to her;
* according her the status of an artist and employing artistic styles, strategies, and modes of expressions that afford her a stake in meaning construction; and
* including research information in the back matter that adds credibility to the story.

To establish trustworthiness in this study, I attempted to "balance between description and interpretation" (Zhang & Wildemuth, 2009, p. 5), and situate the analysis within specific theoretical frameworks. Critical content analysis is an appropriate qualitative research method for this type of study. It affords one the opportunity to analyze literary texts by examining carefully how meaning is constructed, using coding strategies that assist in the creation of analytical categories to further discuss these constructions in ways that are beneficial to communities of scholars and educators. Paired with a critically conscious framework, the method and theory also serve my interest in issues of social justice in texts, of which literature is one type.

Children's literature about conflicts in Africa seems to thrive in the twenty-first century. However, readers rarely read about female characters like Amira who not only survive, but also refuse to be perceived as victims. Such characters believe that in spite of their limitations by virtue of their age, gender, cultural histories, race/ethnicity, class, religion, continent of origin, sexuality, marital status, and more, there is always a way to subvert in order to get ahead. This subversion reverberates key tenets of third world feminisms—the recognition of multiple forms of oppression that females from developing economies face. Art is one way through which one can subvert. In fact, as Amira's father imparts to her, the question should be: *What else is possible?* The spirit of never giving up regardless of the hurdles in one's path would benefit many youth plagued with a myriad of challenges in today's global society. In addition, the use of poetry as an outlet for such messages offers readers an alternate form through which narratives could appear, and Pinkney's *The Red Pencil*, a novel in verse, can serve as an exemplar.

The novel ends in an open-ended manner, creating opportunities for students to rewrite and further illustrate the story as they see fit. As Amira imagines herself flying like the sparrow seeking alternate ways to self-actualize, it is not clear yet what awaits her beyond; but the future *ought* to be better than what she is leaving.

No longer restricted by local traditions that curb her ambitions or by geographical location the world is hers. With her newfound wings and voice and strong belief in her abilities *in spite of where society has positioned her*, she may harness her creative energy to self-actualize.

The novel does not sensationalize violence; neither does it glamorize poverty nor undermine the struggle of being an Other. Rather, it stays steadfast to its mission of shedding light on the human condition, constructing human suffering and possibilities through art in ways that readers can empathize and emulate the actions of the artist/narrator to emancipate the self. Educators can capitalize on the power of such texts that create opportunities for personal and collective growth, and augment potentials for intellectual and emotional development through art in classroom settings. This is one way to engage in a social justice project of possibilities. If all strategies to help students to become well-rounded citizens and empathetic, creative, and critical readers/writers/thinkers fail, rather than giving up and holding everyone else accountable, perhaps we, as educators, should contemplate the question: *"What else is possible?"*

References

Alcoff, L. (1998). What should white people do? *Hypatia, 12*(3), 6–26.

Asian University for Women (2013). *Main tenets of third world feminist theories.* Retrieved from https://sites.google.com/site/anthologyauw/non-fiction/bonus-articles/main-tenets-of-third-world-feminist-theories

Cairnie, J. (2011). Reading across borders: Canadian girls reading African girls' stories. *Jeunesse: Young People, Texts, Culture, 3*(2), 175–189.

Collins, P. H. (2009). *Black feminist thought: Knowledge, consciousness, and the politics of empowerment.* New York: Routledge.

Crenshaw, K. (1991). Mapping the margins: Intersectionality, identity politics, and violence against women of color. *Stanford Law Review, 43*, 1241–1299. Retrieved from http://socialdifference.columbia.edu/files/socialdiff/projects/Article__Mappingthe_Margins_by_Kimblere_Crenshaw.pdf

de Waal, A. (2007). *War in Darfur: And the search for peace.* London: Global Equity Initiative, Justice for Africa.

Gangi, J. (2014). *Genocide in contemporary children's and young adult literature: Cambodia to Darfur.* New York: Routledge.

Human Rights Watch (2015). *World Report 2015.* Retrieved from http://www.hrw.org/world-report/2015/country-chapters/sudan

Khorana, M. G. (2014). Deconstructing the memoirs of African child soldiers published in the West. *Sankofa: A Journal of African Children's and Young Adult Literature, 13*, 106–120.

Kuntz, P. (2015). *Children's Africana Book Award database.* Retrieved from http://archives.africaaccessreview.org/Huwudui/showitem2.cfm?itemid=3089

Mackey, A. (2013). Troubling humanitarian consumption: Reframing relationality in African child soldier narratives. *Research in African Literatures, 44*(4), 99–122.

Mohanty, C. (2003). *Third world.* Durham, NC: Duke University Press.

O'Neill, K. (2012). *The decolonizing potential of local and metropolitan literature of the Rwanda genocide.* Calgary, Alberta, Canada: University of Calgary.

Oyewumi, O. (Ed.). (2011). Decolonizing the intellectual and quotidian: Yoruba scholars(hip) and male dominance. In O. Oyewumi (Ed.), *Gender epistemologies in Africa* (pp. 9–33). New York: Macmillan.

Smith, S. (2013/2014). Black feminism and intersectionality. *International Socialist Review*, Issue 91. Retrieved from http://isreview.org/issue/91/black-feminism-and-inter sectionality

Spivak, G. (2006). *In other worlds: Essays in cultural politics*. New York: Routledge.

South Sudan Profile: Overview. (2015, May 20). Retrieved from http://www.bbc.com/news/world-africa-14069082

Sudan Profile—Timeline. (2015, June 18). Retrieved from http://www.bbc.com/news/world-africa-14095300

Willis, A. I., Montavon, M., Hall, H., Hunter, C., Burke, La., & Herrera, A. (2008). *Critically conscious research: Approaches to language and literacy research*. New York: Teachers College Press.

Yenika-Agbaw, V. & Sychterz, T. (Eds.). (2015). *Adolescents rewrite their worlds: Using literature to illustrate writing forms*. Lanham, MD: Rowman & Littlefield.

Zhang, Y. & Wildemuth, B. M. (2009). Qualitative analysis of content. In B. Wildemuth (Ed.), *Applications of social research methods to questions in information and library science* (pp. 308–319). Westport, CT: Libraries Unlimited; https://www.ischool.utexas.edu/~yanz/Content_analysis.pdf 1(2): 1–12.

Children's Literature References

Kent, T. (2011). *Stones for my father.* Toronto: Tundra Books.

McKay, S. & Lafrance, D. (2013). *War brothers: The graphic novel.* Toronto: Annick.

Pinkney, A. (2014). *The red pencil.* New York: Little, Brown and Company.

Roberts, N. (2012). *Far from home.* London: Frances Lincoln.

9

THE SIGNIFICANCE OF THE ARTS IN LITERATURE

Understanding Social, Historical, and Cultural Events

Janelle Mathis

Art in its many forms not only provides a semiotic system for communicating and comprehending in unique ways, but also offers insights into culture, history, and social issues. As educators expand literacy to include the many ways we understand and communicate with the world, the role of the arts is critical in building knowledge of past and present cultures and understanding the sociocultural contexts that frame the extent and depth of our knowledge. Children's literature provides significant access to the arts through the creation of illustration and text that invite readers into complex issues. These issues are often perceived more clearly and comprehensively through artistic means. Such opportunities afford students a greater understanding of themselves and their position in a global society as they consider issues from multimodal perspectives using multiple sign systems to interpret cultural and historical events.

The inquiry in this chapter, while keeping with a critical content analysis frame that utilizes questions of authenticity, power, voice, and perspective, is offered from an intuitively positive perspective on the role of literature in the lives of readers. With the goal of identifying excellent resources, this inquiry considers the potential of literature that is richly endowed with artistic representation and so offers insightful perspectives on social issues, history, the arts, and culture. Framed by the theoretical lenses of social semiotics and New Historicism that address the role of the arts in society as integral texts in everyday interactions, this critical content analysis of *Sweethearts of Rhythm, The Story of the Greatest All-Girl Swing Band in the World* by Marilyn Nelson (2009) with illustrations by Jerry Pinkney examines the intersection of poetry, the visual arts, and music in framing insights for readers.

This story by an award-winning poet and illustrator is that of an all-female American swing band that originated at Piney Woods Country Life School in

Mississippi. The band performed from 1935 to 1945, and the story offers readers a complexity of understandings about this era that includes a delightful mixture of verbal and visual images, somber attention to the contemporary message of war's effects on a nation and the resiliency that moves it forward, reminders of the powerful effects of music, and insights into the lack of equality for women and people of color. A poetic picturebook for all ages, *Sweethearts of Rhythm* positions readers at a place in history where other texts have left a gap and provides poetry and art that support an exploration into topics that help to fill this gap in understanding U.S. history.

Through the voices of instruments situated in a New Orleans pawn shop in August 2005, the setting creates a connection between the sociocultural issues of the 1940s and more recent events, such as Hurricane Katrina. Issues of war and conflict, racial inequity, gender inequity, and the Great Depression are woven throughout the book. These issues provide a context for both poet and illustrator to present perspectives that enhance historical and cultural understandings through counter-narrative artistry. Such narratives offer readers opportunities to see beyond the dominant cultural interpretations of an event or story and contemplate other voices within society.

Theoretical Frames of New Historicism and Social Semiotics

Key to my focus on this literary work is viewing the arts as integral to understanding and contextualizing historical events and the culture of their times. The theoretical lens of New Historicism helps to frame the beliefs about the arts that undergird this analysis. New Historicism argues that there is no single story and a historical account is an ongoing discussion involving multiple histories. This belief paves the way for inclusion of all people in these accounts—those who are acknowledged by current history, those marginalized, and those whose voices have been previously omitted. Contradictions and gaps become significant as close inspections of history "complicate generalizations" (Gillespie, 2010, p. 86), thus pointing to the critical lens required for this content analysis.

To continue building on a critical frame, *Sweethearts of Rhythm* fills historical gaps and gives voice to women of color, who played significant roles during their lived historical era, but were omitted from historical accounts of World War II. With roots in the everyday, New Historicists consider literary texts significant only as they weave through other cultural representations, social contexts, and power relations of an era. Drawing from the work of Foucault who questions the ways our social order has been produced and how it might be transformed, three premises are significant: "history is discontinuous; a given period is better understood as a site of conflict between competing interests and discourses than as a unified whole; and the role and function of power is redefined" (Malpas, 2013, p. 67).

The use of art reflects another tenet of New Historicism. "Only by refusing to separate artistic expression from other forms of social and cultural interaction, New Historicists have argued, can art or literature come to be meaningful or important to us at all" (Malpas, 2013, p. 67). New Historicism is framed around the interdependence of the arts and culture, a concept that is reflected in *Sweethearts of Rhythm*. Art and literature are shaped by the beliefs and desires of society and actively sustain and challenge them as sites of power and resistance (Malpas, 2013). The various artistic forms become documentary texts providing insight into an event or historical era. At the intersection of Marilyn Nelson's poetry, Jerry Pinkney's art, and the music of the Sweethearts of Rhythm, readers are reminded of the integral role of the arts in life, culture, and history.

Another theoretical lens that undergirds this inquiry is social semiotics. Semiotics is the study of how we use sign systems, such as music, visual arts, language, and dance, and the processes underlying communication and representation. Social semiotics focuses on how people use sign systems within particular historical and cultural social settings (van Leeuwen, 2005). "This implies a dynamic, reflexive relationship between text and context in which individuals acting with text shape and are shaped by their participation in activities" (Siegel & Rowe, 2011, p. 206). According to van Leeuwen, social semiotics takes on significance as a theory when aligned with other forms of social theory as well as theories from fields that speak to specific contexts and issues.

A social semiotic approach is also significant in this inquiry since it "compares and contrasts semiotic modes, exploring what they have in common as well as how they differ, and investigating how they can be integrated in multimodal artefacts and events" (van Leeuwen, 2005, p. xi). Such multimodal approaches to literacy offer unique potentials of meaning. The use of multiple sign systems in illustrated books for young readers enhances the potential for understanding social and cultural events and issues from which students are distanced by geographical location and historical eras. As they position themselves in other contexts in unique multimodal frames, they can potentially become more aware of their own identities.

Thus, the basic tenets of New Historicism supporting this research are:

- historical accounts as ongoing discussions involving multiple perspectives and histories thus allowing for the voices of those previously marginalized;
- the interdependence of art, culture, and social contexts including power relations; and
- the significance of multiple sign systems within historical, social, and cultural scenarios to negotiate understanding, a tenet shared with social semiotics.

These tenets intertwine throughout this analysis.

Research Methodology

Each poem and illustration in this book offers a different perspective on the story of the Sweethearts as embedded within the sociocultural history of the United States during World War II. Therefore, my approach to analysis began by spending time in research to gain a more in-depth understanding of the history and historical perspectives of the time. In seeking to bring not only theory but contextual knowledge to the analysis, I engaged in reading historical pieces of this era, interviews, and other literature set in this time period. I focused as well on establishing knowledge of the author and illustrator that included conversations with them. These conversations not only informed me further about the era from the perspectives of individuals within the African American culture, but they positioned the creators' ideologies within the text and images of *Sweethearts of Rhythm*, thus supporting and strengthening the findings.

I began the critical content analysis by examining each poem in terms of artistic use of poetry and the visual representations that accompany the poems. During this examination through the lens of New Historicism and social semiotics, specific terms and phrases were identified and coded that reflected historical significances, artistic insights (considering both visual art and music), and author perspectives. Questions that reflected a critical stance undergirded this close examination:

- Whose perspective is predominant in this book?
- Whose voices are heard or omitted?
- How is the story contextualized in various historical sociocultural influences?
- How are the arts shown in relationship to the historical events of the story?
- How do the author and illustrator make clear their perspectives?

The same approach was taken for the illustrations using a coding method by Albers and Harste (2007), educators who are also artists. They have approached reading illustrations using the work of Kress and van Leeuwen (2006) to interpret the visual design of the artist by considering the placement of the image by the artist on the top and bottom halves as well as the left and right. Also of importance is how the artist has framed the center as well as used vectors, color, gaze, and exaggeration. The belief that all signs are purposeful is evidenced in the work of counter-narrative art and artists, such as this book, as they offer new perspectives on taken-for-granted, dominant motifs (Harste, 2014). Counter-narratives often speak back to the prevailing interpretations or assumed themes of the dominant culture.

My analysis process consisted of constructing an understanding of the overall organization of the book, described in the next section, and then closely analyzing each poem. The analysis of one poem is shared as an example of my analysis procedures. The themes that emerged as the text and images of each poem were analyzed through the theoretical lenses of New Historicism and social semiotics form the basis of the findings as related to the overall purpose of this critical content analysis.

Overall Organization of the Book

Sweethearts of Rhythm is organized into a series of 20 poems, each narrated by a personified instrument that reflects on an historical event while sharing its relationship with the particular Sweetheart who was renowned for songs performed with that instrument. The poems chronologically tell the story of this swing band from its inception at the Piney Woods School until the band dispersed following the war's end. As each instrument shares a memoir of its "girl," the recognized closeness of a musician to her instrument is realized in Nelson's creative approach. At the same time, taking the perspective of the instruments allowed Nelson to write to social issues of the time without the personal "baggage" that a well-created character would carry.

The format of the individual poems is similar as each is entitled with a particular song title that was part of the repertoire of the Sweethearts, followed by a subtitle that names the person who played the particular instrument and whose voice is being acknowledged. The voice of each instrument is crafted with words that describe its sound, physical presence, and personal history. Each poem has a reference to the war that was ongoing as well as to other sociocultural issues of the time that speak to inequities of race, gender, and social class. And, each poem poses a reflective question or idea for readers to contemplate long after the poems end—questions that frequently link the poetry to contemporary times. Both the authentic musical references and the multilayered poetry reveal the poet's careful research, attention to detail, and perspective as she interprets culture through the artistry of her words. The illustrator, Jerry Pinkney, noted:

> What I noticed was how compact the poems were in terms of lines, words, and word count, but at the same time Marilyn was able to weave into lines the bigness of that time period and all of the different layers and dimensions that were going on. I thought that was pretty powerful as it was not straight forward narrative but did take you through that time and through the lives and journey of the Sweethearts.
>
> *(Mathis, 2009, p. 15)*

The illustrations, while uniquely relaying the story of each instrument and Sweetheart through visual images, provide insights into the history of this time. Pinkney creates a visual sign system to understand the nature of this swing band, including double-page spreads that use color, tone, shape, space, light and dark to portray joy, movement, music, confidence, and agency. Pinkney is known for his artistic ability to create illustrations that not only serve to complement an author's text but that also provide a visual semiotic experience for readers—experiences that enter cultural and historical eras effortlessly and invite readers to understand from the perspective of the creator. As Leavy (2009) reminds, "All art regardless of medium is a product of time and place in which it is created as well as the individual artist who is an embodied actor situated within the social order" (p. 216).

The illustrations surrounding each poem are multilayered in meaning as they focus on the Sweethearts but position them in a sociocultural context of the time in which they lived and performed. Pinkney's own exuberance around the Sweethearts' role in African American and U.S. history is evident in the depiction of the high energy and joyous movement portrayed by vibrant color in illustrations focused on these women. This joy is in contrast with the solemn images in muted tones of war, inequity, racism, and the Great Depression that are appropriately placed throughout the book. This contrast aligns with Pinkney's insights regarding the contrast of the times: "The democracy of the time was in the music. At a time of great struggle, and a great burden on the shoulders, everybody went out and danced. They were dancing all at the same time. There were whites dancing in clubs in the north and blacks dancing in the south—all dancing at the same time and all dancing well" (Mathis, 2009, p. 14). Pinkney also explored the use of color as he sought answers to his question, "How do I interpret the kind of *color* that we find in music?" (Mathis, 2009, p. 16).

As both artist and poet work to bring alive the swing band, the musical focus of the book provides overarching attention to the arts. Music is unifying and offers resiliency, while swing is a musical genre of joy and energy. So in considering the creation of this book, both poet and artist listened to jazz, swing, and the recordings of the Sweethearts performing as they prepared for the transmediation of taking their response to this music and recreating it through poetry and art. This process of transmediation provided the basis from which each artist worked to create a story that reflected history, culture, and their interpretations, interests, and intents in making connections for contemporary readers. Both artist and poet reflect tenets of New Historicism and social semiotics as each embed their portrayal of the Sweethearts within the sociocultural issues of the era and each relies on the other to uniquely tell the same musical story—through the varying perspectives of artist and poet.

Example of Analysis Processes

The following poem reflects only one of the stories in this book. This example reflects the types of words and phrases that were dominant in coding the poems through the theoretical lens of New Historicism and social semiotics.

"Take the 'A' Train: Ernestine 'Tiny' Davis on Trumpet"

Every swing tune tells a story without words:
The truth of people breathing in unison,
The democracy of harmonies and chords,
Unique, disparate voices raised as one.

I led the band in an artillery
of wittily syncopated quarter notes,
or with the buttery longing her strong lips drew from me
until a warbling April morning filled my throat!

Hey, a little forgetfulness was a good things,
a respite from the battle-to-battle news.
The ultimate give-and-take is right there in swing:
the improvised melodic objective of jazz.

Whose music is "truer"? Your bald-eyed protest songs,
or the waves of joy in which people drowned their despair?
Forgetfulness, or a recitation of wrongs?
Shoot, taking the 'A' Train was a form of prayer.

The first paragraph speaks of a country striving for "unity," "democracy," "harmony," "raised as one"—a story told through swing music. Music aligning with democracy is evident in the use of shared terms such as harmony and unity. The second paragraph, reflective of an earlier poem, contrasts two types of trumpet sounds. The first, "wittily syncopated quarter notes," reflects a previous life when this trumpet was played by a military man while the contrasting tones of "with buttery longing her strong lips drew from me / until a warbling April morning filled my throat!" reflects its newfound life in the hands of a Sweetheart. The notion of her strong lips speaks to a powerful, confident woman while the idea of her drawing from this trumpet reflects the relationship that a player has with the instrument. "Hey, a little forgetfulness was a good thing / A respite from the battle-to-battle news" speaks to the music's offer of resiliency. The third paragraph speaks to the improvised melodic give-and-take of jazz. The concept of improvisation somewhat parallels a little forgetfulness in that one might improvise when the need to mentally leave the realities of battle is necessary though never straying totally from the issue at hand, or as in jazz leaving the key melody. And so, a question is asked by the poet: "Whose music is 'truer'?—the blatant realities of protest songs, reciting wrongs, or drowning despair in joy in an effort to forget? For this question an answer is provided by the poet, "Taking the 'A' train was a form of prayer." The music carries as much significance to this writer as the words of protest.

The image accompanying this poem is a couple engaged in an 'A' Train dance movement with both faces looking out from the center in a gaze of pleasurable engagement. Because of the image catching the couple in the midst of a circular flip, the young man's face is positioned in the upper half and his gaze, slightly to the right, gives off anticipatory energy of what is to come—perhaps a show of hopefulness. The musical notes and titles create a circle of torn collage indicating the circular movements of the dancers. The dark background highlights the illuminated figures whose faces and clothing of red, white, and blue colors are proudly illuminated. This image is reflective of the waves of joy that Nelson addresses in the poetry—in contrast to the songs and demeanor of protesters.

Themes Evolving from New Historicism and Social Semiotics

After analyzing each poem by identifying phrases that speak to how this book provides insights into history, four themes were noted from the poems and illustrations of the *Sweethearts of Rhythm*. These themes speak to the role of situated contexts and the arts in understanding historical events and eras.

The Significance of History Becomes Apparent in the Sociocultural Context of the Time that Includes the Weave of Numerous Events, Voices, and Perspectives

As the story of the swing band unfolds, so do the historical events that give the story significance. With some attention in the book's early poems to the girls' beginning at Piney Woods Country Life School, the war is introduced as "Some days the earth seems to reverse its spin" and thus provides rationale as to how this band of females could succeed in a time when the male gender ruled swing bands. The poem concludes with a metaphorical line that positions the music as a prayer for peace, change through music. This imagery leads to Pinkney's two-page spread in which the left side of his collage shows the words "peace" being tossed about by an explosion. The right illustration is an image of a twin playing the sax with a dove holding a branch of musical leaves instead of an olive branch. She is centered with eyes closed and an illuminating white glow that provides a peaceful presence. Another introduction to the onset of war is that of another two-page spread in sepia tones showing soldiers on the right marching with band instruments, then soldiers on the left marching with rifles.

Throughout the book, poems and images continue to focus on war with frequent text and images that work to position swing music as that of resilience in maintaining the spirits of a nation at war. In "It Don't Mean a Thing, Pauline Braddy on Drums," we read, "The jitterbug was one way people forgot the rapidly spreading prairie fires of war." In the poem "Black and Tan Fantasy, Johnnie May Rice on Guitar," a question is asked: "Was it democratic music, making every toe tap / and every heart lifting toward courage again, over fear?"

Another sociocultural issue that impacted the Sweethearts' ability to perform was the Jim Crow laws that did not permit racially mixed performing groups or even audiences. Jim Crow laws are introduced as having an "eye upon them" because the Sweethearts traveled back roads and highways, practicing in the country, playing in the city. Members of the Sweethearts were diverse and had a few white band members who had to darken their faces in order to perform. One poem "Lady Be Good" tells of a time when band member Roz Cron wailed so hard her make-up came off and she had to flee to the next town. While this event is described in a somewhat humorous way as triumphing over the Jim Crow laws, Pinkney created a full spread illustration of water fountains, in somber tones, labeled white and colored on facing pages—a reminder that such laws impacted the daily lives of many U.S. citizens.

Additionally, other perspectives within the era are presented as the guitar gives voice to those of the Dust Bowl—acknowledging that while swing offered resiliency and joy to some, others were victims of the natural disaster of drought coupled with the 'hard times' economics of the World War II era. This poem, "The Hard Luck Blues, Roxanna Lucas on Guitar," is somewhat of an anomaly as the guitar celebrates his glory days, yet downplays the spirit of *swing* as representing the whole nation, even calling it a form of denial. However, the premise of music offering resiliency is maintained as the guitar speaks of "playing ballads and talking blues"—a solemn way that farmers and others affected by the Dust Bowl could tell their story and find solace in song. A two-page spread illustration of a dust-covered farm reveals the depressed state of some of the country— still with notes floating as bits of collage seem to soothe the viewer.

Including others who faced prejudice on the home front of this historical era, both poet and artist solemnly reference the Japanese internment camps. Pinkney's image is in muted tones with guards facing to the right outside a fence. Behind the fence are images of Japanese people with baggage with some viewed as potentially from African American descent.

Additionally, those soldiers who faced internal "gloom" from the war they witnessed are acknowledged as the Sweethearts give a USO tour at the end of the war and the poem gives credit to swing for renewing the smiles of soldiers. Pinkney's image of soldiers is in the same muted khaki tones as the uniforms of the Sweethearts. The background is bright yellow indicating the bright times ahead beyond the battlefield. The performers and audience of soldiers face the page center, uplifted in the top half of the page. In some cases the soldiers' arms are raised in joy as music restores their smiles.

Other historical insights speak to the continuous role of this book as a counter-narrative that fills gaps in history where only the dominant culture is traditionally acknowledged. Black women serving in the role of riveters, an image that has been preserved as an iconic Caucasian figure, is described in light of the trombone section as, "Like dark Betty Grable Rosie the Riveters, felt their way, tune after tune to the absolute / unchanging fable of the universe." The accompanying image is that of a trombonist holding her instrument and sharing the page alongside a parallel picture of an African American female riveter—each centered in a stately position efficiently holding her instrument or tool. Images and words pointedly reveal the involvement of African American women in supporting their country.

A brief line referencing the Victory Gardens is found in "Red Hot Mama" as it discusses the rationing of food and resulting "victory" vegetable plot. This inclusion of African Americans in growing Victory Gardens is an image Pinkney included in his pictorial counter-narrative—a topic that he also addresses in an interview when speaking of *all* U.S. citizens participating in war efforts and resilience. According to Leavy (2009), "Visual art may serve as a vehicle for transmitting ideology while it can as effectively be used to challenge, dislodge, and transform outdated beliefs and stereotypes. Visual images can be used as a powerful form of social and political resistance because the arts, and perhaps the visual arts in particular, always retain oppositional capabilities" (p. 102).

Gender is another social issue that creates a contextual consideration of this era. The Sweethearts formed a swing band that performed nightly and was sold out in significant venues. The sociocultural attitude of the time is revealed through Nelson in lines found in "Bugle Call Rag, Nova Lee McGee on Trumpet." This poem paid tribute to the powerful musicianship of McGee as the trumpet first bemoans having to be played by a female until she "blasted the rafters" and the trumpet realizes his potential went far beyond the marches he had played in the army.

The Sociocultural Context of Any Historical Era Includes the Influences and Role of the Arts in All Its Forms

This second theme is a major theoretical tenet of New Historicism. While the first theme includes examples of this second theme, the impact of the arts deserves to be highlighted because of ways in which Nelson and Pinkney attend to this focus. Detailed descriptions of the tones of the instruments and how they reflected the times are seen in each poem. In "That Man of Mine, 'Tiny' Davis on Trumpet" the poetry describes the war's end proclaimed through the instruments as "a shimmering texture of sound that was shot through with joy" and "a musical edifice shaped out of air."

In a concluding poem, Nelson traces the movement of music to reflect new times, ideologies, and innovations as seen in the stanzas from "Mercy, Mercy, Mercy, Julian 'Cannonball' Adderley on Alto Sax." "The Age of Anxiety" produced a fragmented fast-paced and intense bebop as described in this poem. The end of the war is reflected through poems about the dissolution of the Sweethearts as the men returned home to assume musical positions and the women married and put aside instruments for family responsibilities. In addition, the historical change in music styles and the entry of the juke box took the place of bands in some places.

Despite universality, music is a cultural product imprinted with material and symbolic aspects of its point of production as well as the musical conventions prevalent in that time and place. Music is created in cultural and historical contexts and thus varies across time and space. Although popularly thought of as a universal language, "music only unites people within certain contexts and can also identify differences across cultures and ethnicities and comment on those differences" (Leavy, 2009, p. 102). Further, music can help "access/shed light on social experience that other textual or visual forms may fail to capture" (Leavy, p. 106). Through Pinkney's art, the role of dance and movement is felt as those listening use music to release their tensions during conflict, their joy as armistice is declared, and to accompany the hard times as in the image of the young man playing a guitar on a railway car situated in the Dust Bowl.

Any Retelling of History Is Influenced by the Perspectives and Voices of the Author and Illustrator as Well as Those Individuals Involved in an Event or Experience

The third theme is acknowledged by both Nelson and Pinkney. Nelson's stance on each instrument's story positions universal truths as well as intertextual notions of equity. An example is seen in "She's Crazy with the Heat, Helen Jones, Ina Bell Byrd, and Judy Jones on Trombone":

> That good exists, that love prevails over fear,
> that hate and war are eventually kenneled again.
> Yea, our music told this story to all who could hear.
> Yeah: Love will prevail. Yeah. (Don't ask us when.)

These lines reveal universal concerns for peace. Even the setting of the story, a pawn shop in New Orleans, links the ongoing role of music across eras in obvious ways while implying a connection to notions of equity and human rights. The pairing of music with sociocultural issues of conflict and equity seemingly parallels the association of New Orleans music with issues related to Katrina, implied in subtle ways.

Pinkney articulates the pride and elegance of these young women in interviews and depicts their sense of agency in illustrations with centered positioning of the individuals, serious and knowing when playing their instruments, and attractive in how they present themselves with confidence and stately demeanor. His concern that African Americans have not been represented in many aspects of history is seen in his depiction of the girls as well as those individuals listening to their music as jubilant and confident. His depiction of soldiers on the field and his image of the Victory Gardens put forth his insight that all U.S. citizens were undergoing similar reactions to the war and to the resulting economic and social situations. Leavy (2009) reminds readers that "Visual imagery does not represent a window onto the world but rather a related perspective" (p. 215). This perspective includes the vantage point of the artist, the lens through which he looks, and the context in which a picture/photo is viewed. Visual art opens up multiple meanings determined not only by the artist but also the viewer and context of viewing—both immediate circumstances and larger sociocultural context.

Taking a Social Semiotics Perspective in Understanding History Provides Multiple Ways for Both Those Creating a Book to Share Their Interpretations and for Those Reading the Book to Personally Engage in the Complexity of a Story

A final theme addresses the role of social semiotics in acknowledging the various sign systems that constitute any social context as well as the potential for artists, such as Pinkney and Nelson, to transmediate their understandings of the time through signs—both in a receptive and expressive mode. The artist and illustrator used the venue of this book to share their perspectives on the role of these African American women. Using the signs of language and visual art, both artists engage readers deeply and authentically through the complexity of semiotics that contextualizes this era and this poetic narrative. Leggo (2008) states, "Where prose often seems transparent and is taken for granted, poetry invites the writer and the reader to pay attention to the semiotics of figurative language, sound effects, texture, voice, rhythm, shape on the page, line breaks, and stanzaic structure. In a poem, everything signifies" (p. 169). She continues discussing poetry as invitations to experiment with language, to create, to know, to engage creatively and imaginatively with experience.

Visual art, as well, provides invitations for multilayered approaches to understanding that include evoking stories, questions, and empathetic understandings (Weber, 2008). However, the metaphoric nature of revealing the ineffable nature of visual images invites personal connections to events from history or from places that are distant to the lives of readers. In *Sweethearts of Rhythm*, readers can easily acknowledge the significant role of the visual as Pinkney's work energizes the poetry and reveals a clear perspective of both the swing band and the African American communities involved in listening, dancing, and participating in supporting their country during a time of war.

Music communicates a variety of information to the society, including insights into particular historical periods, power relations, social struggles or movements, social or political resistance, and personal or collective experience related to many circumstances (e.g., racial or gender inequality, the experience of war, violence, sexuality). The particular power of music as a vehicle of information is consistently acknowledged, and it makes sense that other semiotic systems, through transmediation, offer diverse ways of acknowledging the complexities of the stories being told and how those telling the story have engaged in the historical context.

Conclusions

This critical content analysis, while supporting the role of the arts to inform both culturally and historically, also points to the potential of literature to provide historical texts that are significant for readers in speaking to the contextual social issues of the time. The perspectives and voices of the Sweethearts are gleaned from the research of both author and illustrator. Readers hear the voices of those creating the story—their perspectives, concerns, and interests are authentically shared through their art. Such books are important for readers to access a comprehensive perspective of history that invites them to understand history's intrigue and role in contemporary lives. Pinkney himself reminds us of this critical need:

> It is getting harder to talk about things that happened in the past and it doesn't have to be that far back in the past. I try to connect it to what decisions and lives the children are living today—to speak about a time in such a way that students are interested in the topic and how it affects them. I think that is the thing that often times is lost to young people, especially in areas like music. . . . Children should know about swing music and what swing music meant at the time. They should also know about the creativity that was part of that time and how people expressed themselves in terms of dance, body movement. It is important to me that they understand the relevance and that they don't see their lives as this little isolated capsule . . . It is fascinating how we've been able to overcome challenging situations of the past as well as maintain our joys, especially the lineage of music.
>
> *(Mathis, 2009, p. 15)*

Leggo (2008) notes the power of discourse to structure readers' sense of reality as well as their own identities. By challenging "the discursive patterns and frames that society permits and authorizes, on the one hand, and excludes and prohibits, on the other" (p. 168) through literature that situates historical events in comprehensive contexts, we invite students to understand, interpret, and respond in diverse ways. This kind of critical content analysis serves teachers by providing an awareness of texts that challenge existing discursive patterns limiting readers' insights. Through identifying examples of counter-narrative texts, educators develop an awareness of "how singularly words, speech, language and phrase shape consciousness and define reality" (Brueggeman, 2001, p. 164). This awareness supports a critical stance toward book selection, how literature is strategically used, and how history is taught.

Poetry, as a more specific form of artistic text, can invite readers to look at something in a new way, a stance critical to raising consciousness and social change as young readers are asked to see something differently. bell hooks suggests that poets can capture intensely subjective truths as well as their relation to the larger context and states that art can be a site of exclusion but also can be transformative as it resists and dislodges stereotypes (Leavy, 2009). Identifying books that serve this subjective and transformative role is a potential outcome of critical content analysis. As we look to the possibility of social change, such texts can propel people to look at something in new ways, to see differently through a consciousness raising that may not be possible through written text alone.

Another important implication of this content analysis is the relationship of the arts and culture in relating and positioning historical events. Hybridity is referred to as a place in which cultures, eras, genre, and other sociocultural elements merge to create a new space for negotiation and insights regarding culture. This "third space" (Bhabha, 1990) provides a place to examine issues of identity, power, equity, and resilience from shared and differing perspectives:

> All forms of culture are continually in a process of hybridity. But for me the importance of hybridity is not to be able to trace two original moments from which the third emerges, rather hybridity to me is the "third space" which enables other positions to emerge. This third space displaces the histories that constitute it, and sets up new structures of authority, new political initiatives, which are inadequately understood though received wisdom. The process of cultural hybridity gives rise to something different, something new and unrecognizable, a new area of negotiation of meaning and representation.
>
> *(p. 211)*

Marilyn Nelson captured the notion of space in "Chattanooga Choo-Choo, Twin Ione or Irene Gresham on Tenor Sax," when she says "She was pushing herself through me to an open space / Where people can be one." An image by Pinkney frames one twin contemplatively placing the reed in the sax with an illumination surrounding her to indicate that space.

In its broadest sense, third space is a flexible concept that can be used to make sense from multiple perspectives of a "constantly shifting and changing milieu of ideas, events, appearances, and meanings" (Soja, 2008, p. 50). It is a space "where issues of race, class, and gender can be addressed simultaneously without privileging one over the other" (p. 50). The potential of taking a multimodal approach to learning history becomes apparent as a learner's understanding is enhanced through parallels and interweaving of poems, songs, and art. Just as our "real life" awareness comes from the multiple sign systems with which we come in contact daily, so an awareness of history comes alive through the perspectives and connections offered by the arts in literature.

Each classroom has the potential to be a space where literacy learners address and negotiate the complexities of text and the sociocultural events that serve to create and are recreated by these texts. Critical content analysis not only serves the teacher but also provides a frame with which students can question texts and become immersed in a more comprehensive understanding of a sociocultural or historical situation. The use of multiple sign systems affords a multimodal approach that offers a diversity of perspectives—not only those of the author, illustrator, and historical context of the time, but perspectives offered by the arts. In classrooms where such perspectives are valued, students recognize the arts as sources of insight to the communities in which they participate as well those they discover through literature.

Scholars of children's literature frequently undertake critical content analyses to create an awareness of issues of power that place the dominant cultural ideology at the forefront to the exclusion of other voices and perspectives. This inquiry into the *Sweethearts of Rhythm* points to the alternate role of such analyses in providing a resource that serves to fill historical gaps as a counter-narrative in both its poetic text and illustrations. Such authentic texts do exist in our growing children's literature field as authors and illustrators position themselves as educators of young readers. Critical content analyses can serve to identify these texts.

References

Albers, P. & Harste, J. (2007). The arts, new literacies, and multimodality. *English Education, 40*(1), 6–20.

Bhabha, H. (1990). *Nation and narration*. New York: Routledge.

Brueggeman, W. (2001). *The prophetic imagination*. Minneapolis, MN: Fortress Press.

Gillespie, T. (2010). *Doing literary criticism: Helping students engage with challenging texts*. Portland, ME: Stenhouse.

Harste, J. (2014). The art of learning to be critically literate. *Language Arts, 92*(2), 90–102.

Kress, G. & van Leeuwen, T. (2006). *Visual images: The grammar of visual design* (2nd ed.). New York: Routledge.

Leavy, P. (2009). *Method meets art: Arts-based research practice*. New York: Guilford.

Leggo, C. (2008). Astonishing silence, knowing in poetry. In J. G. Knowles & A. L. Cole (Eds.), *Handbook of the arts in qualitative research* (pp. 165–174). Thousand Oaks, CA: Sage.

Malpas, S. (2013). Historicism. In S. Malpas & P. Wake (Eds.), *Routledge companion to critical and cultural theory* (2nd ed., pp. 62–72). New York: Routledge.

Mathis, J. (2009). Swinging with the Sweethearts: A conversation with Marilyn Nelson and Jerry Pinkney. *Journal of Children's Literature, 35*(2), 9–16.

Siegel, M. & Rowe, D. W. (2011). Webs of significance: Semiotic perspectives on text. In D. Lapp & D. Fisher (Eds.), *Handbook of research on teaching the English language arts* (3rd ed., pp. 202–207). New York: Routledge.

Soja, E. W. (2008). Thirdspace: Toward a new consciousness of space and spaciality. In K. Ikas & G. Wagner (Eds.), *Communicating in third space* (pp. 49–61). New York: Routledge.

Van Leeuwen, T. (2005). *Introducing social semiotics*. New York: Routledge.

Weber, S. (2008). Visual images in research. In J. G. Knowles & A. L. Cole (Eds.), *Handbook of the arts in qualitative research* (pp. 41–54). Thousand Oaks, CA: Sage.

Children's Literature Reference

Nelson, M. (2009). *Sweethearts of Rhythm, the story of the greatest all-girl swing band in the world*. Illus. by J. Pinkney. New York: Penguin.

10

THE RIGHT TO PARTICIPATE

Children as Activists in Picturebooks

Kathy G. Short

The willingness to take action in order to make a difference in the world is a critical component of intercultural understanding, but moving from a discussion of social justice into meaningful action appropriate to young children is difficult (Short, 2011). Although service learning is receiving increased emphasis in schools, these projects often take the form of volunteering or charity where children "give a handout to the poor and unfortunate" instead of inquiring into the underlying social and global conditions and developing strategies for action. In addition, these service learning projects are often directed by adults, with children making few decisions about their focus or implementation (Cowhey, 2006).

Novels and picturebooks that portray children taking action for social change in local and global settings are a source of demonstrations of authentic social action and children's rights and responsibilities. Books, such as *Hope Springs* (Walters, 2015), focus on children who live in situations where they fear for their safety or are concerned for the well-being of others. They are willing to engage in the "risky business" of activism with others in order to transform their lives or the world in some way, rather than wait for adults. These books provide demonstrations that children, not just adults, are responsible for and capable of social action.

The question remains, however, whether these demonstrations are limited by the same adult constraints as often occur in action projects in schools. Many adults assume that children will make valuable contributions to society in the future, but currently need adult guidance and protection (Hart, 1992; Young-Bruehl, 2012). The rights of children to be heard and taken seriously often are not recognized, leading to limited expectations about children's ability to participate and make contributions. The issues go far beyond what is authentic social action for children to larger issues of how adults view children and their capabilities.

As educators, we are responsible for examining the demonstrations offered by the books we share with children to determine whether they support children's development of agency and voice or provide further evidence of adult domination. A critical frame that combines children's rights with social justice perspectives provides a lens for examining underlying assumptions about children and what constitutes social action in picturebooks where children take action.

Theoretical Frames of Critical Pedagogy and Childism

The two critical theories that frame this analysis are childism and critical pedagogy. Childism provides insights into the ways in which children are discriminated against by adults, particularly in assumptions about children's reasoning abilities and rights and their development of agency (Young-Bruehl, 2012). Critical pedagogy addresses the question of authentic action for social justice and the need for problem-posing strategies as well as problem-solving (Freire, 1970). Both frames are essential to a critical content analysis of picturebooks where children resist injustice and engage in social action.

Childism and the Rights of Participation

The United Nations Convention on the Rights of the Child (1989) was based in the belief that children have rights, and that adults and governments have obligations to uphold those rights. These rights of provision, protection, and participation involve provision of children's basic needs for food, clothing, and shelter along with their rights for protection of safety and health and their rights of participation in decision making and self-determination. Elizabeth Young-Bruehl (2012) argues that this statement of children's rights also provides the basis for a critique of childism, defined as prejudice against children rooted in the assumption that children are the possessions of adults and so have no rights. She identifies two basic types of prejudice, acts of abuse or neglect and the more subtle lack of respect for children's abilities and capacities to make decisions about their life circumstances and to make contributions to society. This latter type of childism can lead to overprotection that limits children's enactment of agency and restricts opportunities for children to contribute to society in the present moment, not just once they become adults.

Young-Bruehl (2012) argues that adults often construct a child as immature and so underestimate and underappreciate children's contributions. She believes that adults have used the natural dependency of children as an excuse to deny children agency and capacity for choice and expression of their interests or reasoning. By declaring that children do not have these abilities, adults make it difficult for children to develop these aptitudes, leading to a self-fulfilling prophecy. Young-Bruehl challenges adults to listen to the voices of children, to prioritize their needs, and to respect their agency and capacity for choice, within a developmental rather than deficit perspective. Essentially, she asks that adults take children and their abilities seriously. Children should not be expected to act alone without adult support, but can do so when necessary. Their dependence on adults does not negate their ability to reason and for their voices to be considered in making decisions that affect their lives.

Maria Nikolajeva's (2010) concept of aetonormativity further develops childism through her argument that the norms of literature for children are those of adults, not children. The issue of children's oppression is also raised by Perry Nodelman (1992) in his article on children's literature as a form of colonialism. He points out that the adults who write, read, and review children's books often view children as incapable of speaking for themselves and as inferior to adults. Adults underestimate the capabilities of children and write books that provide children with the values and images they believe are important, such as obedience. By speaking for children as the "other," adults silence children and use their knowledge to dominate. In essence, adults ask children to accept their view of childhood and to gradually evolve into becoming "human" by becoming more like adults, instead of viewing childhood as a valid perspective and way of being in the world.

Roger Hart (1992) challenges this view of children and argues for participation as the process of sharing in decisions that affect people's lives and the lives of their communities. He argues that participation is embedded in power relations and that all children deserve opportunities to participate in decisions that directly influence their lives. His research on action projects led to development of the Hart Ladder of Participation, which identifies eight levels of children's participation. The first three levels of manipulation, decoration, and tokenism occur when adults use children to benefit their causes in a manner that patronizes children and silences their voices. The next three levels are based in adult initiation but engage children in some degree of choice in that children may be assigned but informed or consulted and informed or the action project may be adult-initiated with shared decisions with children. These degrees of participation are all valid depending on the nature of the project and children's knowledge and experiences.

Hart's final two rungs of the ladder involve projects that are child-initiated and child-directed or are child-initiated with shared decisions with adults. Shared decision making is the highest rung because Hart (1992) believes that collaborative action uses the unique contributions of both children and adults to most effectively take action. Hart's ladder is frequently employed as an evaluation tool for community programs for teens and provides an effective tool to connect children's rights and participation with social action through the lens of critical pedagogy.

Critical Pedagogy as a Frame for Action

Critical pedagogy is based in the work of Paulo Freire (1970), particularly his theories about challenging domination and oppression through examining the sociohistorical conditions that produce inequities and influence thought and relationships within a community. The goal is to go beneath the surface to understand the deeper meanings and causes of any action, event, or discourse. Through conscientization, individuals realize their consciousness by critiquing and disrupting accepted practices of power to challenge oppression through action.

The critical awareness that comes through critique is based in questioning the status quo and not accepting problems as "just the way things are." Instead, Freire (1970) urges individuals to ask *why* problems exist and to identify the underlying issues and root causes and who benefits from things staying the same. Critique alone can lead to paralyzing guilt unless paired with hope, imagining "what if" in order to consider alternative ways of living and to develop a vision of equity and justice. Out of critique and hope grows action for social justice and change.

Critical consciousness is put into motion by dialogue where individuals reflect on their views of reality and become problem-posers. Freire (1970) argues that the person who poses the problem is the one who remains in control. A problem-poser questions the questions posed by others, instead of automatically working to solve those questions. Both problem-posing and problem-solving are essential to taking action for social change and are embedded in collaboration as individuals engage in joint efforts toward liberation from oppression.

Critical pedagogy connects to childism through valuing children's voices and abilities as thinkers who can critique society. Freire (1970) believes that children become truly participatory members of a society as they create and re-create that society to increase freedom from oppression for themselves and others.

Critical Content Analysis through the Lens of Childism

Childhood studies (Hunt, 1991) has a long history of research of examining the ways that cultures construct childhood in children's literature. Galbraith (2001) argues that an emancipatory approach to childhood studies focuses on childhood experiences first and foremost, recognizing the significance of children's desires within human community. She points out that children's books provide a means of critiquing the dilemmas of childhood in an adult-dominated world, such as adults who don't stop to hear children's calls of distress. Only recently, however, have critical content analysis studies used childism as a critical theory frame for analysis.

Nance-Carroll (2014) uses childism and aetonormativity in an analysis of *The Composition* (Skármeta, 2000), a picturebook about the political involvement of a nine-year-old boy, Pedro, and his parents during Pinochet's dictatorship in 1970s Chile. He argues that Pedro's parents view children as apolitical, believing this position shields children from political attacks. Pedro not only teaches his parents that they have naïve views about childhood but that a political life is a necessity for a child living in a dictatorship and their protective stance has endangered him and themselves. Benevolent but limiting attitudes of adults construct children as deficient simply because they are children and, despite being well-meaning, put children in danger.

Nance-Carroll (2014) states that positioning Pedro as an average child, rather than exceptional or heroic, allows Skármeta to make visible that children frequently have to make moral and political decisions without access to the advice of adults. The book depicts childhood as "fraught with events from which children have the right—but not the opportunity—to be shielded" (p. 281). Adult perspectives are often childist and harmful even though they do not reflect cruelty. Nance-Carroll argues that viewing children as needing protection does not have to lead to the assumption that they lack the capacity for difficult decisions. Pedro's actions show children that they are not merely extensions of their parents, but "are instead active participants in the political world" (p. 284).

Joosen (2013) uses childism to study how adults are portrayed as characters in children's books by Guus Kuijer, a Dutch author. Kuijer published a critique of adulthood, arguing that children should be given respect for what they are now and not what they will become as adults. His children's books depict a "variety of positions that adults can take toward children, with varying degrees of childist features" (p. 205), offering positive and negative role models of adults in relationships with children through a child's perspective, a demonstration to both adults and children as readers.

The portrayal of adults as childist takes a nasty turn in Roald Dahl's *The Witches* (1983), which Curtis (2014) argues is based in child-hatred as a present danger hidden under the disguise of acting in the best interests of children. Curtis provides evidence that Dahl exposes the conflicting attitudes of adults who admire and resent children because of their frustration that they can never return to the "innocence" of childhood. Child-hatred takes the form of extreme neglect and abuse by the witches and is countered by the grandmother who respects and listens to the boy's opinions and ideas. Curtis points out that this book uncovers the connection between child-protection and child-hatred and the troubling ambivalence of adults toward childhood.

Todres and Higinbotham (2013) use a law perspective on childism to examine the work of Dr. Seuss, arguing that his child-centered, imaginative, and self-determining books challenge the supremacy of adult perspectives as inherently superior in setting rules for children's own good. Instead, his books offer portrayals of children gaining power and agency on their own terms, in ways appropriate to the actions and thinking of a child. They provide evidence that Dr. Seuss's books, particularly *Horton Hears a Who!* (1954) and *Yertle the Turtle* (1958), establish the child as a distinct individual who has rights, including the right to non-discrimination, the right to survival and development, and the right for participation and to be heard—the foundational principles of the Convention on the Rights of the Child (1989).

Todres and Higinbotham (2013) use their analysis of Dr. Seuss as well as their knowledge of the law to argue that, while children may lack the full autonomy of adults, they have the right to be heard. Children's voices are not the only voices in a decision, nor necessarily the determining voice, but they have the right for an opportunity to participate in the process. They also point out that Dr. Seuss shows that children's rights come with responsibilities to respect and protect the rights of others through action. In addition, his books contain adult characters who recognize and act to ensure the rights of children and who work collaboratively with children to enable children to "articulate their needs and realize their rights" (p. 36).

These scholars draw from childism to examine how children's books can take on a child's perspective of the world and resist the imposition of adult views. Their research provides strategies and theoretical insights that inform my analysis. In addition, the studies offer a lens for critiquing the plot of books, such as *The Tale of Peter Rabbit* (Potter, 1902), in which children are taught that they must obey adults and conform to adult expectations and rules for their own good.

Critical Content Analysis as a Research Methodology

This critical content analysis of picturebooks in which children are portrayed as taking responsibility for social action is based in the frame of childism and critical pedagogy, specifically pulling from the theoretical tenets of:

- children's rights for participation in decisions about their life circumstances and in making contributions to society;
- children's right to be heard and their views considered in interactions with adults;
- children's development of critical consciousness to critique oppression in everyday life; and
- children's movement from critique to hope before moving to action—from questioning "what is" to considering "what if" and then acting.

Although novels contain many depictions of children engaging in action, I decided to focus on picturebooks since these books are read by younger children who are more vulnerable to adult assumptions about their abilities to participate in taking responsibility for action. Also, picturebooks can easily be shared with children to provide a range of images of social action.

Twenty-nine picturebooks published and/or distributed in the United States between 1990–2010 were identified for analysis with some books first published in other countries (see Appendix A). The selected picturebooks are ones in which children take action and where they act to benefit others as well as themselves. Books in which children took action only for themselves, such as standing up to a bully, were excluded from analysis in order to examine whether the books portrayed children's responsibilities to others as well as themselves. The contexts are ones where children fear for the safety of themselves and others, but vary from dangerous political conflicts to interactions with bullies and compassion for animals and plants.

The critical theory frames of childism and critical pedagogy along with a literature review on service learning and social justice using sources such as Kaye

(2010) and Wade (2007) were used to analyze classroom data from K–5 classrooms on inquiries about human rights and hunger. Data from field notes, transcripts of literature discussions, and student artifacts were analyzed to identify principles for authentic and meaningful action in elementary classrooms (Short, 2011). The question then turned to whether or not these same principles were present in picturebooks depicting children taking action. The assumption was that if these principles are essential in children's inquiries to support authentic action, then they should also be present in the books read with children to provide demonstrations of action.

Definitions for each of the seven principles were developed from the action research and refined during analysis of the picturebooks, particularly with the addition of a childism frame. An analysis chart was developed for each book around the seven principles. After analyzing each book separately, the charts were used to identify patterns and anomalies across the books for each principle. This process also involved multiple returns to the theoretical constructs and literature review in order to use theory to think with the data.

Depictions of Children Taking Responsibility for Action

The analysis of classroom data indicated that authentic action develops out of inquiry and experience and meets a genuine need recognized by children. That action is based in collaborative relationships and leads to mutual exchanges between everyone involved in that action. The action is also based in a cyclical process of problem-posing and problem-solving that involves children in taking responsibility throughout the process so that their voices and choices are always considered. Finally, this action grows out of children's understandings of their responsibility for social justice and of the root causes for social problems.

Develops through Inquiry and Experience

When the action that children take is grounded in their lives and experiences and in their knowledge about the context for that action, the action is no longer completely dependent on adult knowledge. Kaye (2010) argues that meaningful service in a community must be combined with academic content so that the content that children are exploring through inquiry informs service and the service drives further learning and inquiry. Action goes beyond volunteering to collect trash in a neighborhood park, for example, to include analyzing that trash, figuring out the sources and reasons for the trash, and working with the community to reduce pollution. Students need time for reflection, inquiry, and learning values, strategies, and content.

If the action taken by children is carefully grounded in their life experiences, their inquiries grow from their interests, tensions, and understandings. The inquiries of children in this set of picturebooks did emerge from daily life, with the exception of one book. In these books, children did not necessarily have a strong knowledge base from which to act. Tension was not an isolated issue imposed by adults but something children were concerned about from their lives.

Two types of tensions were identified in the books. One set of tensions emerged from everyday events, such as teasing or bullying behaviors, an encounter with a homeless person, the desire to own a pair of popular shoes, or noticing an injured bird. An interesting tension in *Tricycle* (Amado, 2008) occurred when a Guatemalan child with plenty observes a child who has little take her tricycle and decides not to claim ownership of the tricycle. A second type of tension was that of war and conflict in which characters respond to dictators, a bombing, or ongoing adult conflicts, as in *First Come the Zebra* (Barasch, 2009) about two boys on opposite sides of a long-term conflict between hunters and grazers in Kenya.

Children's actions in a third group of books grew out of their need for hope as they struggle with extreme poverty and look for ways to bring hope into their family. The main character of *The Caged Birds of Phnom Penh* (Lipp, 2001) searches for a way to find a bird that will carry her family's wishes for the future into the sky. This need for hope stands in contrast to the desire to do good found in the final two books. In *Paulie Pastrami Achieves World Peace* (Proimos, 2009), Paulie goes through the day engaged in small acts of kindness at his home, school, and community in order to achieve world peace. The final book, *Give a Goat* (Schrock, 2010), involves a class project to raise money to purchase a goat for a family in Africa. In both books, the tension is the characters' desire to do good for others, rather than knowledge about the problems, a problematic stance that became more apparent in considering other principles.

Meets Genuine Needs

Authentic action meets an actual need that is recognized by children. Children need time to research and understand the issue from multiple perspectives by investigating whether the need actually exists and the nature of that need (Vasquez, 2004). Determining a need is not enough—children must also see that the need is significant. In all of the books except two, children were shown as responding out of a strong sense of need that they recognized and valued. They were not responding to an adult-imposed view. The two books that were exceptions were *Paulie Pastrami Achieves World Peace*, where Paulie skips from person to person doing good without stopping to determine an actual need and *Give a Goat* where the children are depicted as liking the idea of a gift that keeps giving. Their need is to raise money but the book does not depict whether they understand the needs of the people for whom they are trying to purchase a goat. Paulie reflects an adult view of the innocence and natural compassion of children, while the class acts out of an adult view of need without the opportunity for children to develop recognition and intent.

The types of needs depicted in the rest of the books ranged from:

*   misuse of power and authority (bullies, Border Patrol, generals);
*   threat of danger or the experience of oppression (war, child labor);
*   love of nature (plants, animals, birds, fish);
*   desire for peace and hope (breaking walls, making wishes); and
*   poverty and basic needs (food, shelter, clothes, toys).

One problematic pattern was the difference in level and type of need based on the global setting. Most of the books based in the United States and Western Europe were ones in which children took action out of compassion for plants and animals or concerns for friends, while those in Asia, Africa, and the Middle East took action out of fear based on dictators, war, and poverty. Although there were a few books showing homelessness and poverty in the United States, the type and level of need are strikingly different from other global settings. From a critical pedagogy perspective, these books do not question existing stereotypes of global settings; instead, they reinforce the view that these countries are places of conflict and oppression, in contrast to the safety of the United States. Poverty in the United States is shown from the perspective of those who have plenty, for example, the child who shares with a homeless person, rather than those living with poverty as in the global books.

Builds Collaborative Relationships

Reaching out to work *with* others through partnerships and shared responsibility with community members, parents, organizations, and students is essential to effective action; particularly in creating the potential for dialogue that Freire (1970) argues is necessary for transformation. These collaborative relationships involve learning about and with each other and gaining mutual respect, understanding, and appreciation. The books show a range of types of relationships:

*   children acting alone (8 books);
*   children taking action with other children (6 books);
*   children acting with adults (11 books); and
*   children acting within a group of people (4 books).

Subway Sparrow (Torres, 1993) depicts a group of people working together on a subway across languages and ages to rescue a sparrow caught in the underground, while *Sélavi/That Is Life* (Youme, 2004) tells the true story of homeless children who create a movement to build an orphanage and radio station in Haiti. These books show children who act with adults and peers on important issues in their worlds, the top rung of Hart's Ladder of Participation (1992). Individualism is a strong value in American culture and often leads to heroic depictions of one person, referred to as the Rosa Parks myth that she acted alone as a tired anonymous seamstress rather than as a long-standing activist within an organized movement. Kohl (1995) argues that not everyone can see themselves acting alone as a hero, but can imagine themselves as participating in a community effort against injustice.

Results in Mutual Exchanges

Many action projects in schools take the form of charity—"let's help the poor and unfortunate." Students raise money to send away to those experiencing hardship, resulting in giving that goes in one direction while students remain distanced from those whom they are helping (Cowhey, 2006). Authentic action occurs when there is a mutual exchange of ideas, information, and skills among *all* participants. Each person views others as having something to share and everyone gains from the experience (Wade, 2007).

The immediacy of the experiences in these books showed children gaining from interactions in different kinds of exchanges. The only two books where some type of mutual exchange did not occur were *Paulie Pastrami Achieves World Peace* and *Give a Goat* where the focus is on children as givers to "others." The rest of the books show children gaining from their interactions in several ways:

- Children gain from relationships, including friendship and the survival of living things.
- Children gain hope, through expressing wishes or being able to attend school.
- Children gain through joining with others to challenge inequity, such as child labor or government oppression.

Freire (1970) argued that dialogue is the key to transformation and the majority of the books depict characters engaged in dialogue with each other and those with and for whom they are taking action, creating a perspective of respect as collaborators. This dialogue shows children as capable and as being heard. In *Wanda's Roses* (Brisson, 1994), adults join Wanda in converting a trash-filled lot into a space for plants and flowers, offering her water and other resources and, in the process, gaining hope from her determination and faith. In *Friends from the Other Side* (Anzaldúa, 1993), a girl hides a boy and his mother who are undocumented immigrants in the United States. The girl realizes she must develop a relationship with the boy before offering help so that her action is based in relationship, not charity. The book also shows a moment of connection with a Border Patrol agent, instead of depicting him as an unfeeling oppressor.

Includes Action and Reflection

Authentic action grows out of children having responsibility throughout the process, including witnessing the outcome of their action when possible. A continuous cycle of action and reflection spirals throughout the process—identifying a problem, researching to understand, planning, anticipating consequences of the action, taking action, observing what happens, reflecting on what occurs, accepting responsibility for consequences, and then acting again. Dewey (1938) argues that when learners do not have the time to reflect on action, they lose much of the learning potential from an experience. A balance of action and reflection allows children to be aware of the impact of their work on their thinking and life as well as on others, essential to mutual exchanges. This emphasis on action and reflection recognizes children's ability to reason and challenges childism.

All of the books show the characters engaged in active problem-solving with only the children in *Give a Goat* not reflecting on their actions as problem-solvers, except in relation to how to raise money, and, of course, Paulie who is too busy doing good to reflect. In the rest of the books, the characters reflect on the problem before taking action and work to understand the situation in order to determine how to act. Several books show characters in a cycle of reflecting, acting, and then reflecting again on the response to that action before taking further action as in *Yasmin's Hammer* (Malaspina, 2010), where Yasmin tries to figure out a way to afford school and for her father to hear her voice on why education matters for her.

The type of reflection and action varies with most books showing a *direct action* where the child's action directly involves the recipients of that action, as when a Protestant girl in Belfast takes action to assist a Catholic girl who has to walk through her neighborhood each day in *Walking to School* (Bunting, 2009). Only one book depicted *indirect action*, where there is no direct interaction with the recipient even though the action benefits others. Indirect action often characterizes school projects so it's no surprise that this book was *Give a Goat* on a school project to raise money. Several books show *advocacy for action*, including *The Video Shop Sparrow* (Cowley, 1999), where two children advocate to various adults to open a closed shop where a sparrow is trapped. Other books include *research for action* as in *How to Heal a Broken Wing* (Graham, 2008) where a boy researches how to help a bird with a broken wing.

Invites Student Voice and Choice

Action projects in schools are often conceived and directed by adults, with little room for student voice or choice. Young-Bruehl (2012) and Hart (1992) argue that children have the right to participate meaningfully in the decisions that affect their lives and in the "behind the scenes" thinking that determines those choices. The valuing of individual voice is balanced by recognition of responsibility to the group so that one voice does not silence other voices, but is still heard and considered. Freire (1970) argues that dialogue provides an opportunity for children to learn to act with conviction and courage in expressing their views while keeping an open mind to the views and needs of others.

In relation to Hart's Ladder of Participation (1992), all of the books except *Give a Goat* show the action as child-initiated, with half of the titles depicting the child as acting with adult support. Adults respond to children's requests for help, the top rung of Hart's ladder, rather than imposing their beliefs onto a child. These books directly challenge the belief that children are not able to take responsibility for action. Children do not ask permission in these books; they act.

A closer examination of the role of adults, however, reveals that they are often the cause of the problem. While some adults act with children, many other adults are the direct cause of the situation that requires children to take a stand. Sometimes adults cause the conflict between opposing groups and expect children to continue those animosities as in *Walking to School* on the Belfast conflict. Other times adults are oppressors as in *Freedom Summer* (Wiles, 2001) where adults opposing the end of segregation fill in the town pool to prevent African American children from swimming with White children.

Two interesting patterns that reflect more subtle childism involve adults who underestimate or dismiss children. In *The Composition* (Skármeta, 2000), Pedro's parents withhold information about their involvement in resistance to a dictator, underestimating his ability to discern when that information could be dangerous. The book ends with the parents recognizing his competence. In *The Video Shop Sparrow*, the adults whom the children ask for assistance in opening a closed shop dismiss the children's request because they do not value the life of the sparrow. The children's persistence eventually leads them to an adult who listens, but the book effectively portrays the ways in which adults dismiss children's concerns. Finally, in *Sparrow Girl* (Pennnypacker, 2009), a young girl in China quietly resists Mao's demand that all sparrows be killed as pests by hiding birds in her barn. Her compassion and resistance are recognized by adults when insects eat the crops due to the absence of sparrows. These books highlight children's voices and resistance to being underestimated and protected or dismissed by adults.

Involves Civic/Global Responsibility for Social Justice

Civic engagement is often viewed as being a good citizen by voting, volunteering, and engaging in political activities that do not involve challenging the status quo (Banks, 2004). Taking civic or global responsibility from a social justice perspective (Freire, 1970) puts the focus on issues of power and oppression by looking at the social conditions within local and global communities through questions of critique, hope, and action that go below the surface of a problem to get at root causes, social contexts, beliefs, and consequences of that problem.

Children learn to problematize by questioning what is assumed to be "normal" by society and by developing critical consciousness. They do not just serve lunch in a soup kitchen; they also analyze the reasons for poverty in the community. They may visit seniors in a nursing home, but they also explore why the elderly are isolated in our society. The canned food drives in many U.S. schools reinforce stereotypes of the poor, oversimplify problems and solutions, and fail to teach an understanding of the causes of poverty. Instead of pity or charity, civic engagement challenges stereotypes of those who live in poverty, developing an understanding of the complex causes of poverty, introducing activists who work at these causes, and removing the stigma of poverty (Cowhey, 2006).

Civic engagement is not just focusing on local or global needs, but encouraging children to question prevailing practices and to develop strategies for making the world a better place. Their focus is social change, not just filling a gap in services or donating money, but questioning the conditions in society that create a need and seeking to alter those conditions. The goal is promoting change and transformative practices (Freire, 1970).

In using these theoretical frames to analyze the books, one immediate observation is that they depict children as willingly involved in challenging the status quo and questioning existing conditions within society in a number of ways:

- Children challenge the inequity of homelessness, child labor, poverty, discrimination.
- Children challenge the ways in which adults view their status as children and insist that their concerns be taken seriously by adults.
- Children challenge how adults value living things, such as birds, plants, animals, and fish.
- Children challenge the conflicts of adults and take a stand for peace.
- Children challenge traditional notions of ownership, asserting their right to give something they "own" to someone else with a greater need.

It is no surprise that the one book in which children do not challenge the conditions of society is *Give a Goat*, since this book focuses on the children's efforts to raise money. Other books, such as *First Day in Grapes* (Pérez, 2002), show a child taking action to counter the prejudice of adults and children toward him as a migrant and a Latino. The homeless children in *Sélavi* challenge the throwaway status they have been given by adults and create awareness through a radio program. A young boy in *Gleam and Glow* (Bunting, 2001) gives goldfish a chance to live by dumping them in a pond as his family flees conflict. *Sami and the Time of Troubles* (Heide & Gilliland, 1992) considers the role of children in organizing a peace march to end the constant bombing and conflict in Beirut. *Those Shoes* (Boelts, 2007) depicts a child challenging ownership by giving his prized sneakers to a child who has even less than he, while two girls in *Four Feet, Two Sandals* (Williams, 2007) share ownership of the same pair of shoes.

Children's willingness to challenge existing conditions within society is offset, however, by the lack of attention in these books to the root causes of those conditions—the underlying conditions of society that have led to these problems. Although a few causes can be inferred in several books, for the most part, references to root causes are omitted. Picturebooks do not provide space for extended discussions, but the absence of any reference to the social conditions that led to the problems that children are responding to within the books signals a deeper issue of childism.

Conclusions

Overall, books portraying children taking action provide more effective and authentic demonstrations of action than the service learning projects that occur in many schools. In fact, the book that was most problematic portrayed action within a school setting. On one hand, the children in *Give a Goat* are working to raise money for a sustainable project that provides space for agency by recipients. On the other hand, the book provides little insight into the reasons why this action matters. Beyond two problematic books, the books show children taking responsibility and initiating action in collaboration with others to address real needs in their environments out of a sense of community and respect for others, not pity.

Concerns with this set of books include the depiction of the sole hero acting alone rather than in collaboration with others and distinctions between issues that lead to action within global and Western societies. These concerns are ones that teachers can counter by the conversations they engage in with children around these books and by pairing these books with others that provide a wider range of portrayals of global and local communities.

The major concern is that these picturebooks show children challenging the conditions of society without examining the root causes of those conditions. This lack of attention to root causes appears to be based in the beliefs of the adults who write and illustrate about the limits of children's understandings. Ironically, while these picturebooks provide many positive portrayals of the rights of children to participate in making decisions and contributing to the world, the authors stop short of recognizing children's ability to understand *why* these problems exist. A lack of understanding of the root causes puts children in the position of taking action on the surface, on the most visible sign of the problem, instead of exploring underlying root causes and addressing the real issues. In doing so, authors fall victim to the societal assumptions about children's rights for participation that they are challenging.

This lack of focus on root causes requires the use of additional resources and inquiries with children. The recent CitizenKids books from Kids Can Press provide one source of books that address root causes, and novels written for children, such as *A Long Walk to Water* (Park, 2011), address these issues in greater detail. For a short read aloud, teachers can share background information on reasons why particular problems exist as part of class discussion. Longer units of inquiry provide the opportunity to use multiple fiction and nonfiction resources so that children can build deeper understandings across sources. The hunger inquiry mentioned at the beginning of this chapter engaged children in using Internet data, nonfiction books on famine, a simulation drama, film clips, picturebooks, a novel, and guests to explore the multiple causes of hunger (Short, 2012).

Children are constructing themselves as human beings by developing the ways in which they think about and take action within their lives and world. Dialogue about literature can play a key role in building on children's lived experiences and developing their sense of agency and strategies for action. Books can help children reflect on and connect to their own life experiences, immerse them in the lives and thinking of global cultures and places, offer new perspectives by taking them beyond their life experiences and challenging their views of the world, and provide demonstrations of ways that they might work with others to take action.

The lives of children in books provide a demonstration that the voices of children can make a difference in the world and that there are multiple ways in which children take action. They are able to try on perspectives and actions beyond their own by living in the story world of characters whom they have come to care about. Through engagements with literature, children can develop complex understandings about global issues, engage in critical inquiries about themselves and the world, and take responsibility for action. The significance of these experiences is that children move from a position of powerlessness to a position of possibility as they claim their rights for participation.

APPENDIX A

Text Set of Picturebooks in Which Children Take Action for Social Change

Book Title	Author/Illustrator	Setting of Book	Publisher/Date
The Caged Birds of Phnom Penh	Frederick Lipp (U.S.) Ronald Himler (U.S.)	Cambodia	Holiday House, 2001
The Can Man	Laura E. Williams (U.S.) Craig Orback (U.S.)	U.S.	Lee & Low, 2010
The Carpet Boy's Gift	Pegi Shea (U.S.) Leane Morin (U.S.)	Pakistan	Tilbury House, 2003
A Child's Garden: A Story of Hope	Michael Foreman (UK)	Global (unnamed)	Candlewick, 2009
The Composition	Antonio Skármeta (Chile) Alfonso Ruano (Spain)	Chile (1970s, Pinochet)	Groundwood, 2000
The Curious Garden	Peter Brown (U.S.)	U.S. (urban)	Little Brown, 2009
First Come the Zebra	Lynne Barasch (U.S.)	Kenya (Masaai & Kikuyu)	Lee & Low, 2009
First Day in Grapes	L. King Pérez (U.S.) Robert Casilla (Latino)	U.S. (Mexican American migrant)	Lee & Low, 2002
Fly Free!	Roseanne Thong (Hong Kong) Enjin Kim Neilan (Korean American)	Vietnam	Boyds Mills, 2010

(Continued)

Book Title	Author/Illustrator	Setting of Book	Publisher/Date
Four Feet, Two Sandals	Karen Lynn Williams & K. Mohammed (U.S.) Doug Chayka (U.S.)	Afghanistan	Eerdmans, 2007
Freedom Summer	Deborah Wiles (U.S.) Jerome Lagarrigue (African American)	U.S., 1964	Atheneum, 2001
Friends from the Other Side	Gloria Anzaldúa (Mexican American) Consuela Méndez (Venezuelan American)	U.S. (Latinos, border with Mexico)	Children's Book Press, 1993
Give a Goat	Jan West Schrock (U.S.) Aileen Darragh (U.S.)	U.S.	Tilbury House, 2010
Gleam and Glow	Eve Bunting (U.S.) Peter Sylvada (U.S.)	Bosnia-Herzegovina	Harcourt, 2001
How to Heal a Broken Wing	Bob Graham (Australia)	Australia (urban)	Candlewick, 2008
The Lady in the Box	Ann McGovern (U.S.) Marni Backer (U.S.)	U.S. (urban)	Turtle, 1997
Paulie Pastrami Achieves World Peace	James Proimos (U.S.)	U.S.	Little Brown, 2009
Rebel	Allan Baille (Australia) Di Wu (Chinese Australian)	Burma	Houghton Mifflin, 1994
The Recess Queen	Alexis O'Neill (U.S.) Laura Huliska-Beith (U.S.)	U.S.	Scholastic, 2002
Sami and the Time of Troubles	Florence Heide & Judith Gilliland (U.S.) Ted Lewin (U.S.)	Beirut, Lebanon	Clarion, 1992
Sélavi: A Haitian Story of Hope	Youme Landowne (U.S.)	Haiti	Cinco Puntos, 2004

(Continued)

APPENDIX A (Continued)

Book Title	Author/Illustrator	Setting of Book	Publisher/Date
Sparrow Girl	Penny Pennypacker (U.S.) Yoko Tanaka (Japanese American)	China (Mao Tse-Tung, 1958)	Disney Hyperion, 2009
Subway Sparrow	Leyla Torres (Colombia)	U.S. (urban)	Farrar, 1993
Those Shoes	Maribeth Boelts (U.S.) Noah Z. Jones (U.S.)	U.S. (urban, African American)	Candlewick, 2007
Tricycle	Elise Amado (Guatemalan Canadian) Alfonso Ruano (Spain)	Guatemala	Groundwood, 2008
The Video Shop Sparrow	Joy Cowley (New Zealand) Gavin Bishop (Maori)	New Zealand	Caroline House, 1999
Walking to School	Eve Bunting (Irish American) Michael Dooling (U.S.)	Belfast, Ireland	Clarion, 2009
Wanda's Roses	Pat Brisson (U.S.) Maryann Cocca-Leffler (U.S.)	U.S. (urban)	Boyds Mills, 1994
Yasmin's Hammer	Ann Malaspina (U.S.) Doug Chayka (U.S.)	Bangladesh	Lee & Low, 2010

References

Banks, J. (2004). *Diversity and citizenship education.* New York: Wiley and Sons.

Cowhey, M. (2006). *Black ants and Buddhists.* Portland, ME: Stenhouse.

Curtis, J. (2014). "We have a great task ahead of us!": Child-hate in Roald Dahl's *The Witches. Children's Literature in Education, 45*(4), 166–177.

Dewey, J. (1938). *Education and experience.* New York: Collier.

Freire, P. (1970). *Pedagogy of the oppressed.* South Hadley, MA: Bergin & Garvey.

Galbraith, M. (2001). Hear my cry: A manifesto for an emancipatory childhood studies approach to children's literature. *The Lion and the Unicorn, 25*(2), 187–205.

Hart, R. (1992). *Children's participation: From tokenism to citizenship.* Florence: UNICEF.

Hunt, P. (1991). *Criticism, theory and children's literature.* Oxford, UK: Basil Blackwell.

Joosen, V. (2013). The adult as foe or friend?: Childism in Guus Kuijer's criticism and fiction. *International Research in Children's Literature, 6*(2), 205–217.

Kaye, C. (2010). *The complete guide to service learning*. Minneapolis, MN: Free Spirit.

Kohl, H. (1995). *Should we burn Babar? Essays on children's literature and the power of stories*. New York: The New Press.

Nance-Carroll, N. (2014). Innocence is no defense: Politicized childhood in Antonio Skármeta's *La Composición/The Composition*. *Children's Literature in Education, 45*, 271–284.

Nikolajeva, M. (2010). *Power, voice, and subjectivity in literature for young readers*. New York: Routledge.

Nodelman, P. (1992). The other: Orientalism, colonialism and children's literature. *Children's Literature Association Quarterly, 17*(1), 29–35.

Short, K. (2011). Children taking action within global inquiries. *The Dragon Lode, 29*(2), 50–59.

Short, K. (2012). Children's agency for social action. *Bookbird, 50*(4), 41–50.

Todres, J. & Higinbotham, S. (2013). A person's a person: Children's rights in children's literature. *Columbia Human Rights Law Review, 45*(1), 1–56.

United Nations (1989). A Summary of the United Nations Convention on the Rights of the Child, 1989. *UNICEF*. Retrieved from http://www.unescocentre.ulster.ac.uk/pdfs/pdfs_uncrc/uncrc_summary_version.pdf

Vasquez, V. (2004). *Negotiating critical literacies with young children*. Mahweh, NJ: Erlbaum.

Wade, R. (2007). *Social studies for social justice*. New York: Teachers College Press.

Young-Bruehl, E. (2012). *Childism: Confronting prejudice against children*. New Haven, CT: Yale University Press.

Children's Literature References (see also Appendix A)

Park, L.S. (2011). *A long walk to water*. New York: Harcourt.

Potter, B. (1902). *The tale of Peter Rabbit*. New York: Warne.

Seuss, Dr. (1954). *Horton hears a Who!* New York: Random House.

Seuss, Dr. (1958). *Yertle the turtle*. New York: Random House.

Skármeta, A. (2000). *The composition*. Toronto: Groundwood.

Walters, E. (2015). *Hope springs*. Illus. by E. Fernandes. Toronto, CA: Tundra.

11

BLURRED LINES

The Construction of Adolescent Sexuality in Young Adult Novels

Melissa B. Wilson

And that's why I'm gon' take a good girl
I know you want it
I know you want it
I know you want it
But you're a good girl
　　　　"Blurred Lines" written by Pharrell Williams and Robin Thicke

The sexuality of young people is problematic for American society. A constructed dichotomy is evident in popular culture in which girls are objectified as "wanting it" while at the same time pressured to be a "good girl" by society. The song "Blurred Lines" encapsulates this ambivalence well (Trust, 2013). This kind of double standard is especially poignant when examined in 2015, the 40th anniversary of the young adult novel, *Forever* (Blume, 1975). Long regarded as liberating, *Forever* was the first young adult (YA) text to explicitly describe a heterosexual encounter, and seen as dangerous for the same reason (Knowles & Malmkjaer, 1996). Young adult literature was new at the time of its publication, and *Forever* can be seen as a harbinger of what was to follow in its wake (Marcus, 2008). As Coats (2011) writes, "Young adult literature may be seen as a distinct genre because of its inclusion of sexuality; . . . if a book has sex in it, it's YA; if it doesn't, it is preadolescent" (p. 322).

Adolescent sexuality cannot be separated from adult tacit theories about youth and, in turn, about what literature for younger people should be. Examining these "theories" offers insights into culture, history, and power. Challenging tacit theories is also useful to disrupt a dualistic discourse in which younger females are seen as innocents/seductresses and younger males as predators/victims (of the seductress). As Foucault (1990) argued, whatever is made can be unmade.

Young adult literature provides an excellent foray into a study of adolescent sexuality by reading closely for what is said and, maybe more important, what is unsaid. While children's texts serve the double purpose of writing explicitly for the age group (pseudo addressees) but implicitly for adults (real readers), this "purpose" is more complex in the realm of YA literature where the "real readers" are adults as well as teenagers who often have the agency to purchase their own reading material far from the watchful eyes of adults (Hunt, 2004; Nodelman and Reimer, 2003). Conversely, it could be argued that adults are also the pseudo addressees, as many novels are purchased for use in a school setting. This double audience requires a double purpose, in which the story is a relatable one for the teenaged reader, and for the adult an "appropriate" read, with the novel attempting to bridge the gap between generations.

The inquiry in this chapter is a critical content analysis of recent *The New York Times* bestselling young adult novels to examine how teenaged sexuality is constructed in this culture at this moment in books that adolescents are consuming both in and out of school. The books were chosen by their popularity, except for *Forever*, which was selected as a starting point from which to compare and contrast changes in constructions. For this chapter I will be limiting my scope to two texts from the set: *The Fault in Our Stars* (Green, 2014) and *If I Stay* (Forman, 2010). Both of these novels made it to number one on the bestseller list. These texts, as befits their genre, also have sexuality in common, although this is not the central preoccupation of either book. For this study, sexuality is defined as comprising emotional, cognitive, behavioral, and physical experiences, needs, and desires by all humans that relate to the lived human experience of the erotic (Hill, 2014, p. 4).

Postcolonial Studies and Youth Lens

This research is undergirded by the belief that YA literature is a space in which to examine the ideals and ideas of what adolescence should be/is, the social construction of adolescence. In addition, the position of younger people in relation to adults can be examined as one in which the subaltern are controlled by the oppressors, in this case through the hegemony of adult-sanctioned literature (Cannella & Viruru, 2004; Nodelman & Reimer, 2003). Youth lens offers the researcher a stance from which to analyze young adult literature by introducing a set of guiding principles about adolescence (Petrone, Sarigianides, & Lewis, 2015).

Postcolonial Theories

The need of adults to control and monitor youth activities makes postcolonial theories a helpful lens for YA literature. Postcolonial critiques are ways of thinking that acknowledge an absence of one "truth" and look at the world as a complex and random place where competing ideas can and do coexist. Tacit theories are critiqued to disrupt the accepted discourses that are used to control the subaltern. Placing younger people in the category of "colonized," or subaltern, makes sense, in that like all traditionally colonized groups, which includes women, people of the "third world," and people of color, there is a belief that this group is not fully formed, is ignorant and weak, and is in need of guidance and protection from those who have the knowledges and strength. "Psychology and science have created 'children' as the perfect objects of the Empire, those who would be defined, described, known, and controlled" (Cannella & Viruru, 2004, p. 97).

A postcolonial theoretical approach is also significant in this inquiry in that it focuses in part on the borders between the oppressed and the oppressors (Anzaldúa, 1987). YA texts are where adults and younger people meet. It is a place where what youth wants to read and what adults want them to read collides. In 1975, youth were given an explicit novel about an adolescent falling in love and losing her virginity, while at the same time, the reader had the opportunity to learn about birth control and the perils of not using it. Currently, the bestselling *The Fault in Our Stars* has a very discreet mention of sex between the two main characters who are both dealing with terminal cancer, which happens after a romantic Make-a-Wish date in Amsterdam. While this encounter could have consequences such as an unplanned pregnancy, the characters' relationship is doomed with or without intimacy. In *If I Stay*, the main character, Mia, who is a classically trained musician, speaks of her sexual encounter in terms of playing a cello. The analogous description is far from explicit. While she may have had an orgasm, "the swirl of sensations hit a dizzying crescendo" (p. 62), it is so couched in romance that it is hard to tell. In today's frontier between adult and youth, pornography is rampant, anything can be looked up, viewed, and experienced through media, but YA literature has become less explicit as adults seem to be trying to protect children more and they have more to protect them from.

Youth Lens

Youth lens, while not a theory per se, is a theoretical stance that looks at YA texts for representations of adolescents and adolescence (Petrone et al., 2015), arguing that adolescence, like childhood, is a construct that was "invented" at the turn of the last century. These "truths" about teenagers have the consequence of standardizing adolescence. Outliers who do not conform with the idea may be overlooked or stigmatized. Of especial interest for this study is the youth lens statement that adolescence serves as a symbolic placeholder, meaning that teens stand in for the zeitgeist (Petrone et al., 2015).

In the case of Katherine, in *Forever*, she is the "new liberated woman" who can experience sex and sexual fulfillment without fear of an unwanted pregnancy thanks to the pill. Her ambivalence toward sex may also reflect the nation's unease with this liberation. The younger women in the more recent novels may symbolize the backlash of women's liberation as well as our highly sexualized societal yearning for "love relationships" rather than "hookups" by making the romance of falling in love center stage and leaving explicit descriptions of the sexual act in the wings.

From these theories of youth lens and postcolonialism, I developed the following tenets connected to adolescence that guided my analysis:

- Teenagers may have some agency but are still colonized subjects of the adult world.
- Adolescence isn't a biological truth but a historical/social/cultural construction.
- Adolescence/adolescents serve as a symbol for the culture's zeitgeist.

Recent Research

The valuing of romance is discussed in Kokkola's research (2011) in which she analyzes the *Twilight* series and finds that these novels, while including sex, give status to agapic over erosic love (p. 170). In other words, while the erotic is found in this series, the undying romantic love of partners is the focus. This focus may occur because adolescents are expected to know all about sex anyway. In a later study with colleagues, Kokkola contends that until this century in the English-speaking world sexuality has largely been missing from YA literature. And while these texts may be very direct, they assume the readers know who does what to whom. These readers are called "knowing children." The actual mechanics of sex do not need to be discussed as they were in older books like *Forever*, because younger people are familiar with the mechanics of the sexual act (Kokkola, Valovirta, & Korkka, 2013). These same themes seem to be present in the texts I analyzed.

Research Methodology

Each of the three novels offered a different construction of sexuality as I transacted with the text and created my own interpretation (Rosenblatt, 1978) using postcolonial theory and a youth lens. I employed both a meta-analysis and a microanalysis. I read the texts aesthetically to experience the story in its entirety and then read them again as a whole from an efferent stance looking to answer the following questions:

1. How is sexual activity portrayed?
2. Who is in control in the sexual relationship?
3. How is the story contextualized in various historical sociocultural influences?
4. How is desire portrayed?
5. What are the consequences (if any) for having sex?
6. How are the adult perspectives shown in the books and what are they?

Next, I did a close reading of key passages that spoke to the above questions. I analyzed key passages for themes. Once I looked at all three texts, I analyzed the themes as a whole using the two theoretical frames and research stance to guide and focus the analysis.

For this project, critical content analysis consists of a close reading of the whole text, parts of the text, and the text set as a whole, from a hermeneutic, reader-response-oriented research stance. My goal is to make abductive inferences, to take the particulars from one domain, the novels, and to apply them to another domain, in this case youth lens and postcolonial theories. The analytical process consisted of constructing a description of the overall plot of each book that spoke to the focus questions and then closely analyzing passages and plot details. The themes that emerged from the close readings were analyzed through a youth lens and postcolonial theory and form the basis of these findings as related to the over-all purpose of this critical content analysis. The following provides an example of this process, simplified, as it is recursive and time-consuming.

Plots of the Three Novels as Related to This Study

This section describes my second meta-efferent reading where I focused on the parts of the plot that helped to answer the research questions. This is a very specific way of reading and leaves many characters and plotlines out, as they are not pertinent to this particular study.

In *Forever*, Katherine is a virgin at the beginning of the novel and has had one serious relationship in the past that ended because, "Sex was all he (ex-boyfriend) was interested in, which is why we broke up—because he threatened that if I wouldn't sleep with him he'd find somebody who would" (pp. 14–15). She meets Michael at a New Year's Eve party and is attracted to him. They have a date the next weekend during which Katherine feels desire for him. They go back to her house as her parents "always invited my boyfriends home" (p. 20). They fool around a bit but it stops when Michael asks if she's a virgin. They continue to see each other and Katherine insists that Michael go slowly into sex with her. By page 65 they still haven't had sex but Michael tells her he loves her. On page 106 they have intercourse and Katherine is no longer a virgin. Although they have both climaxed previously, sex is a let down (at least for Katherine) as evidenced by the following passage:

> He stopped moving, "It wasn't any good for you, was it?"
> "Everybody says the first time is no good for a virgin. I'm not disap-pointed." But I was. I'd wanted it to be perfect. . . .
> "Next time it'll be better . . . we've got to work on it. Did you bleed?"
> "I didn't feel anything."
>
> *(p. 106)*

At her grandmother's urging Katherine goes into the city to Planned Parenthood to procure birth control. She doesn't tell Michael and tells the counselor and the reader, "I think it's my responsibility to make sure I don't get pregnant" (p. 125). They continue to have less-than-satisfying sex and then are separated for the summer. Katherine meets another boy she is attracted to and she and Michael end their relationship as the new one is on the horizon.

In *The Fault in Our Stars*, Hazel is 16 years old and dying of cancer. Her mother worries about her depression and makes her attend a cancer support group where she meets Gus, who has survived cancer. There is an immediate attraction. Hazel, the narrator, says, "Look, let me say it: He was hot" (p. 9). They start to flirt and Hazel becomes more intrigued. "Honestly, he kind of turned me on. I didn't even know that guys could turn me on—not, like, in real life" (p. 17). Despite Hazel's reluctance to form a close relationship and hurt Gus, they grow close and hang out at each other's homes under the watchful eyes of parents. When they start to go in the basement to watch a movie Gus's father says, "So just show Hazel the basement . . . and then come upstairs and watch your movie in the living room" (p. 29). Hazel's father worries too when he tells Gus, "You have to understand that Hazel is still sick . . . and will be for the rest of her life. She'll want to keep up with you, but her lungs—" (p. 83).

Hazel is obsessed with a novel and her greatest wish is to meet the author to learn the fate of the characters, but the author lives in Amsterdam. Gus, who saved his "wish" (as in the Make-a-Wish Foundation) uses it to pay for a trip to Holland for Hazel, her mom, and him. Hazel worries that Gus will expect her to sleep with him in exchange. When he tries to touch her she backs away because:

> So of course I tensed up when he touched me. To be with him was to hurt him—inevitably. And that's what I'd felt as he reached for me: I'd felt as though I were committing an act of violence against him, because I was.
>
> *(p. 101)*

Hazel becomes too ill to travel and in a phone conversation Gus reveals he is a virgin and will die one as he only has one leg. They become closer and Hazel tells the reader that she "fell in love the way you fall asleep: slowly, and then all at once" (p. 125). Despite Hazel's poor health they risk the trip. Hazel and Gus end up having their first "make out" session at the Anne Frank House and later that day they have sex and both lose their virginity. Hazel propositions him, "Me: 'We could go to your room.'" The sex scene takes 18 lines start to finish and is the only time they have sex because Gus is dying. The remainder of the novel is a slow death scene, made more poignant by the fact that Hazel and Gus may have had a great love if it weren't for fate—"the fault in their stars."

In *If I Stay*, Mia is 17 years old and just found out she is accepted to Julliard when she and her family get into a car accident with Mia, the only survivor, in a coma. Mia narrates the story from the ICU with flashbacks about her life. She has a boyfriend, Adam, who is in an up-and-coming band, and their relationship is failing because she is leaving him in Oregon to pursue her studies in New York City. We learn about how they first fell in love. Adam takes Mia to see Yo-Yo Ma out of the blue and she feels as if he is "too cool" to date a classical music geek like herself. But he likes her and when he goes to kiss her she is surprised by his ardor and by her desire.

> And it took me by surprise how much I wanted to be kissed by him, to realize that I'd thought about it so often that I'd memorized the exact shape of his lips, that I'd imagined running my finger down the cleft of his chin.
>
> *(pp. 39–40)*

Mia's parents allow her to have Adam in her bedroom where their only sexual encounter that is recounted occurs. This encounter is told in musical metaphors making it lyrical but less than transparent. The encounter lasts for approximately four pages and involves Adam asking Mia to play him like a cello, which she does and enjoys. "I looked at the bow, looked at my hands, looked at Adam's face, and felt this surge of love, lust, and an unfamiliar feeling of power" (p. 61). Next, he plays her like a guitar, making her feel like "the swirl of sensations hit a dizzying crescendo, sending every nerve ending in my body on high alert" (p. 62). That is the only semi-overt mention of sex. Mia is a virgin before meeting Adam, according to Mia, Adam is not, and her mother prepares her for a sexual relationship by giving Mia "ten bucks to start my supply (of condoms)" (p. 113). The rest of the novel is about Mia deciding whether or not to stay (to live) without her family.

Doing Critical Content Analysis

Meta-Analysis of the Novels

In this meta-read I focused on the research questions, noticing that sexuality was written about in a clear and overt way in *Forever* a number of times, while in the other two novels the context of sex was described but the actual act was not explicitly reported. Question two about who is in control in the sexual relationship was more complex and required a close reading of specific passages in order to answer the question fully. The next question pertaining to historical sociocultural influences also garnered a closer reading, as did the question about how desire is portrayed.

It was easier in this more general reading to pinpoint the consequences of sex, since there were none discussed in the novels. The relationships didn't end because of sex nor did intimacy cement a long-lasting relationship. Also, sex didn't conclude with unwanted pregnancy, sexually transmitted diseases, shunning, or slut shaming. The parents in all three novels were not overtly anti-sex. The mothers in *Forever* and *If I Stay* were very matter-of-fact in viewing sex as a normal part of an adolescent relationship. The parents in *The Fault in Our Stars* were more intrusive on the surface insisting that the teens not have alone time in bedrooms and being sensitive to public displays of affection. However, they were willing to let their sick children go out on a date in a foreign city and leave them alone long enough to have intercourse. This dichotomy may be explained by the knowledge that the children are sickly and need to be cared for closely and, at the same time, they will die at a young age and should be allowed to experience as much of life as possible while still able to do so.

Microanalysis of a Passage

After this more general and efferent read I went back to the texts to look closely at passages that spoke to the questions that were more complicated to answer. One example of this microanalysis occurred with *Forever* in examining passages that might indicate who was in control of the sexual relationship. I looked for instances in the text, where Katherine and Michael are "fooling around" or discussing sex, for places to find the answers to my questions. While Katherine takes the bold step of going into the city alone to Planned Parenthood and ultimately controls her own destiny, it is Michael's sexual agenda that takes precedence. On the first night they are together Katherine stops the intimacy, "We sat on the sofa for an hour. Michael moved his hands around on the outside of my sweater but when he tried to get under it I said, 'No. . . . let's save something for tomorrow'" (p. 21). His response is to ask her if she's a virgin. This question flusters Katherine and she answers, "'Yes, I am . . . does it matter?' He answers, 'No . . . but it's better if I know'" (p. 21). Michael goes on to tell Katherine that being a virgin is nothing to be ashamed of. Later that night Katherine muses that "If I hadn't been one then he probably would have made love to me" (p. 22).

Katherine is not ready for as much sexuality as Michael and his question is patronizing in that he assumes that the only reason Katherine would refuse his advances is because she hasn't had intercourse. Because Katherine is interested in Michael she worries that he may lose interest in her and takes the passive voice when wondering if he would have made love *to* her. The pattern of their sexual forays is Michael wanting more than Katherine and then reacting in a passive-aggressive way as illustrated by this passage:

> He touched me and we kissed until the same record had played three times. But when he fumbled with the snap on my jeans I sat up and said, "No. . . . not now . . . not with them in the other room."
> Michael rolled over on his stomach and kind of groaned. I bent down and stroked his hair. "You're not mad, are you?"
> "No."
> "You're sure?"
> "Yeah . . . but this is really rough."
>
> *(p. 27)*

Michael is not "mad" but following Katherine's wishes is "really tough" and he leaves immediately after this exchange. This kind of manipulative behavior is seen on page 41 when Katherine wants to change alone and Michael responds by asking her, "Are you ashamed of your body?" He goes ahead and watches her change and offers to hook her bra but instead, "he slid his hands around to my breasts and kissed the back of my neck." Katherine tells him to stop and it is only a knock on the door from her sister that does stop this interaction.

This closer reading of *Forever* allowed me to answer my question transactionally (Rosenblatt, 1978). I read what Judy Blume had written and transacted with the words, creating my own "poem" or interpretation infused by my own experiences. As a 46-year-old woman rereading a book that was important to me in my youth I (re)experienced Katherine as less of a liberated female and more as a girl who needs to be constantly vigilant in order to curb Michael's desire. I went into this study thinking that *Forever* was an example of a text that reflected the possibilities of the women's movement in 1975 and ended up seeing it as the same old story of a girl's needs succumbing to the needs of a boy.

Themes Evolving from a Youth Lens and Postcolonial Studies

After analyzing each text by doing both a meta-analysis and a microanalysis, three themes were identified that speak to how teenaged sexuality is constructed in these novels. These themes gave me the opportunity of looking at the construction of adolescence by examining the female protagonists' sexuality in terms of power, ideology, and history. Conversely, by examining these books, the disciplinary nature of children's literature was also illuminated.

Ambivalent Girls

These novels show sex in a specific way that reflects society's beliefs about being a teenager. There seems to be a script that is palatable to adults, one that maintains the "truth" that they want to believe and pass on. That script begins with the female protagonist as a virgin, speaking to the ideal that childhood is a time of innocence and virginity signals this for girls. These characters are not only innocent for having an intact hymen, but they are also ambivalent about their own sexuality. They have desire, but it is dampened by other issues.

For Katherine her desire isn't allowed to blossom but is held in check by Michael's insistence that they go further than she is ready to go. This is illustrated in the following excerpt:

> "I want you so much," he said.
> "I want you too," I told him, "but I can't . . . I'm not ready, Michael . . ."
> "Yes, you are . . . you are . . . I can feel how ready you are."
> "No . . ." I pushed his hand away and sat up. "I'm talking about mentally ready."

(p. 50)

Mia, in *If I Stay*, feels power when she plays Adam's naked body like a cello but spends most of the novel worrying about if she is "cool" enough to hold his attention, reducing her self-confidence. She dresses up for a Halloween concert like a punk rock girl to impress and seduce him. Adam reassures Mia that she is cool just the way she is. Her response is, "After that, whenever I started to doubt Adam's feelings, I'd think about my wig, gathering dust in my closet, and it would bring back the memory of that night. And then I wouldn't feel insecure. I'd just feel lucky" (p. 101).

Mia's statement speaks to the idea that the story is different for boys. There is an expectation that they will be more experienced than the girls as evidenced by the matter-of-fact way Mia says, "I *was* a virgin, but I certainly wasn't devoted to staying that way. And Adam certainly wasn't a virgin" (p. 58). I am left to believe she assumes his experience, as she never specifically asks him about it. Nor does Katherine in *Forever* after Michael confronts her about her virginity when he is sexually frustrated. In *The Fault in Our Stars*, Hazel also assumes Gus is experienced. "'You're a virgin?' I asked, surprised" (p. 119).

This assumption speaks to our society's long-held beliefs that "boys will be boys" and "nice girls, don't" (except within a loving relationship). Katherine's mother in *Forever* explains this when she says, "In the old days girls were divided into two groups—those who did and those who didn't" (p. 37). Katherine's reaction speaks to this adult-sanctioned script, when she says "It's true that we are more open than our parents but that just means that we accept sex and talk about it. It doesn't mean we are all jumping into bed together" (p. 37).

Katherine's words hold up in the later texts as well. While younger people see more than their parents did through the Internet and social media, they (at least girls) are not jumping into bed, but have sex within the confines of a loving, parent-approved relationship. In all three novels sex happens only after the boy tells the girl he loves her. The sexual relationship is constructed as the product of love. The parents must also approve of the girl's choice.

This "approval" is analogous to the adult-normative approval of these texts being "appropriate" for younger people to read. In *If I Stay* Adam bonds with Mia's dad over basketball and in *The Fault in Our Stars*, most of the dates consist of family dinners. In *Forever*, Katherine's grandmother makes sure that birth control is used. When Katherine's parents start to worry about her attachment to Michael, she is forced to teach tennis at a far away camp. Even though she is about to enter college, Katherine's parents are still calling the shots and protecting her.

While these texts have sex, they also have portrayals of family values replete with babysitting for younger siblings, long intimate chats with understanding moms, and teenagers who are not rebelling. These values reflect the values our society tries to maintain in mainstream media despite (or because of) the increasingly easy access to pornography and the current experiences of a hookup culture.

These inscribed values are a way of dealing with younger people as the postcolonial objects who are defined, described, known, and controlled (Cannella & Viruru, 2004, p. 97). The protagonists are defined and described as "good girls" and the boys as "aggressors." The adults are given the knowledge of their daughter's fledging relationships in order to control what does and does not happen. And what power the parents cannot exert, the boys fill in as they are in the hierarchy as males over females.

Horny Boys

These novels position boys in the power role. In these novels the girls are the recipients of the boys' advances, and it is their job to fend the boys off or to give in. This is seen in the language of the novels where the girl is the passive participant. In the first line of *Forever*, "Sybil Davidson has a genius I.Q. and has been laid by at least six different guys" (p. 1), this is especially apparent. For despite being a genius Sybil *has been laid*, she is the passive participant in a sexual act, it is being done to her, not with or by her. Katherine fends off Michael's many advances partially because she is afraid that she won't satisfy him. She admits she doesn't know how to please him when she says, "Well . . . the thing is . . . I don't know exactly how to do it . . . satisfy you, I mean" (p. 51). There is no further discussion, it must be noted, about him learning how to please her.

This power inequality plays out in *If I Stay* when Mia longs for Adam to kiss her. Instead of kissing him, she waits for him to make the first move as she does when he asks her to play him like a cello. But there is power inequality seen in non-sexual, but romantic ways as well. Mia can't believe that Adam would like *her*, "'Why?' I asked. 'Why me?'" (p. 39). He goes on to explain why but there is no parallel discussion of why she is drawn to Adam.

In *The Fault in Our Stars* this inequality plays out differently. Gus pursues Hazel but not in a sexual way. He controls her through his offer to use his wish on her. Or that is how Hazel sees it:

> Then I found myself worrying I would *have* to make out with him in Amsterdam, because (a) It shouldn't've even been a *question* whether I wanted to kiss him, and (b) Kissing someone so that you can get a free trip is perilously close to full-on hooking. . . .
>
> *(p. 93)*

Hazel seems to have bought into the tacit theory that boys only do nice things for you if you are willing to give them sexual favors in return. Gus echoes this idea when he is disappointed when it seems that Hazel is too sick to go on the trip and says, "my grand romantic gesture would have totally gotten me laid" (p. 118). Again, this is couched in the girl's passivity, with no mention of Hazel getting "laid" as well.

There is no reason to assume that the authors of these texts are purposely putting the male in the power role. However, their plots speak to tacit theories about the girl as innocent and the boy as aggressor and don't allow the female characters to have agency in their sexuality. In *Forever* Michael introduces Katherine to his penis whom he has named Ralph. There is no reciprocal meeting of Katherine's unnamed vagina. Mia, in *If I Stay*, believes that her relationship with Adam is falling apart because she has the opportunity to study in New York, and doesn't take into account that Adam's refusal to move is also a problem. Gus's imminent death is kept from Hazel in *The Fault in Our Stars* as a way for him to control his last weeks, by revealing his prognosis only after they have had intercourse.

This discourse of girls being subservient to boys' desires both in and out of bed, while denying their own, seems to be a never-ending story. This may be a surprise to scholars who work under the tacit belief that our society is post-patriarchal, because the analysis suggests that female bodies still belong to others and are objects of discipline (Foucault, 1979).

Delicate Sexuality

This adult discipline is seen as well in the portrayal of sex as still mysterious. In today's novels sex may be what separates children's literature from the young adult novels, but while we are more inundated with sex through the media, books are still quite chaste. This theme is epitomized by Hazel's description of her intercourse with Gus. "The whole affair was the precise opposite of what I figured it would be: slow and patient and quiet and neither particularly painful nor particularly ecstatic" (pp. 207–208). The "whole affair" is alluded to but not described, leaving more questions than answers. This is also seen in *If I Stay*, where the recount of sex reads like a concert. *Forever*, on the other hand, reads in parts like a YA how to have sex manual:

> "I'm trying, Kath . . . but it's very tight in there."
> "What should I do?"
> "Can you spread your legs some more . . . and maybe raise them a little?"
> *(p. 105)*

These differences may signal an adult need for YA literature to keep the "mystery" of love and sex in the midst of the pornography boom and so represent the zeitgeist in which these novels are being produced. When *Forever* was published, younger people had little access to representations of sex. These discrepancies may also have arisen out of the backlash against Blume's frank prose that continues to this day with *Forever* having the distinction of being one of the most banned and challenged books in the United States for the past 40 years (Marcus, 2008).

In her *New Yorker* article, Talbot (2014) quotes a YA publisher as saying that, "Green writes books that are appropriate for teen-agers and for the adults who want books to be appropriate for teen-agers" (n/p). This is a telling statement that buttresses the idea that children's fiction has two audiences and is a space where adult-normative ideas control what can and cannot be said to and about younger people.

These themes suggest that, to (mis)quote an old cigarette ad, "we haven't come a long way, baby." Forty years after the International Year of the Woman, girls may have desire but it is tempered by their male partner's needs. Younger females are still subject to the control of adults and males in the three novels examined in this study. And younger people are still being disciplined through the mainstream media that adults are able to control. Girls may "want it" but only in the ways that tacit theories see as being "good."

Conclusions

Stone (2006) asserts that, "Books are possibly the safest place for them to learn about sex—not just the physical part but also the complex web of emotions that accompanies it" (p. 463). Books can be a safe place to learn and to experience all kinds of situations. Part of the power of literature is its ability to give the reader the chance to rehearse parts of life before they happen. The act of writing for a group of people who are not seen as "complete" or able to care for themselves may also be viewed as an oppressive act. The adult author, like a colonizing government, is taking on the role of educating and shaping lesser humans, children, through literature (Freire & Macedo, 1987).

Since adults are supplying these scripts it is important that we look at what we are giving younger people. Teenaged sexuality is a subject many people are uncomfortable with and they have various ethical/moral issues that muddy the waters. But despite our adult reticence, teenaged sex happens. Younger people have sex and they deserve books that teach them about the physical and the emotional parts of intimacy.

We seem to be failing at publishing these books. Wood (2010), in her explorations of YA literature from the perspective of a librarian, found that the genre tries to push morals instead of offering younger people an opportunity to live through the narratives of sex. Pattee (2006) echoes this call when she writes; "Teenagers deserve to have the option of seeing positive representations of sex in the books they are reading" (p. 38). It seems as our culture is becoming more sexualized, younger people are denied the opportunity to work through sex prior to experiencing it. The irony is that while pornography may show sex, it doesn't offer the younger person the opportunity to live through the experience.

Using critical content analysis allows the researcher to go beyond the story and to use texts as a space to explore how teenage sexuality is constructed. The books that are given to our youth should be critiqued, and, as adults, we should take the opportunity to rethink our own tacit theories about youth and sexuality and how these ideas influence our work.

References

Anzaldúa, G. (1987). *Borderlands: La Frontera*. San Francisco: Aunt Lute Books.

Cannella, G. S. & Viruru, R. (2004). *Childhood and postcolonization: Power, education, and colonization*. New York: Routledge.

Coats, K. (2011). Young adult literature: Growing up, in theory. In S. A. Wolf, K. Coats, P. Enciso, & C. A. Jenkins (Eds.), *Handbook of research on children's and young adult literature* (pp. 315–329). New York: Routledge.

Foucault, M. (1979). *Discipline and punish: The birth of the prison*. New York: Pantheon.

Foucault, M. (1990). *Politics philosophy culture: Interviews and other writings 1977–1984*. New York: Routledge.

Freire, P. & Macedo, D. (1987). *Literacy: Reading the word and the world*. New York: Praeger.

Hill, C. (2014). Introduction: Young adult literature and scholarship come of age. In C. Hill (Ed.), *The critical merits of young adult literature: Coming of age* (pp. 1–25). New York: Routledge.

Hunt, P. (2004). Children's literature and childhood. In M. J. Kehily (Ed.), *An introduction to childhood studies* (pp. 39–58). London: Open University Press.

Knowles, M. & Malmkjaer, K. (1996). *Language and control in children's literature*. London: Routledge.

Kokkola, L. (2011). Virtuous vampires and voluptuous vamps: Romance conventions reconsidered in Stephanie Meyer's "Twilight" series. *Children's Literature in Education, 42*, 165–179.

Kokkola, L., Valovirta, E., & Korkka, J. (2013). Who does what to whom and how: "Knowing children" and depictions of prostitution in Anglophone young adult literature. *Children's Literature Association Quarterly, 38*(1), 66–83.

Marcus, L. S. (2008). *Minders of make-believe: Idealists, entrepreneurs and the shaping of American children's literature*. New York: Houghton Mifflin.

Nodelman, P. & Reimer, M. (2003). *The pleasures of children's literature* (3rd ed.). New York: Allyn and Bacon.

Pattee, A. (2006). The secret source: Sexually explicit young adult literature as an information source. *Young Adult Library Services, 4*(2), 30–38.

Petrone, R., Sarigianides, S. T., & Lewis, M. A. (2015). The *youth lens*: Analyzing adolescence/ts in literary texts. *Journal of Literacy Research, 46*(4), 506–533.

Rosenblatt, L. M. (1978). *The reader, the text, the poem: The transactional theory of the literary work*. Carbondale, IL: Southern Illinois University Press.

Stone, T. L. (2006). Now and forever: The power of sex in young adult literature. *Voice of Youth Advocates, 28*, 463–465.

Talbot, M. (2014, June 9). The teen whisperer: How the author of "The Fault in Our Stars" built an ardent army of fans. *The New Yorker*. Retrieved from http://www.newyorker.com/magazine/2014/06/09/the-teen-whisperer

Trust, G. (2013). *Robin Thicke's "Blurred Lines" is Billboard's song of the summer*. Retrieved from http://www.billboard.com/articles/news/5687036/robin-thickes-blurred-lines-is-billboards-song-of-the-summer

Wood, E. (2010). Pushing the envelope: Exploring sexuality in teen literature. *The Journal of Research on Libraries and Young Adults*, 11. Retrieved from http://www.yalsa.ala.org/jrlya/2010/11/pushing-the-envelope-exploring-sexuality-in-teen-literature/

Children's Literature References

Blume, J. (1975). *Forever.* New York: Atheneum.

Forman, G. (2010). *If I stay.* New York: Speak.

Green, J. (2014). *The fault in our stars.* New York: Penguin.

12

A POSTSTRUCTURAL DISCOURSE ANALYSIS OF A NOVEL SET IN HAITI

Deborah Dimmett

My deep interest in the culture, history, and politics of Haiti began with my first visit in 1997. Since that time, I have visited Haiti every year for extended periods of time, providing professional development to primary and secondary teachers, working with community human rights councils, participating in prisoner extractions with a human rights advocacy group, organizing a youth development program, leading a medical mission in rural areas, and developing needs assessment models after Haiti's historic earthquake in 2010. Even with this immersion in different aspects of Haitian life, I do not consider myself an expert on Haiti with sufficient expertise to warrant being identified as an author or sufficient experience to construct a collective view of Haiti. Using a poststructural discourse analysis approach, however, allows me to mobilize my knowledge of Haiti in a way that is transparent to researchers and proposes the reader as a constructor of a text rather than just a simple receiver of a text.

If reader response wrestles meaning production away from the intentionality of authorship in order to produce a text that is unique to an individual reader yet shared within a community of readers, what is the contemporary mechanism that allows an author to state intentionality and to presume a homogenous readership for the constituted text? Although intentionality might occur in the form of a memoir, country of origin, political identity, or any episteme that consolidates meaning, this question challenges many long-held assumptions about authors and readers and redirects attention to discourse. In this chapter, my goal is to address this question by demonstrating a poststructural discourse analysis approach to a young adult text. While some literary critics view children's or young adult (YA) texts as not sufficiently complex for such an analysis, I argue that these texts support complex ideologies that need to be rendered transparent.

Serafina's Promise (2013) by Ann E. Burg is one such YA text. After the 2010 earthquake in Haiti destroyed much of the country's infrastructure, a number of children's and YA books, including *Serafina's Promise*, were published target-ing young readers who knew little about Haiti. Authors who had never visited Haiti felt a connection to the plight of the Haitian people and wrote stories for a predominantly non-Haitian readership. This lack of traditional authenticity is not problematic, per se. Poststructural discourse analysis does not evaluate authenticity as much as attempt to constitute a text that is vital to the concerns of the popula-tion being represented and to identify what readership population is being hailed, or constituted, by the ideology presented in a text.

The Concept of Poststructuralism

Generally, books exist in a political economy in which they have to produce something for someone. Poststructuralism is less useful for writing book reports but very effective at identifying the power relations that contour discourses. Book reports tend to reify the primacy of texts using familiar tools for unpacking those texts. An examination of the power relations that form a text is central to any definition of critical content analysis. When presented with a story, it is reason-able and desirable to use established reading strategies to unpack the narrative. When presented with a text, it is important to understand that the text (and the author and the reader) was and is being formed through discourses. Derrida (1972/1991) argues that a text is "no longer a finished corpus of writing, some content enclosed in a book or its margins, but a differential network, a fabric of traces referring endlessly to something other than itself, to other differential traces" (p. 127). Few would argue against the proposition that we come into being through language, yet there is anxiety when it is suggested that we maintain our position in a social structure through something as fluid as discourse.

Poststructuralism constitutes a different type of text for the purpose of con-ducting a different type of analysis that focuses on discourse. Those who practice poststructuralism often reject the acquisition of power and the textual coercion that inevitably holds that power in place (Foucault, 1980). Ironically, poststructur-alists are often charged with attempting to ruin the aspiration to power of others, which is construed as an attempt to gain power for themselves. Fundamentally, the practice of poststructuralism is highly ideological in that it seeks to identify how power is supported by some discursive formations while other possible discourses are elided.

The poststructural emphasis on transparency is part of a methodology of rejecting how a text is supposed to operate in order to produce some small con-sideration for its master. Poststructuralist theory offers alternatives to traditional conceptions of author and reader by constituting a different kind of text produced by a combination of discourses rather than by a traditionally conceived author. It is not sufficient for an author to assert that, while all subject positions are fractured, a homogenous readership exists for that author's unique hybridity. Poststructuralists reject questions that are considered "commonsense" and "normal" within other disciplines and "argue that their very 'normalcy' gives them a troubling power to shape thought and to hinder the posing of other questions" (Bové, 1990, p. 52).

A poststructural methodology implies one more crucial perspective, regarding whether the ontology of a text, the first cause, resides with the author or the reader or both, and whether participants are constituted through discourse prior to the formation of a text. My analysis is not about *Serafina's Promise* as a story; it is about applying a poststructural methodology to analyze *Serafina's Promise* as a text that mobilizes discourses and the ideological ramifications of privileging some discourses over others. In particular, this analysis raises questions such as, Why are certain discourses (such as 'poverty' or 'tragedy') often mobilized in stories set in a third world or ethnic/urban settings, while other discourses are considered peripheral to the 'real' story?

The Theoretical Frame of Discourse and Episteme

The act of identifying is to state that something is or something is not. A poststructural literary approach can be used to identify the discursive formations that are structuring a text and, simultaneously, the discursive formations that could structure the same text, using the same discourses in that text, if a different reading is desired. Poststructural literary critics cope with the metaphysics of this critical reading strategy by arguing, "Textuality being constituted by differences and by differences from differences, it is by nature absolutely heterogeneous and is constantly composing with the forces that tend to annihilate it" (Derrida, 1979/1991, p. 257).

A single text can have multiple readings by multiple readers, but can a single text have multiple valid readings by a single reader? How does the latter position critique the validity of the concepts of author and text? In 1969, Michel Foucault gave a speech to La Societe Français de Philosophie titled *What Is an Author?*, in which he argued,

> The author is not an indefinite source of significations that fill a work; the author does not precede the works; he is a certain functional principle by which, in our culture, one limits, excludes, and chooses; in short, by which one impedes the free circulation, the free manipulation, the free composition, decomposition, and re-composition of fiction.... One can say that the author is an ideological product, since we represent him as the opposite of his historically real function.
>
> *(Foucault, 1969/2013, p. 292)*

Foucault raises the possibility of the reader being considered the primary author of a text, an authorship that acknowledges the free circulation of signification.

This chapter employs a critique of cultural aspects in the poststructuralist work done by Foucault. Poststructuralism has been applied to a variety of fields, using many different approaches. The key poststructuralist elements addressed include the source of authenticity of a text (author and/or reader), how a text is constituted (through truth or invention, and/or discourse), and how or if a text can be sufficiently 'frozen' to be an object of analysis. The author figure identified by Foucault is so powerful a cultural construct that it undermines the discourse approach that this chapter advocates. The contemporary inclination toward identity politics elevates the author figure as a primary authenticity rather than emphasizing discourse as the 'author' of a text. Foucault's critique of the author figure is challenged by Jeanne Willette (2014) as related to women and people of color and social criticism. Willette is an example of the perspective that my emphasis on discourse will have to negotiate.

The final theoretical frame used in this chapter is the work done by Foucault with respect to the episteme. In *The Order of Things*, Foucault (1971) states, "In any given culture and at any given moment, there is always only one *episteme* that defines the conditions of possibility of all knowledge, whether expressed in a theory or silently invested in a practice" (p. 168). The episteme, like the author figure, seals texts from the examination of discourse analysis. While the power relations that form a discourse are subordinate to the beliefs, values, and goals provided by the biographical lens of the author figure, the discourses that constitute an episteme are naturalized and avoid examination based on this status. When attempting to analyze an episteme, it is helpful to consider that "it's not a matter of emancipating truth from every system of power (which is a chimera for truth is always power) but of detaching the power of truth from the forms of hegemony, social economic and cultural, within which it operates at the present time" (Foucault, 1980, p. 133). Like handling a snake during a church service, applying poststructuralism is an act of faith that one's most cherished and fundamental beliefs are extricated from the power relations that framed those beliefs. The snake always bites.

Reading poststructuralist theory is like being slapped, hard, in the face, and as the burning intensifies, all you can remember is the sharp sound of the slap. Foucault's ideas threaten to ruin the textual meaning party for his detractors and promise a self-immolation for his supporters as they fall into a bottomless pit of meaning, all the while losing their position in relation to that meaning. The process identified by Foucault is truly a reframing perspective in that the authenticity of the author is examined—not as an investigation of the veracity or intentionality of the author, but as an examination of the discourses through which the author produces meaning. An examination of how discourses come into being and are maintained is a strategy to open opportunities for social action that are more productive than simply identifying the intent of the author figure or the apparent content of a text. Ozan Örmeci (2010) describes this process of analyzing discourses, saying:

> Discursivity unlike textuality, not only deals with the 'text', but also with the 'context'. Discursive researchers focus on the question of 'how' rather than 'why'. They do not look for causal explanations but instead, they try to

understand the working of an incredibly complex mechanism that creates subordinations and produces hierarchical power relations.

(para. 2)

As noted by Willette (2014), there are widely accepted discursive constructions that are not part of poststructuralist thinking. Is gender or ethnicity an ontology to the extent that these categories remain constant across socioeconomic class position, culture, history, etc.? Is it discursively viable to "interpret a statement in the context of gender and race" as defined through the author figure (Willette, 2014, para. 10)? Clearly not in poststructuralist thinking. Across cultures, the discourses are going to be a function of the unique domestic power relations that formed them. This type of discursive analysis can be done with texts from the United States, depending upon how many discursive variables are elided to accommodate the formation of gender or ethnicity categories as embodied in an author figure. It takes a lot of effort and knowledge to faithfully analyze global discourses. But, in the best tradition of reciprocity, we as participants in Western culture can shed the unwieldy and unproductive discourses that we use to lens the world.

Central to gender or ethnicity as a political subject position is the right to speak an authenticity, to manifest an author figure. According to Willette (2014), "In the end Foucault imagined that in the future the author function and/or the author him or herself would disappear in a proliferating discourse. But as was usual in Foucault's writings, the actual mechanisms of such a change are never explained." Willette goes on to note that Foucault ended *What Is an Author?* by stating: "What difference does it make who is speaking?" (para. 9). Willette (2014) responds,

To women and people of color, who have been denied the privilege of writing, "who" writes makes a difference. . . . It is important to know "who is writing" in order to interpret a statement in the context of gender and race. Without this contextual tool, critique becomes difficult and Foucault, as did his colleagues, carefully neutered critique and rendered social criticism mute, coincidentally or not, at the time of a struggle for the rights of women and people of color.

(para. 10)

In Willette's binary system, if you are not part of the solution, you are part of the problem. How often do variables that do not reify the author figure escape the gravity of the author figure and get put into discursive play? Foucault (1969) argues, "The author is therefore the ideological figure by which one marks the manner in which we fear the proliferation of meaning" (p. 230). When competing approaches of discursivity and textuality gridlock, it seems to come down to what ideology we need for a text to produce; like Alvy Singer's statement about relationships at the end of the movie *Annie Hall* (Joffe & Allen, 1977): "They're totally crazy, irrational, and absurd, but we keep going through it because we need the eggs."

Literature Review

Much has been written about authenticity in children's and young adult literature. Elizabeth Howard (1991) identified a set of criteria for judging the cultural authenticity of a text. Although other scholars have also tried to identify authenticity, simply developing a list of criteria does not take into account the myriad of discourses that inform the reading and writing of cultural texts. *Stories Matter* (2003), edited by Dana L. Fox and Kathy G. Short, is a comprehensive collection of essays about authenticity in children's literature. In the first essay, Short and Fox (2003) discuss the need for dialogue on authenticity and the possible contentiousness of such debates. They argue that children and teachers need to be able "to take negotiated and oppositional positions in their interpretations of literature and to analyze the authenticity of a book and the perspectives it presents to the reader" (p. 22).

Howard (1991) provides a foundational definition of an authentic text as:

> one in which a universality of experience permeates a story that is set within the particularity of characters and setting. The universal and specific come together to create a book in which "readers from the culture will know that it is true, will identify, and be affirmed, and readers from another culture will feel that it is true, will identify, and learn something of value."
>
> *(p. 92)*

Short and Fox (2003) problematize this definition of authenticity by stating that reading is transactional:

> Given that each reading of a book is a unique transaction which results in different interpretations (Rosenblatt, 1938/1995), and given the range of experiences within any cultural group, this definition of cultural authenticity immediately hints at why there are so many debates about the authenticity of a particular book.
>
> *(p. 5)*

Serafina's Promise qualifies as an authentic text in many aspects when discussed within the parameters of Howard's frame and within a reader response frame for a domestic readership (to the cultural context of the text). It is not clear if these conceptions of authenticity allow for readership to be fractured along, for example, gender or ethnicity or if reception in either culture is considered to be homogeneous. Can some readers from a culture perceive universality and some readers from another culture perceive universality, and so the common text is both authentic to a domestic culture and appreciated as authentic by another culture? This discussion quickly takes a poststructural turn with respect to the question of where to position authenticity.

Methodology

According to Martin Heidegger (1943), the original meaning and essence of 'truth' was unconcealment, or the revealing or bringing of what was previously hidden into the open. In this chapter, a poststructural methodology emphasizing transparency identifies texts that are authentic to the purpose of discourse analysis using two criteria. The first criterion is to identify the lens or framing through which the text is to be considered authentic. A reading may be 'valid,' not based on the political economy value of the text but on the clarity of the framing. In critical evaluative terms, some of these framings will be inspiring and some will be considered quite dull. As a middle school teacher for 30 years I have observed endless ways to frame a text, but I also have learned to never turn a text into a carnival act where students suckle at the most obvious cultural aspects and the teacher feigns astonishment at the truth of the revelations generated by the text. A secret truth revealed about a marginalized culture is still a point of conflict/ resolution in a classical Western narrative. A poststructural analysis emphasizes the conditions that produce or maintain the secret truth.

A second criterion is to determine the discourses that produced a transparent text and the discourses that are produced or extended through the text. The question, What are the power relations that produce the discourses that constitute a text?, is essential in this process of analysis.

When Willette (2014) says that it is important to interpret a statement in the context of gender and race, she appears to suggest that women and people of color can function as signifiers for a context of gender and race. Is this true, for example, about all women, in every culture, across history? What is being signified? The right to speak, the authority to be an author of a text? The authority to include and exclude significations in a text; and, in so doing, to order the boundaries between author, text, and reader? I argue that it is not a sufficient textual practice to begin with an ontology of signifiers, to coerce meaning in a text, and then to pronounce authenticity largely based on the formation of the ontology.

The text that is the focus of this analysis is authored by Ann Burg, an out-sider to Haiti who has written a YA story with Haitian characters set in Haiti. Being female, Burg fulfills one signifier congruent with the story of *Serafina's Promise*. Burg writes about a young girl, Serafina, growing up in rural Haiti during the period marked by the earthquake. On January 12, 2010, at 4:53 p.m., the sixth-deadliest earthquake in recorded history flattened much of Haiti's capital city, Port-au-Prince. Burg had not previously visited Haiti and developed her ideas by watching news reports about the devastation caused by the earthquake. Burg read articles and watched news programs about the earthquake's impact, and reflected on the image of a small Haitian girl leaning against a wall and crying, stating, "I just couldn't get her out of my mind, so I decided to write about her" (Dellon, 2013).

Serafina lives in the Haitian countryside just outside of Port-au-Prince with her parents, baby brother, and *gran manman*, Gogo. She describes her life from dawn to dusk helping her mother with the difficult chores that must be done first so that she can then cook, clean, and take care of her baby brother, Pierre. The family is very poor, and Pierre dies from malnutrition. In her prayers, Serafina makes a promise that she will work hard to become a medical doctor so that she can heal the sick and so that no more baby brothers will die needlessly. A series of natural disasters (flooding and the earthquake) function as both obstacles and motivation to her goals.

The representation of content such as extreme poverty or political instability is difficult to render in a narrative form, and such a representation tends toward the melodramatic or clichéd. Burg effectively uses the device of verse instead of prose to suggest a sustaining rhythm of life for the people in Haiti's countryside:

> Papa says that nobody buys
> Haiti rice anymore.
> Why should they?
> Miami rice costs less money.
> *(Burg, 2013, p. 65)*

Burg incorporates Haitian proverbs throughout the story, embedding them in conversations between the characters:

> Cheap is not better,
> Gogo always says,
> Shrugging her shoulders.
> But an empty sack cannot stand.
> *(p. 65)*

"An empty sack cannot stand" is a colloquial Haitian expression still in use to express the difficulty of advancement given the burden of daily life.

One of the official languages of Haiti is Creole, which Burg stylistically combines with verse to continue the idea of a sustaining rhythm of life:

> Together we walk
> down our hill of dirt and roots,
> across a field of rock and grass.
> Down one mountain, up another.
> Dèyè mòn gen mòn, Gogo says.
> *(p. 163)*

Discussion of Analysis

Much in *Serafina's Promise* deserves a positive critical reception. Connections to prose and poetry forms, the language of the everyday expressed in proverbs, the rhythm of Creole troped as the consciousness of a particular socioeconomic class of Haitian (much as the Song of the Family functions in John Steinbeck's *The Pearl*) are all expertly rendered by Burg. The book has received over 10 nominations or awards as a story of compassion for Serafina and children like Serafina, set in the engaging context of Haiti. Many adolescent and adult readers will find that this sentiment is a worthy topic for YA literature.

Burg's story of Serafina is also a Horatio Alger character or Gunga Din (Kipling, 1890) story that never rises above any cogent identification of context to address complex third world socioeconomic problems that could affect Serafina's success in achieving her goals. Burg situates the potential resolution of the story's problems with notions of rugged individualism and personal sacrifice that are unreasonable when applied to Serafina as a character, a real Haitian female, or Haitians as a population. However, the story's resolution is very reasonable if the effect is to remind a first world audience of what was once a fundamental first world ideology. Writing about Haiti, or writing on the Haitian Other? Alger is Alger and Din is Din precisely because they are exemplars; they are hegemony's poster kids. As individuals, Alger and Din do not comprise a society, and certainly not a diverse society, or a reasonable address to larger social problems. I do not intend for my comments to reflect on Burg. I am questioning the investment in and coercion to maintain a type of textual practice that would have Serafina's motivations be congruent with the sentiment, "You're a better man than I am, Gunga Din!"

Serafina is often given advice on how to succeed. Her grandmother tells her to sit on her own eggs if she wants them to hatch and her father tells her she must work extra in order to go to school. Antoinette Solaine, the medical doctor who befriends Serafina, explains the evolution of social change:

> Maybe someday,
> when you're grown-up,
> you can help change things
> so that children will learn
> in their own language.
> But for now,
> we must deal with things as they are.
> We must not let
> learning French
> stand in the way
> of helping people.
>
> *(p. 256)*

Gogo is proud that Haitians were former slaves who revolted and formed their own republic.

However, what is the status quo of their freedom? Following the earthquake, Solaine tells Serafina that she can help once things are normal. Serafina wonders, "Will things ever again be normal?" (p. 258). Given the economic circumstances experienced by rural girls, like Serafina, her status quo might teeter toward the status quo of her friend, Julie Marie, who experiences life as a restavèk. She runs away from her employer because:

> She only wanted me
> to cook and clean.
> And when I asked about school,
> she beat me.
>
> *(p. 262)*

Serafina's Promise is a very different text when examined through the lens of post-structural discourse analysis. This critical reading approach repurposes *Serafina's Promise* without attempting to produce a definitive reading of the text. A poststructural methodology informed by Foucault (1971) deconstructs privileged ideology, which has led to the complaint that poststructuralism destroys meaning. Poststructuralism is a methodology that reveals the diversity of meaning in the process of textuality by untethering the significations that combine to produce meaning.

At this point in demonstrating a poststructural reading of *Serafina's Promise*, the reader could be viewed as the 'author' of the text as reader response theorizes a reader who in some way produces meaning that alters the reception of a text in process. Ironically, Foucault might object to the artificial boundary created by acknowledging a reader who is already constituted in discourse. It is the responsibility of the reader of this chapter to determine if the discourses I have chosen to address form a reasonable reading formation based on the significations put into play through *Serafina's Promise*.

Stephanie Newell and Onookome Okome (2014b) discuss the role of popular arts in fulfilling the ambitions of emerging social groups with respect to the formation of a social consciousness (p. 6). This position strikes me as similar to how Foucault (1971) conceives of the meaning production in a social sphere with all meaning being constituted and constituting simultaneously. Serafina occupies a fixed social position and aspires to participate in an emerging social group. Especially for the experience level of a YA target audience, *Serafina's Promise* needs to include a context of the ambition of emerging consciousness, rather than a simple Western goal of upward mobility. Serafina wants a mobile social position, and most from the capitalist West understand this sentiment. *Serafina's Promise* does not contain sufficient context, however, to identify the conditions that motivate 'why' Serafina wants social mobility or 'how' she might achieve it. In third world countries, what is the discourse of 'ambition,' what does it mean to 'emerge'? Is emergence perceived as a solitary or collective act, and how can these respective discourses be incorporated into a text?

Extrapolating to Haiti a discourse of emerging female self-determination that Newell and Okome (2014a) identify in relation to Africa from a story by Ogali A. Ogali, *Veronica My Daughter* (1956):

> [Veronica] is merely happy to have her own man in place of the old, illiterate chief that her father wants her to marry. Such narratives leave little

space for the option of not marrying at all: Veronica merely moves from one regime of male hegemony (that of the father) to another—that of the husband. . . . What emerges from this is not just the anxiety of the men who wrote these texts, but a fear associated with the awareness of a new and emerging female consciousness that emphasized self-worth and pride in decision-making.

Would a Haitian reader, female or male, interpret *Serafina's Promise* as a text that opens up a legitimate space for emerging female self-determination or conclude "that ain't gonna happen"?

As someone engaged with Haitian culture for over 10 years, I have made yearly visits to Haiti providing teacher seminars. In that time, I have never been able to attract more than three or four Haitian women to the seminars, even though the men have returned multiple times. Early on, I asked the men why more women educators did not attend. Always, I was told that the women just could not attend because they had things to do. Drawing on my own cultural bearings, I suggested a women-only seminar and was told, as if I had not heard the first time, that the women educators had things to do.

What was so casually clear to these male Haitian educators while I was still trying to brainstorm new options? *Dèyè mòn gen mòn* ("Beyond mountains, more mountains") is a popular Haitian proverb that can be interpreted as bountiful opportunity or endless obstacles. A real-life Serafina from her socioeconomic class position would perform daily tasks that have to be accomplished at a certain time of day and, likely, in a certain order. A real-life Serafina would be considered fortunate to have such a gainfully productive day compared to those who have been cast aside by Haitian society. Gender issues intertwined with extreme poverty produce a subject whose sense of self-worth is economically maintained on a day-to-day basis. A real-life Serafina would be rooted to the physical day as a reality and would fear losing her place in the physical by projecting her identity into an abstract future. I would have preferred to observe "anxiety" or "fear" in the male Haitian educators because it could indicate that the "complex mechanism that creates subordinations and produces hierarchical power relations" (Örmeci, 2010) was rattling apart, producing fissures, cracks. As it was, the calm and self-satisfied tone of the male educators might as well be saying, "What a beautiful summer day."

Returning to Örmeci (2010), *Serafina's Promise* offers some formal textual elements: a 'why' discussion about Serafina's character motivation to become a doctor; a 'how' question about gender roles organizing the activities of the everyday and producing a female identity in a specific socioeconomic class; and a 'how' question about two types of consciousness (ambition to emerge versus Western upward mobility). The choice of a single discourse, gender or education or consciousness, will eventually result in a discussion of 'how' power relations produce a subordinate class and hierarchical power relations. Once the 'how' apparatus is identified, it is possible to analytically address how the apparatus is configured and then ascertain how changes in the apparatus might produce different political results.

The criteria of authenticity for third world cultures is often characterized by some discourse of race, ethnicity, nationalism, politics, poverty, gender, etc. Ironically, both an in-group and out-group identification of discourses for third world countries mimics Captain Renault (Claude Rains) at the end of *Casablanca* (Warner & Curtiz, 1942) who directs his men to "round up the usual suspects." The most familiar topics seem to be both critically and politically vibrant, but they do not engage the nuanced discourses of contemporary cultural reality in third world countries. Authenticity is often used as a holistic belief suggesting that some cultural values are unanimously agreed upon and knowable monolithically across a contemporary culture and sometimes across the history of a culture. The emphasis should not be on the author or content of the text, but on the process that coalesces content into a discourse that is meaningful to an individual or group.

For example, the choice of 'poverty' as a discourse is inherently an episteme that results in the general agreement that poverty is a bad thing and that it should not exist. Poverty can seldom demonstrate how it came into being or the nature of its contours. It certainly does not explain why it exists in such a prominent position or the role it plays in ordering other discourses. The single address to the poverty episteme is to care (whatever form caring takes). Ironically, once the poverty episteme comes into being, there is no longer an actionable discourse representing a global lack of caring. The episteme of poverty means 'to care.' To not care is to be demonized without articulation of the demonized position. Unfortunately, the political results are generally to shield the discourses that thrive on global poverty from visibility.

Epistemes do not respond to interrogation. Broad suggestions, such as a new system of economics that more equitably distributes resources to end poverty, do not engage the episteme. Less radical suggestions are simply absorbed and become part of the discursive formation of the episteme. For example, Serafina is inspired to become a doctor by interacting with the character Dr. Antoinette Solaine. However, the discourse of Serafina's medical education is absorbed by the tragic events of Pierre's death and the natural disaster of the catastrophic earthquake—neither of which have anything to do with Serafina successfully becoming a medical doctor. Pierre isn't suffering from a disease that needs medical attention, per se. He and his mother are victims of the political and economic distribution of the goods and services that humans need to thrive. An earthquake victim does not need a medical opinion regarding the health risks of having a poorly constructed building collapse on him or her. The epistemes of 'poverty' or 'third world catastrophe' have appropriated a complex discursive discussion of Serafina's medical education. In the contemporary United States, this type of appropriation of discourses by an episteme is known as the 'politics of hope.'

Serafina's Promise is a tangle of multiple discourses in the manner that discursive formations actually exist in relation to four intertwining contexts: consciousness, education, economics, and Haitian expatriates (a person who lives outside of his or her native country). With respect to the discourse of consciousness, in *12 Years a Slave* (McQueen & Northup, 2013) plantation owner William Ford gifts Solomon Northup with a violin. This uncomfortable moment is made more so in comparison to a selection from Northup's 1853 memoir: "The influences and associations that had always surrounded [William Ford] blinded him to the inherent wrong at the bottom of the system of Slavery" (p. 90), even though Northup goes on to praise Ford as a person outside of his role as plantation owner. This is an example of how consciousness is an amorphous, slippery, yet highly structuring discourse that critical readers must negotiate into our interactions with global texts. Not all global gender or ethnicity positions will correspond to those in the United States, or reinforce our domestic political emphasis for gender or ethnicity. Not all global discourses for a similar topic will correspond to the same discursive formation. We critically read global texts not 'even though' there are differences, but precisely because there are differences. We have attempted to distance ourselves from the imperialist practice of exclusively viewing global countries as the producers of raw materials for our manufacture of finished goods. Critical reading can enable the citizens of first world countries to understand the complexity of global culture, rather than appropriating that culture to construct a domestic ideological product.

The chances that Serafina will ever become a medical doctor are greatly reduced by her gender and general access to education. One third of girls over the age of six never go to school (Haiti Partners, 2015). The prohibitive cost of school fees in Haiti keeps many children, male and female, out of school (Basic Education, 2015). With luck, Serafina will complete classical school and then will likely become an expatriate whether or not she attends medical school in Haiti or overseas. Unlike Western societies that have large middle-class populations, Haiti's middle class is about 14% (Pauyo, 2011; UNICEF, 2009). More disturbing is the distribution of income in Haiti. Eighty-five percent of the Haitian population lives in absolute poverty (earning less than two U.S. dollars per day) or extreme poverty (earning less than one U.S. dollar per day) (Haiti Partners, 2015). Twenty percent of the richest 1% in Haiti receives 64% of the country's available income (Charles, 2014). Once Serafina acquires her medical education, she would find that Haiti does not have a sufficient middle class to compensate her for her services or an adequate medical infrastructure to allow her to practice medicine to her professional best. Like many highly trained Haitian engineers, mathematicians, and medical doctors, Serafina would likely become an expatriate.

Woch Nan dlo pa Konnen Doule Woch Nan Soley

"The rock in the water does not know the pain of the rock in the sun." Expatriates are suffering rocks in the water. They have escaped poverty but they have often escaped without family, friends, and most important, without a consciousness of what it means to be Haitian in an ever-changing Haiti. Even the emotions of alienation that expatriates feel can be conceived as luxuries compared to the limited emotional response that the everyday conditions in Haiti allow the average Haitian. With respect to consciousness, being an expatriate from a third world country, such as Haiti, has a different dynamic than being an expatriate from a first world country.

This discursive formation provides a lens from which to inquire 'how' some Haitian expatriates contribute humanitarian aid to Haiti. I have worked with a number of Haitian expatriates in a humanitarian aid context, and they each conceive of the structure of aid within the parameters of how they perceive their own best traits or achievements as their connection to the ever-changing face of Haiti and to their identity as Haitian subjects. Extending the dilemma of the education discourse from *Serafina's Promise*, I was engaged in preliminary talks with an expatriate Haitian medical doctor who does great humanitarian work funding education-related resources in Haiti. The dialogue was strained when I indicated that Haiti's colonialist-based French education system needed a major overhaul. The doctor is a product of that older system, and he emotionally needed for a holistic destiny to be reified in younger Haitians following his same path. His conception of humanitarian aid to education is structured by his expatriate consciousness. In my opinion, Haitian education should focus less on highly educated gatekeepers (the colonialist/imperialist model) who end up leaving Haiti as expatriates and should, instead, address those students who can fill and expand the ranks of a middle class, reside in Haiti, and who can provide some normalizing structure for the country. Once this occurs, then highly educated expatriates may find that it is viable for them to return to Haiti.

Conclusion

YA literature is sometimes perceived as being less complex because of its assumed lower lexile levels or simplified discourses. I believe that outstanding YA literature tries to present the 'how' of discourse rather than the 'why,' and provides at least a skeleton of discursive formations whether or not those formations are fully fleshed out. For example, 'economics' or 'consciousness' can almost always be connected to dynamic discursive formations, whereas 'poverty,' fulfilling the category of an episteme, cannot.

The act of critical reading tends to work out the theoretical complexities of Foucault if my second criterion of authenticity is strictly adhered to: What are the power relations that produced the discourses that constitute a text? The configuration of power relations is what is being sought. When incorporating poststructuralism in a classroom, a critical reading lesson does not begin with what the educator considers most politically liberatory and then backtracks to the discourses that support that position. An analysis of discourses, identifying the 'how' rather than the 'why,' is the strategy to identify power relations.

This reading of *Serafina's Promise* employs a different model of textuality than Burg's organization of discourses in order to emphasize different nuances in the text. My reading is authentic to the poststructural lens I chose to analyze this book, yet the question of what prevents someone from producing a fictitious or appropriative reading of a text through the selection of discourses needs to be asked. Other than the observation that this occurs regularly, the discourses (other than epistemes) that a reader employs to structure a text will produce meaning for that reader. Situating the diversity of meaning with the most complex component of textual meaning production (a reader) has the potential to produce a transparency where the text is not just constituted, but is presented for examination. Applying poststructuralism is an act of faith that one's most cherished and fundamental beliefs are extricated from the power relations that framed those beliefs. A poststructuralist practice does not destroy knowledge as much as it makes possibility visible.

References

Basic Education Coalition. (2015). *U.S. basic education assistance to Haiti.* Retrieved July 18, 2015 from www.basiced.org

Bové, P. (1990). Discourse. In F. Lentricchia & T. McLaughlin (Eds.), *Critical terms for literary study* (pp. 50–65). Chicago: University of Chicago Press.

Charles, J. (2014). Haiti sees drop in poverty rates, but inequality remains. *The Miami Herald.* Retrieved March 31, 2015 from www.miamiherald.com

Dellon, S. (2013). *Author Ann E. Burg Talks "Serafina's Promise."* Retrieved April 19, 2015 from www.combinedbook.com/blog/author-ann-e-burg-talks-serafinas-promise/

Derrida, J. (1972/1991). Plato's pharmacy. In P. Kamuf (Ed.), *A Derrida reader: Between the blinds* (pp. 112–139). New York: Columbia University Press.

Derrida, J. (1979/1991). Living on border lines. In P. Kamuf (Ed.), *A Derrida reader: Between the blinds* (pp. 256–268). New York: Columbia University Press.

Foucault, M. (1969, February 22). *What is an author?* Lecture for La Societe Français de Philosophie. Retrieved August 20, 2015 from www.case.edu/affil/sce/authorship/Foucault.pdf

Foucault, M. (1969/2013). What is an author? In D. Lodge & N. Wood (Eds.), *Modern criticism and theory* (pp. 281–293). New York: Routledge.

Foucault, M. (1971). *The order of things: An archaeology of the human sciences.* New York: Pantheon Books.

Foucault, M. (1980). *Power/knowledge: Selected interviews and other writings, 1972–1977.* New York: Vintage Press.

Fox, D. & Short, K. G. (2003). *Stories matter: The complexity of cultural authenticity in children's literature.* Urbana, IL: National Council of Teachers of English.

Haiti Partners. (2015). Website. Retrieved July 18, 2015 from www.haitipartners.org

Heidegger, M. (1943). *On the essence of truth.* Trans. J. Sallis (1961). Retrieved September 7, 2015 from www.aphelis.net

Howard, E. (1991). Authentic multicultural literature for children: An author's perspective. In M.V. Lindgren (Ed.), *The multicolored mirror: Cultural substance in literature for children and young adults* (pp. 91–99). Fort Atkinson, WI: Highsmith.

Joffe, C. & Allen, W. (1977). *Annie Hall.* Los Angeles: United Artists.

Kipling, R. (1890). *Gunga Din and other favorite poems.* New York: Dover.

McQueen, S. (Director) & Northup, S. (Writer). (2013). *12 years a slave* [Motion picture]. Los Angeles: Bass Films and Monarchy Enterprise.

Newell, S. & Okome, O. (2014a). Popular culture in Africa: The episteme of the everyday. In S. Newell and O. Okome (Eds.), *Popular culture in Africa: The episteme of the everyday* (p. 6). New York: Routledge.

Newell, S. & Okome, O. (2014b). *Popular culture in Africa: The episteme of the everyday.* New York: Routledge.

Örmeci, O. (2010). *Michel Foucault and post-structuralism.* Retrieved June 28, 2015 from www.ydemokrat.blogspot.com

Pauyo, N. L. (2011). *Haiti: Refoundation of a nation.* Bloomington, IN: AuthorHouse.

Rosenblatt, L. (1938/1995). *Literature as exploration* (5th ed.). Chicago: Modern Language Association.

Short, K. & Fox, D. (2003). The complexity of cultural authenticity in children's literature: Why the debates really matter. In D. Fox & K. G. Short (Eds.), *Stories matter: The complexity of cultural authenticity in children's literature* (pp. 3–24). Urbana, IL: National Council of Teachers of English.

Steinbeck, J. (1947). *The pearl.* New York: Penguin Books.

UNICEF. (2009). *At a glance: Haiti—The big picture.* Retrieved July 18, 2015 from http://www.unicef.org/infobycountry/haiti_2014.html

Warner, J. & Curtiz, M. (1942). *Casablanca.* Los Angeles: Warner Bros.

Willette, J. S. M. (2014, January 24). Michel Foucault: "What is an author?" (Part Four). *Art History Unstuffed.* Retrieved June 10, 2015 from www.arthistoryunstuffed.com

Children's Literature Reference

Burg, A. (2013). *Serafina's promise.* New York: Scholastic.

13

CONNECTING CRITICAL CONTENT ANALYSIS TO CRITICAL READING IN CLASSROOMS

Holly Johnson, Janelle Mathis, and Kathy G. Short

This final chapter addresses the "so what" question that researchers ask (and worry about) at the end of any study in considering how their research might inform the broader field. Clearly, given our focus on research methodology, there are many implications for researchers from our work, but we are educators and so the question we find most compelling is how this research might inform teachers and students beyond a critique of specific global and multicultural books. In particular, we are interested in how strategies used for research purposes might inform teachers and students in their critical reading of books in K–12 and teacher education classrooms. Each researcher reflected on the processes, questions, and strategies used in our studies to consider the implications for critical literacy. The three of us also read carefully across the studies, identifying strategies and processes to explore connections to critical literacy in classroom settings.

Critical literacy is the theoretical and curricular frame through which teachers engage with critical content analysis in classroom settings. In this chapter, we discuss our understandings of critical literacy and then reflect on our experiences with research to consider how to support readers in critically engaging with texts in classrooms. Strategies and processes employed by each researcher are discussed in terms of their potential for classroom readers and teachers. In light of current expectations of literacy, we also argue that there are significant parallels between the requirements of close reading and the use of a critical content analysis stance in reading.

The Transformative Potential of Critical Literacy

Critical literacy involves taking a critical stance as reader. Although there are a number of approaches that fall under the critical literacy umbrella, all view language and texts as a primary means for representing and reshaping the world and what is possible in society. Thus, readers assume a critical lens to analyze texts for the intent of transforming themselves and the world. This transformation occurs by disrupting inequitable practices that contribute to an unjust world and replacing inequity with ways of representing and constructing both texts and the world through a social justice perspective (Lewison, Leland, & Harste, 2014).

The concept of *critical* can be traced to the work of Paulo Freire (1970), and addresses a lens through which teachers and students come to understand that the world and its texts are socially constructed and read through perspectives that differ from one reader to another. Each person transacts with a specific text in unique ways based on her/his lived experiences, value systems, and cultural understandings (Rosenblatt, 1938). Texts can be "revised, rewritten, or reconstructed to shift or reframe" meaning, and thus are never neutral (Vasquez, 2012, p. 466). Texts are written from a particular perspective to convey particular understandings of the world, and authors use language to position readers in a particular way so as to gain an intended meaning from the text. Because of this positioning of author and reader, the perspectives of each should be questioned as well as the discourses within which they locate the text and themselves. The concept of critical therefore requires a questioning stance when reading the word and the world (Freire & Macedo, 1987).

Typically this questioning stance focuses on social issues involving race/ethnicity, class, and gender, and the ways language is used to shape the representations of others who could be similar or dissimilar to the intended audience. The language used can impact perceptions of readers about specific groups of people and by extension influence the power those within particular groups may or may not have within a society. For instance, women are often portrayed as more sensitive in the United States and thus often held suspect when considered for powerful roles.

A critical stance includes questioning the concept of "truth" and how it is presented, by whom, and for what purposes. In addressing these issues, other questions also emerge around whose values, texts, ideologies, and concepts of normative should be privileged so as to achieve a more just and equitable world (Luke, 2012). A critical stance focuses on voice and who gets to speak, whose story is told and in what ways, and who is silenced or misrepresented. Groups marginalized on the basis of gender, language, ethnicity or nationality, race, and sexual orientation are often the focus of a critical lens due to a long history of misrepresentation and bias.

Teaching from a critical stance involves supporting students in making connections between the texts they read and their lives, thus linking critical analysis with a focus on connecting language and power (Janks, 2009). Furthermore, students are taught to examine texts for who might benefit and who is disadvantaged by taking into account the social effects of texts and their representations as well as noting what choices authors and readers make either in their writing or their behavior in response to a specific set of truths (Janks, 2014). Learning to read through a critical stance allows readers to see what is privileged, what is hidden, and what can be made possible in their lives or others' lives if they question what is assumed and might be disrupted in respect to individual racial, gendered, or socioeconomic circumstance.

Critical Literacy in the Classroom

Given these theoretical understandings and goals for critical literacy, our question is what insights can be carried from our research with critical content analysis into engagements with literature in classrooms. We believe that the strategies and processes we used within critical content analysis can be adapted and used within K–12 classrooms and teacher education settings to encourage critical thinking around a book or text set. A range of strategies is described that provides possibilities for critical literacy in classrooms so that teachers can select the ones most relevant to their purposes and students.

Identify a Tension that Provides a Focus for Inquiry

The critical reading of a text goes beyond reading for enjoyment to engaging readers in an in-depth examination of a book and beyond conversation to dialogue, both of which require a focused and long-term investment by a reader. Students are not just exploring a book but investigating a book through a range of systematic processes and strategies. This type of investment occurs when students are inquiring into an issue or tension that is compelling to them and that focuses their investigation in a productive manner.

Critical content analysis is based on finding a research focus that leads to a set of questions and texts. Our research grows out of contexts in which tensions emerge that eventually lead us to a research focus. In turn, critical literacy is rooted in identifying a tension that matters to students and engages them in inquiry as problem-posers and problem-solvers (Freire, 1970). That tension might emerge from questions about a particular book or set of books, an event in the classroom or community, global occurrences, student relationships, or a classroom unit of study. Frank Smith (1983) notes that we can't think critically about something we know nothing about. In this case, we can't think critically about a book unless that book is embedded in a rich context of experiences and inquiry.

Identify a Text or Set of Texts Related to the Inquiry

Identifying the book or set of books to examine through critical reading seems like an obvious process within critical literacy but often is not given enough time and emphasis in classrooms. We spend a great deal of time selecting the texts within our research, often gathering and considering a wide range of texts before deciding on those that will be our focus. Vivian Yenika-Agbaw found that an in-depth focus on a single book provided the best context for exploring her questions on identity, while Kathy Short needed a set of books to explore her questions about patterns in how action is depicted in children's books. Kathy's study also reflects the need to develop a specific set of criteria for text selection.

We believe that these same considerations are important in selecting books for critical literacy experiences in the classroom. The books have to match our inquiry focus, offer layers of meaning that will stand a close look, and be appropriate to the interests and experiences of students. The same processes of considering criteria for what kind of books will best support an inquiry focus and then gathering and considering a wide range of possible books before making a selection are essential to critical literacy.

Read to Experience the Text

As researchers, we first read, not to analyze a book through a particular critical lens, but to immerse ourselves in the story world of that book. We have a purpose for selecting the book, but do not read to *learn about* that text but to *live within* that text (Rosenblatt, 1938). Critical literacy also begins with students immersing themselves in a book, not to answer questions or analyze, but to experience. That reading is followed by a chance to reflect on that experience by writing or talking with others to share initial interpretations and connections.

Explore Critical Theories and Tenets

The purpose for reading a particular book and first responses to that book provide a context for determining a critical lens for in-depth analysis and dialogue. As is evident across our studies, identifying a critical theory and examining that theory to determine several key tenets shape the questions that we ask in looking at a text and give a focus for close analysis. In each study, the selected theoretical lens led to a different set of questions to guide analysis. Janine Schall used intersectionality theory and privilege theory to identify a set of questions for examining her set of picturebooks:

- Where are sites of oppression and privilege?
- How is power and privilege operating in these books across different levels?
- Where are the intersections between identity and social structures? Between identity and power?

In-depth reading of critical theory is not appropriate in most K–12 classroom contexts but teachers can provide students with access to a particular theory as an analytic tool. That access involves teacher guidance in understanding the theory and the key tenets in order to construct a theoretical lens for analysis and to support students in framing questions for their reading of particular texts. The youth lens used by Melissa Wilson and childism lens used by Kathy Short offer critical theories that connect in significant ways to the experiences of youth and so can be particularly generative for critical analysis.

Each chapter in this book provides examples of critical theories and the questions emerging from those theories that teachers can draw upon in critical literacy engagements. In addition, teachers can refer to academic books that have chapters overviewing critical theories (Malpas & Wake, 2013; Tyson, 2015), as well as books like *Doing Literary Criticism* (Gillespie, 2010) and *Using Critical Theory* (Tyson, 2011) that summarize critical theories and recommend ways of engaging students with these theories.

Questions to ask when exploring a theoretical lens include:

- What critical theory seems most useful in examining a particular piece of literature or group of texts given the specific text and the instructional purpose for using that text?
- What key tenets make up a theory? How much background reading about the tenet is needed before examining the literature?
- What examples from the text can be identified as related to the tenets of that theory? Do the textual examples of the tenets change as the novel progresses?
- Are there certain literary elements or features of the texts that have the most potential for insights into the theoretical tenets? For example, is it better to examine tenets through characterization, plots, style, or themes?

Because there are so many different theories through which to examine literature, the possibility of doing comparative analysis is another instructional strategy. Students can read the same book through several different theoretical lenses and see how each lens changes their questions and interpretations. They can also consider whether certain theories focus on different elements of a text or are more useful with particular genres. This comparative analysis can lead students to better understanding not only the text, but the different theoretical lenses through which to explore a text. There are multiple ways of seeing the world and reading a text, and students may find literature more exciting if encouraged to produce meanings that expand beyond the typical.

An additional instructional strategy is to have readers apply the critical theory to their own lives. Through genealogical searches that center on their own family history, students may come to a better understanding of themselves as readers from particular historical and cultural locations that influence their understandings of a narrative. Wanda Brooks found that critical race theory helped her understand the literature she read for her study as well as her strong connection to the storyline through her own family history of land ownership. The questions readers ask situate them in the theory and literature at the same time.

Explore Historical and Sociocultural Contexts and Discourses

The interpretive lens that researchers bring to a text involves not only a critical theory but knowledge of significant sociohistorical or sociocultural contexts essential to understanding that text. Janelle Mathis used New Historicism as her theoretical lens to consider the use of the arts in telling the story of a World War II female swing band, but she also read about the historical context surrounding the swing bands, particularly related to gender and race. In addition, she interviewed the author and illustrator to gain further insights into their historical research and intentions. Janine Schall created a time line of important events in the history of gay rights and mapped them onto the publication dates of the picturebooks she was analyzing. Clare Bradford read anthropological, historical, and geographical sources to create a lens for her critical reading of an Aboriginal picturebook.

In a classroom setting, gathering a text set that includes informational books, news reports, picturebooks, and online sources can provide an important contextual frame to inform students in their critical reading of a text. These texts can be available as independent reading or read alouds to support the ongoing analysis of a particular book. The questions to consider are:

- What is the sociocultural context or historical context in which the narrative is embedded?
- What other texts would be useful to read alongside this text?

Deborah Dimmett argues in her chapter that a poststructuralist lens asks readers to consider the discourses within which both theory and texts are embedded. Questions from a focus on discourses include:

- In what ways do the cultural aspects of the text reveal the conditions that produced it, the discourses that are produced, and the relationship of those discourses to power?
- Are the discourses in a text apparent before the text is critically read? For example, is "poverty" both a beginning and an end point? Do different contexts produce "poverty" in different ways? Is it problematic for the teacher or student critically reading an intercultural text in which the topic of "poverty" is not a universal discourse that can be associated with a political stance?

Through questions that address culture, discourses, and authenticity, readers are better able to explore what a particular story may or may not represent.

Explore the Cultural Locations of Authors and Readers

Although critical content analysis highlights the text, the analysis is conducted by a reader—the researcher—and so it's important to question the reader's stance in connection to a narrative. This questioning affords aspects of critical literacy to enter the relationship of how readers, authors, and texts are situated by their reading (Vine & Faust, 1993) as well as how the author may situate a reader by the language used, the tone in which the story is told, and the assumptions made in respect to the reader. As researchers, we examine our situatedness as readers by looking at the ways in which we interpret the text or make meaning from the text and at how our interpretations are shaped by our own cultural understandings of the world.

Students can also examine their cultural locations as readers and be mindful of how they are reading themselves and their relationship to the culture represented in the story. In addition, they can investigate the author's cultural location in relation to that particular text and how the author's location transacts with their experiences as readers. When working with global and multicultural texts, readers need to remember their own culture may be quite different from the culture represented within the story they are reading. Questions to consider include:

- What is it about my own interests, assumptions, or values that brings me closer to or distances me from the situation or character in the narrative?
- If there is too much distance from a situation/character, how can I close that gap?
- If the situation/character is closely connected to me, how can I distance myself to explore what is not addressed in the situation or character?
- How does the author influence me through the language used in the story?
- What are the author's background and experiences related to this particular text? How do the author's experiences relate to my experiences and position for this text?
- How do I relate to the situation or characters within the book?
- How am I resisting the narrative and why?
- What does this book teach me about another time, place, or people?

Through questioning themselves as readers and how they are situated by the text or outside the world of the text, students garner greater insights into the world, narrative structures, and themselves as readers and citizens.

Decide What to Focus on within a Text

Even given a research focus and interpretive lens, examining a whole text can be overwhelming and so determining a unit of analysis is an important part of our research process. In particular, we determine whether there are key features or literary elements of the text that are particularly useful to examine through the lens of the theoretical tenets. Wanda Brooks found it useful to focus on the protagonist (characterization), after initially coding many examples and illustrations connected to other characters in the novel, settings, general plot events, and idiomatic expressions. This became overwhelming, so she narrowed her analysis to the protagonist.

This same process of determining what passages to focus on within a book also supports critical reading with students so they do not feel overwhelmed and can move into more in-depth analysis. They might examine individual words or phrases, interactions or dialogue between specific characters, key incidents, or other elements of the book that connect to their inquiry. Selecting what element of the text they are focusing on guides them through a more in-depth look at the narrative.

Identifying key words, phrases, or sentences to do a linguistic analysis is one type of unit of analysis within a critical reading. Pulling out these words and phrases and placing them in charts provides a context to quickly look over the data to identify patterns and questions for further analysis or coding. Carmen Martínez-Roldán pulled out the Spanish words used within the text in one chart and the Mock Spanish in another chart. Being able to visually scan the words on the chart provided her with a perspective from which to then return to the text to examine how those words were used within the story. Vivian Yenika-Agbaw identified words, phrases, and sentences related to her focus on the main character's multiple identities and listed these to provide the basis for further coding. Students can use these same strategies of pulling out words and phrases related to their purpose onto a chart to identify possible insights for further analysis in the text.

Examine the Ideology within a Text

Another way of exploring a narrative is through an examination of ideology by identifying the values found within a text. Carmen Martínez-Roldán argues that students gain valuable insight into the world by asking what ideologies are promoted or critiqued in the text (through the description of the characters and the consequences of their actions). Often readers will find competition, commodification, consumerism, the American Dream, and rugged individualism in many narratives from U.S. authors. Suggesting these ideologies to students is an interesting way to discuss the concept of ideology as well as the messages readers might embrace or reject because of the ideologies at play within a story. In connection to competition and commodification, students can ask questions such as:

- Do issues of class play a role in the story?
- How is success defined in the story?
- What do the characters do in response to issues and definitions of class and success?

Carmen also argues that ideology can be revealed through the role humor plays within a story. Questions students could ask when examining a humorous text include:

- Who do you think feels entertained by the humor?
- Does the humor reflect respect for diverse cultures, groups of people, and languages?

- What kinds of relationships are produced among characters in a particular text or between the reader and the text as an outcome to the humor?
- Is the author a cultural insider or outsider and how does that matter when using humor?

Exploring what is funny or not can provide insight into a community's values, and depending on how the humor is used in respect to cultural mores, young readers gain valuable information about a culture and how that humor creates a bridge or a gap to the reader's understanding of the story and perhaps even of the culture represented within the text.

Examine the Text through Analysis Strategies

Each researcher used a range of strategies for the actual close analysis of the text and these strategies reflect different options for teachers and students. This section suggests possible strategies for critical literacy with a brief reference to the researchers whose chapters can be consulted for a more detailed description.

Evaluate Focalization, Social Processes, and Closure

One strategy that we frequently use as researchers is to examine the focalization of the story in order to determine whose story is being told within a particular text and from whose point of view that story is told. These questions can reveal, for example, whether a book in which a main character is a person of color is told through a white person's point of view about that character or the character's own point of view. Carmen Martínez-Roldán used this strategy to determine that the Skippyjon Jones books are told from a white perspective.

Focalization can also include an analysis of the interactions between characters, particularly characters from marginalized groups and those from the dominant culture, to examine who is the focus of the story and what is the narrative point of view. This strategy, for example, allowed Clare Bradford to note that interactions between Muslims and Christians in the Crusade novels were told through the Christian character's perspective and values.

Questions about social processes examine who is portrayed as having power and agency in the book, while closure examines how a story is resolved, particularly who is depicted as solving the conflict or problem at the heart of the plot (Botelho & Rudman, 2009). Questions include:

- Whose story is told? From whose point of view is the story told?
- Who has power? Who has agency to take action for self and others?
- How is the story resolved and who resolves it? What are the assumptions in the story closure?

Compare Texts to an Anchor Text

Intertextual connections provide a comparative strategy for critical reading, particularly if an anchor text is selected that is a counter-narrative, a text that resists common stereotypes around a particular theme, context, or cultural group. By first reading the counter-narrative in-depth and noting characters, themes, and contexts, an anchor point is established from which to compare readings of other texts. Yoo Kyung Sung, Mary Fahrenbruck, and Julia López-Robertson used *Inside Out and Back Again* (Lai, 2011) as their anchor text or counter-narrative to examine the portrayal of immigrant experiences in novels. In their reading of other novels, they noted themes and patterns of important points of difference between the anchor text and the other novels. This strategy seems particularly productive for critical reading in classrooms because the counter-narrative provides an anchor that facilitates identification of significant differences and connections across texts. Students have a place to focus their attention in looking across texts.

Another variation is to read paired texts, with the two texts providing important points of comparison in their portrayal of a cultural group, such as *Homeless Bird* (Whelan, 2001) with *Keeping Corner* (Sheth, 2009) about child widows in India, or reading *When My Name Was Keoko* (Park, 2012) against *So Far from the Bamboo Grove* (Watkins, 2008) about the Japanese occupation of Korea in World War II. In both pairs of books, the authors have very different cultural locations in relation to the same events. The impact of that location on the text is immediately obvious to readers and so provides important insights. Wanda Brooks suggests pairing historical fiction with contemporary realistic fiction to highlight past to present racial connections, for example, pairing *The Land* (Taylor, 2001) with *Hold Fast to Dreams* (Pinkney, 1995).

Identify Themes or Categories

Critical content analysis involves a search for patterns related to the questions that are guiding our reading of texts. As we read through the texts, using the lens of the theoretical tenets, we look closely at particular passages or words and phrases and make notes in the margins or on charts. In some cases, these notes are quickly moved into broad themes and, in other cases, we engage in careful coding that leads to categories and then themes. The key is that we search for patterns and use evidence from the texts related to our theoretical frame to identify those patterns. We go deeper into our initial responses to identify passages, take notes, and use those notes to determine patterns and insights. It is important to note that the theoretical tenets provide a lens for reading and making initial notes and so inform, but do not determine, the actual themes or categories.

Adapting this strategy for classroom use puts the focus on moving beyond initial impressions and conversations about a book to engage in some type of systematic process to identify themes related to the critical lens. In general, that process includes identifying the passages or parts of the book to which close attention will be paid, reading those carefully and making notes, and then using those notes to identify themes or categories.

The analysis strategies included in our chapters make clear that there is a tremendous range in the procedures for how we use our notes to identify themes or categories. Wanda Brooks codes every passage identified from the text related to her research focus and then combines the large set of codes to create a smaller set of categories from which she then develops a few key themes. Many of us use a more holistic process of writing notes about key passages and moving from there to themes. Melissa Wilson began with a close reading of the whole text, followed by a meta-analysis of relevant aspects of the plot and then a microanalysis of identified passages in order to identify themes. Holly Johnson and Becca Gasiewicz found it useful to create a chart of emerging themes to record notes about the themes and relevant passages.

The key issue is that our reading goes beyond only reflecting on our recollections of reading a particular book. Critical literacy involves systematically revisiting a text multiple times to look closely for patterns and themes and to identify evidence from the text around those themes, always within a particular critical lens. Many literature discussions involve students sharing connections and interpretations but not going back to analyze those interpretations in a systematic way around particular issues or themes. Freire (1970) notes that students often walk on the surface of words instead of wrestling with meaning and this distinction is an important difference between the discussions that frequently occur within literature circles and the dialogue that we are calling critical literacy.

Consult Other Expert Perspectives

Researchers often consult additional sources on the book they are analyzing in order to establish the trustworthiness or credibility of their findings. These strategies include collecting multiple sources of information to triangulate or check their emerging findings. In critical content analysis, commonly used strategies include exploring authors' websites and interviews, book reviews, and online blogs. These sources provide additional information that can be triangulated or compared with the researcher's emerging ideas and interpretations of the narrative being analyzed. Another source is other published content analysis studies of the same book or topic or that use a similar theoretical frame to compare findings from these studies or to identify strategies for analysis. These same strategies to establish credibility can be used by students in classrooms.

Read within an Interpretive Community

Another strategy that has possibilities for deepening understanding is reading within a group of students or researchers to apply a particular theory to texts as

Holly Johnson and Becca Gasiewicz did within their research. In our studies, sometimes researchers read and analyzed the same text individually within the same theoretical lens and then compared initial analyses to create a shared interpretation. This approach highlights how readers with the same text and lens construct different interpretations and perspectives that then need to be negotiated. Other times they read and worked at the analysis together as a group instead of individually, a collaborative approach that uses dialogue to provide a supportive structure for critical analysis. Both strategies gradually lead to the formation of an interpretive community where readers share a history and important conceptual understandings as well as ways of interacting that facilitate the analysis.

These same strategies can be used within literature circles in classroom contexts. Once students have developed an understanding of their critical lens, they can revisit the same book, each using that lens to make notes and identify themes that are shared and negotiated within the group. Or they can each read the book and come together with initial notes and responses to engage in a process of dialogue to identify themes and patterns.

Close Reading and Critical Content Analysis

Given that critical content analysis involves the use of critical theories to engage in a close reading of a particular text, this analysis provides an alternative approach to the close reading approaches currently being mandated in many schools. Critical content analysis provides a lens through which students can consider how pieces of literature are products of particular historical and cultural contexts. In close reading, students explore how literary devices are used in the text to garner better understandings of the author's work. By utilizing the complementary analyses of critical content analysis with close reading, teachers and students can examine power relations not just through close reading of the text itself, but also through reading the world in which the text exists. Thus, students engage with the world of the text, but also what is possible in their world outside the text.

Rosenblatt's discussion of New Criticism as close reading in 1938 indicates that the concept of close reading is not new. Current instructional approaches based on the Common Core Standards have emphasized close reading as essential for academic reading practices in schools. The most common definitions of close reading highlight "reading between the four corners of the page" and text-dependent questions to emphasize that readers need to attend to what the text says and how it says that, rather than what a text means to a reader. The reader's perspectives and experiences are seen as interfering with comprehension. Fisher and Frey (2014) argue that discussion should begin by asking, What does the text say?, followed by asking, How does the text work? Only after discussing these questions in-depth is the reader allowed to consider, What does the text mean? Rosenblatt (1938) would argue that this final question is where readers both begin and end a reading event. Beginning by considering what a text means engages the reader and provides a purposeful context from which to consider evidence within the text and the literary devices that support meaning-making.

The use of critical content analysis provides a means of working toward the expected standards while also being allowed an aesthetic response to the reading (Rosenblatt, 1938) and an understanding of the societal issues of power reflected in that text. In addition, critical content analysis directly connects to aspects of close reading, including understanding how language functions in different contexts as well as the use of figurative language and word meanings. With the use of critical content analysis, readers have the opportunity to see examples of particular and purposeful language usage and opportunities to evaluate closely so as to draw conclusions. Readers are also invited to examine how language represents particular worldviews and how those views must be scrutinized so as to examine issues of power in respect to culture, gender, race, and class. Critical content analysis requires readers to conduct close readings of the text, but to move beyond the text to explore how narratives have the power to codify experiences and relationships between peoples that forefront privilege for some, but not for all, and what such privileging and lack thereof might mean for human strivings and cross-cultural endeavors.

In addition, critical content analysis examines the narratives read in classrooms to focus on the way in which language plays a role in hierarchical power relations, an aspect of close reading. Through examination of the sociopolitical functions of the language in texts, classroom communities can analyze the ways in which authors, narrators, characters, publishers, teachers, students, and readers construct their worlds.

Critical content analysis is consistent with criteria for the Common Core English Language Arts anchor standards and can be used concurrently with both literary and informational texts. These standards require students to attend to a vast amount of information as they read, addressing comprehension as well as critique. Students are to "question an author's or speaker's assumptions and premises and assess the veracity of claims and the soundness of reasoning" (NGA, 2010, p. 7). Furthermore, readers come to understand other perspectives and cultures as they, "actively seek to understand other perspectives and cultures through reading and listening . . . they evaluate points of view critically and constructively" (p. 7, para. 8). Secondary readers are to respond to the varying demands of audience, task, purpose, and discipline as they are asked to "appreciate nuances, such as how the composition of an audience should affect tone when speaking and how connotations of words affect meaning" (p. 4). When contemplating these three standards, it is clear that critical content analysis is a tool for textual analysis that would guide students to experiment with and gain critical and analytical interpretive skills and strategies.

With a more critical stance to a story, students find relevance in the readings and see connection to the world around them. Critical content analysis allows readers to see the world in new ways and to move beyond the "what is" to the "what could be possible." As teachers support students in taking a more question-ing stance toward who and what is (or is not) represented within the books they read, they are able to directly address curricular mandates at the same time. The theoretical and analytical tools discussed in this chapter are ones that support close reading from both literary and critical perspectives.

Conclusion

Throughout this volume, we argue for the use of critical content analysis when reading literature written for children and young adults within both research and classroom settings. Utilizing a theoretical stance from which to read the word and the world provides a generative context for reading to create ways of know-ing outside of our own perspectives. As the world becomes a smaller and smaller place, what happens in one country or region can have a profound impact on everyone else around the world, and so it becomes imperative that we understand one another and the cultural contexts within which we live as well as embrace the differences and similarities that make us unique individuals united in our striving toward greater awareness, acceptance, and celebration. The use of global literature gives us this opportunity; however, literature alone cannot accomplish these goals.

Critical content analysis can enhance our reading as well as invite literacy learners of all ages to think beyond the written word as they enter the context of the world through a diversity of perspectives and insights. Our hope is that critical engagement with texts will provide an opportunity for readers to gain stronger understandings and advocacy as more socially conscious global citizens.

References

Botelho, M. J. & Rudman, M. K. (2009). *Critical multicultural analysis of children's literature: Mirrors, windows, and doors.* New York, NY: Routledge.

Fisher, D. & Frey, N. (2014). *Text-dependent questions, grades K-5.* Thousand Oaks, CA: Corwin.

Freire, P. (1970). *Pedagogy of the oppressed.* New York: Continuum.

Freire, P. & Macedo, D. (1987). *Literacy: Reading the word and the world.* Santa Barbara, CA: Praeger.

Gillespie, T. (2010). *Doing literary criticism.* Portland, ME: Stenhouse.

Janks, H. (2009). *Literacy and power.* New York: Routledge.

Janks, H. (2014). Critical literacy's ongoing importance for education. *Journal of Adolescent & Adult Literacy, 57*(5), 349–356.

Lewison, M., Leland, C., & Harste, J. (2014). *Creating critical classrooms.* Mahweh, NJ: Erlbaum.

Luke, A. (2012). Critical literacy: Foundational notes. *Theory into Practice, 51*(1), 4–11.

Malpas, S. & Wake, P., Eds. (2013). *The Routledge companion to critical and cultural theory* (2nd ed.). New York: Routledge.

National Governor's Association. (2010). *Common Core State Standards for English Language Arts.* Washington, DC: NGA.

Rosenblatt, L. (1938). *Literature as exploration.* Chicago: Modern Language Association.

Smith, F. (1983). *Essays into literacy*. Portsmouth, NH: Heinemann.

Tyson, L. (2011). *Using critical theory: How to read and write about literature* (2nd ed.). New York: Routledge.

Tyson, L. (2015). *Critical theory today* (3rd ed.). New York: Routledge.

Vasquez, V. (2012). Critical literacy. In J. Banks (Ed.), *Encyclopedia of diversity in education* (pp. 466–469). Thousand Oaks, CA: Sage.

Vine, H. & Faust, M. (1993). *Situating readers: Students making meaning of literature*. Urbana, IL: National Council of Teachers of English.

Children's Literature References

Lai, T. (2011). *Inside out and back again*. New York: HarperCollins.

Park, L. S. (2012). *When my name was Keoko*. New York: Harcourt.

Pinkney, A. (1995). *Hold fast to dreams*. New York: Morrow.

Sheth, K. (2009). *Keeping corner*. New York: Disney/Hyperion.

Taylor, M. (2001). *The land*. New York: Penguin.

Watkins, Y. K. (2008). *So far from the bamboo grove*. New York: HarperCollins.

Whelan, G. (2001). *Homeless bird*. New York: HarperCollins.

ABOUT THE AUTHORS

Clare Bradford is an Alfred Deakin Professor at Deakin University in Melbourne, Australia. Her books include *Reading Race: Aboriginality in Australian Children's Literature* (2001); *Unsettling Narratives: Postcolonial Readings of Children's Literature* (2007); *New World Orders in Contemporary Children's Literature: Utopian Transformations* (2009) (with Kerry Mallan, John Stephens, and Robyn McCallum); and *The Middle Ages in Children's Literature* (2015). Clare is a Fellow of the Australian Academy of Humanities.

Wanda M. Brooks is an associate professor of Literacy Education in the College of Education at Temple University. She teaches graduate and undergraduate courses related to literacy research, theories, and instruction. Wanda's primary research interests consist of examining the literary interpretations of urban middle school youth as well as conducting analyses of contemporary African American young adult literature. She has published in journals such as *Reading Research Quarterly*, *Children's Literature in Education*, *Research in the Teaching of English*, *The Urban Review*, and *The English Journal*.

Deborah Dimmett is an assistant professor of practice in the Department of Teaching, Learning, and Sociocultural Studies at the University of Arizona. Deborah is the co-founder and executive director of Youth Envision, a nonprofit organization that provides literacy and advocacy programs for youth and youth leaders and teachers in Haiti.

Mary L. Fahrenbruck is an assistant professor in the Department of Curriculum and Instruction at New Mexico State University in Las Cruces, New Mexico. Her research focuses broadly on access to literacy and specifically on comprehension strategies, on children's literature in the classroom, and on the ways children develop as literate beings.

Becca Gasiewicz is a doctoral candidate at the University of Cincinnati. Her research interests revolve around children's literature, particularly informational texts in the early childhood classroom.

Holly Johnson is an associate professor in Literacy and Second Language Studies at the University of Cincinnati. Her interests include reader response theory, young adult literature, disciplinary literacy, and the impact of international literature on young people's understandings of the world. She has co-authored multiple articles and books including *Essentials of Young Adult Literature*; *Creating Confident Adolescent Readers: Key Elements for Building Proficiency*; and *Developing Critical Awareness at the Middle Level: Using Texts as Tools for Critique and Pleasure*.

Julia López-Robertson is an associate professor of Language and Literacy at the University of South Carolina. Her scholarly agenda is built on a commitment to working with children, families, teachers, and preservice teachers in public schools, universities, and communities for the purpose of advancing understandings about emerging bilingual/multilingual students and their families and on the transformation of teacher education to support equitable teaching for all children, particularly English Language Learners.

Carmen M. Martínez-Roldán is an associate professor in Bilingual Bicultural Education at Teachers College, Columbia University. Her research focuses on bilingual children's literate thinking—the various ways Latino children construct meanings from texts and the contexts that mediate their interpretive processes and discourses. She co-authored *Visual Journeys through Wordless Narratives: An International Inquiry with Immigrant Children and The Arrival* (with Evelyn Arizpe and Teresa Colomer).

Janelle Mathis is a professor of Literacy and Children's Literature at the University of North Texas. Her research, publications, and instructional interests focus on international and multicultural children's literature in supporting greater insight for readers to the global community and are centered at the intersection of critical content analysis, the transactional theory of reader response, and multimodality. She is past president of USBBY, the U.S. national section of the International Board on Books for Young People.

Janine M. Schall is an associate professor and department chair of Bilingual and Literacy Studies at the University of Texas Rio Grande Valley. She teaches literacy courses and conducts research in the areas of multicultural literature and children's literature with LGBT characters.

Kathy G. Short is a professor in Language, Reading and Culture at the University of Arizona with a focus on global children's and adolescent literature, intercultural understanding, and critical content analysis. She has co-authored many books, including *Essentials of Children's Literature, Essentials of Young Adult Literature,* and *Stories Matter: The Complexity of Cultural Authenticity in Children's Literature.* She is director of Worlds of Words and is Past President of the National Council of Teachers of English.

Yoo Kyung Sung is an associate professor in Language, Literacy and Sociocultural Studies at the University of New Mexico in Albuquerque, New Mexico. She teaches a range of children's literature courses. Her research includes studies on critical content analysis of global and international children's literature, including global immigrants and diaspora's representations in children's literature.

Melissa B. Wilson, recently an associate professor of Literacy Education at Southwest Louisiana University, is engaged in examining preservice teachers' concepts of race from a critical race theoretical perspective. Her research interests within the literature field revolve around how texts for and about younger people help to construct and dismantle tacit theories about younger people and adults.

Vivian Yenika-Agbaw teaches children's and adolescent literature at the Pennsylvania State University both in the residential and World Campus programs. She has authored or co-edited several books, including *Adolescents Rewrite Their World: Using Literature to Illustrate Writing Forms* (with Teresa Sychterz) and *Fairy Tales with a Black Consciousness: Essays on Adaptations of Familiar Stories* (with Ruth Lowery and Laretta Henderson).

INDEX

Page numbers in *italic* format indicate figures and tables.

Aboriginal literature 10, 23–4, 190
action projects in classrooms 143
adolescent literature 46, 47, 59, 62
adolescent readers 40, 46, 107, 109
adolescent sexuality 155–67
aetonormativity concept 139, 140
African American literature 82–8
agency of characters 35–7
American Dream 64, 192
Anthony Burns: The Defeat and Triumph of a Fugitive Slave (Hamilton) 78
appropriation 65, 69–72
arts: culture and 115–16, 117; gender and 116–17; role of 131–2, 133–6
Ask Me No Questions (Budhos) 32–3, 36, 38, 39
authentic action 138, 144–7
authentic texts 136, 174
authors: cultural locations 190–1; positionality 37–8

Blood Red Horse (Grant) 17–20
bottom-up analysis 20, 22, 65
branding and synergy 63, 65, 72–3

Caged Birds of Phnom Penh, The (Lipp) 144, *151*
Call Me Maria (Cofer) 49, 56
capitalism 62–3, 65
Case for Loving: The Fight for Interracial Marriage, The (Alko) 100

childhood 52, *53*
childism: content analysis studies of 140–2; rights of participation and 138–9, 142
children: action projects by 143; levels of participation 139; overprotection 138; rights of 137–9
Children's African Book Award (CABA) 111, 112, 116
child soldiers 106, 110
civic engagement 148–9
Civil Marriage Act of 2005 92, 100
classroom: arts in literature and 135; critical literacy in 187–96
close reading 11–12, 28, 196–8
colonialism 44–7, 57–8
commodification 61–4, 65
community members 48, 52, *53*, 56
comparative analysis 12, 82, 189
Composition, The (Skármeta) 140, 148, *151*
content analysis 2–4, 82
Copper Sun (Draper) 78
counter-narratives/counter-storytelling 81–5, 86, 88, 89, 125, 131, 194
critical consciousness 5, 110, 140, 142, 148
critical content analysis 4–14, 16–22
critical literacy 185–98
critical multicultural analysis (CMA) 29–31, 34–5, 41–2
critical pedagogy 138–40, 142–3
critical race theory (CRT) 78, 81–90, 189
critical theory 5, 8–10, 188–9

Crusade (Laird) 17–18, 26
cultural locations 190–1
cultural practices 115–16, 117
cultural understandings 5, 123, 186, 191

Daddy's Wedding (Willhoite) 96, 99,
101, 103
Darfur conflicts/war 106–8, 110, 117,
118, 119
Day of Tears (Lester) 78
discrimination 78, 84, 94, 102–3
displacement 31–3, 39, 115–16
Doing Literary Criticism (Gillespie) 189
Do Not Go around the Edges (Utemorrah
and Torres) 23
Donovan's Big Day (Newman) 97,
100–1, 103

Elijah of Buxton (Curtis) 78
*Empire of Magic: Medieval Romance and the
Politics of Cultural Fantasy* (Heng) 19
entitlement and privilege 86–7
Esperanza Rising (Ryan) 48–50, 52–8
Every Day Use (Walker) 64
exoticism 54–5
expert perspectives 195

Fallen Angels (Myers) 78
family 55–6, 114–15
Far from Home (Robert) 112
Fault in Our Stars, The (Green) 156–7,
160–1, 164–6
First Come the Zebra (Barasch) 144, *151*
First Day in Grapes (Pérez) 149, *151*
focalization 11, 20–1, 64, 193
Forever (Blume) 155, 158, 159, 161–6
Four Feet, Two Sandals (Williams) 148, *152*
freedom and security 87–8
Freedom Summer (Wiles) 148, *152*
Friends from the Other Side (Anzaldúa)
146, *152*
Friendship, The (Taylor) 77
Funny in Farsi (Dumas) 34

gays *see* LGBT people
gender issues 115–17, 179
*Genocide in Contemporary Children's and
Young Adult Literature: Cambodia to
Darfur* (Gangi) 110
Give a Goat (Schrock) 144, 146, 147,
149, *152*
Gleam and Glow (Bunting) 149, *152*
Glory Field, The (Myers) 78
Great Depression 48, 77, 123, 127

Haitian life and culture 169–83
Hart Ladder of Participation 139, 145,
147, 148
historical and sociocultural contexts 10,
189–90
Hold Fast to Dreams (Pinkney) 89, 194
Homeless Bird (Whelan) 194
Home of the Brave (Applegate) 32–9
homophobia 95, 102
Hope Springs (Walters) 137
Horton Hears a Who! (Seuss) 141
How to Heal a Broken Wing (Graham)
147, *152*
humanitarian aid 182
hybridity 134–5

If I Stay (Forman) 156, 157, 160–1,
164–6
illustrations in children's literature 96–7,
112–14, 125–7, 129–30
immigration/immigrants 35–9, 44–7,
47–52, 52–8
Indigenous people 22, 23
individualism 145–6, 192
Inside Out and Back Again (Lai) 32–3,
36–7, 39–40, 46–57, 194
intercultural understanding 74, 137
interpretive community 195–6
intersectionality theory 93–5, 97,
108–9, 188
intertextuality 47–53, 58–9

Jim Crow laws 129, 130
Jimi & Me (Adoff) 89

Kalma camp 110, 112, 116, 118
Keeping Corner (Sheth) 194
King & King (de Haan and Nijland) 96,
99–102

Land, The (Taylor) 77–9, 82–4,
87–90, 194
land ownership 77–8, 82, 85, 86, 87, 88
language learning 52, *53*, 56–7
LGBT people 94–5, 98–9, 101–4
Lionheart's Scribe (Bradford) 17–19, 21
literary theory 18, 28, 29
Long Walk to Water, A (Park) 150

marriage equality 92, 94
Marxist framework 62–5, 75
medievalisms 19, 21, 25
Mexican culture 66–75
Mock Spanish 69–73

Mom and Mum Are Getting Married (Setterington) 92, 96, 99, 101, 103
music *see* arts
My Uncle's Wedding (Ross) 96

Never Fall Down (McCormick) 32–4, 36, 38–9
New Historicism 122–4

One Crazy Summer (Williams-Garcia) 78
Operation Marriage (Chin-Lee) 96–8, 100–1, 103
oppression 79, 80, 97, 188
Order of Things, The (Foucault) 172
Orientalism (Said) 18, 20

Paulie Pastrami Achieves World Peace (Proimos) 144, 146, *152*
poems 113, 125, 129
postcolonialism 44–7, 52, 58–9
Postcolonial Middle Ages, The (Cohen) 19
postcolonial studies/theories 19, 97, 156–9, 163–7
poststructural discourse analysis 170–3, 175
poverty 179, 180, 181
prejudice 52, 58, 59, 138
privilege theories 93–5, 97, 188
problem-posing and problem-solving 138, 140, 143, 187
property ownership/rights 83, 84, 86, 88, 89
Proposition 8 96, 100

qualitative and quantitative content analysis 3, 111

racism 78, 82–90
reader response theory 29, 178
readers: cultural locations of 190–1; positionality 37–8
Reconstruction era 77, 82, 84, 86, 87
Red Pencil, The (Pinkney) 106–20
refugee issues 32, 41, 46
research purpose 6–11, 13, 185
research questions 7–8, 11, 82, 111, 159
rights of participation 137–9
Roll of Thunder Hear My Cry (Taylor) 77–8, 87
Routledge Companion to Critical and Cultural Theory, The (Malpas and Wake) 9

same-sex marriage 92–104
Sami and the Time of Troubles (Heide & Gilliland) 148, *152*

Secret Side of Empty, The (Andreu) 32–3, 36–9
Sélavi / That Is Life (Youme) 145
Serafina's Promise (Burg) 169–83
service learning 137, 142, 150
sexuality 155–6, 163–7
sign systems 124, 126, 133
Skippyjon Jones (Schachner) 64, 66–8
Skippyjon Jones Class Action (Schachner) 65, 66, 67, 72
Skippyjon Jones in Mummy Trouble (Schachner) 64
Skippyjon Jones in the Doghouse (Schachner) 61, 64
Skippyjon Jones . . . Lost in Spice (Schachner) 65
social change 134, 140, 149, *151–3*
social justice 29–30, 94, 137–8, 142–3, 148–50
social semiotics 123–4, 129–33
socioeconomic status 37, 52, *53*, 97, 102
So Far from the Bamboo Grove (Watkins) 194
Spanish grammar elements 69–70
Spanish words in series *Skippyjon Jones* 67, *68*, 71
Sparrow Girl (Pennypacker) 148, *153*
Step from Heaven, A (Na) 32–3, 36, 38–9, 50, 53–5, 58
Stones for My Father (Kent) 112
Stories Matter (Fox and Short) 174
Subway Sparrow (Torres) 145, *153*
support networks 35, 36
Sweethearts of Rhythm, The Story of the Greatest All-Girl Swing Band in the World (Nelson) 122–36

Tale of Peter Rabbit, The (Potter) 142
Tango Makes Three, And (Richardson and Parnell) 101
Taylor, Mildred 78–81
Tears of a Tiger (Draper) 82
text analysis strategies 11–12, 16–22, 34–5, 49–52, 64–6, 83–4, 95–7, 112–14, 125–9, 142–3, 161–3, 175–6, 193–6
theoretical frame 11–12
theoretical tenets 10–11
Third Crusade period 17
third world feminisms 107–10, 113, 115–18
top-down approach 16–19, 21–2, 65
Trafficked (Purcell) 32–3, 35, 38, 39
traumatic experiences *see* Darfur conflicts/war
Tricycle (Amado) 144, *153*

Uncle Bobby's Wedding (Brannen) 96, 99–100
Under the Mesquite (McCall) 34
undocumented migration and immigrants 33, 36, 39, 46, 146
unit of analysis 11, 84, 191, 192
Using Critical Theory (Tyson) 189

Victory Gardens 131, 132
Video Shop Sparrow, The (Cowley) 147, 148, *153*
visual arts 122, 124, 125, 131–3
visual images 23, 123, 126

Walking to School (Bunting) 147, 148, *153*
Wanda's Roses (Brisson) 146, *153*
War Brothers (McKay and Lafrance) 106
war trauma 106, 107, 117
Ways of Being Male (Stephen) 25
When My Name Was Keoko (Park) 194
women of color 88, 93, 108, 118, 123
World War II 10, 123, 125, 130, 190
writing as emancipatory practice 106–20

Yasmin's Hammer (Malaspina) 147, *153*
Yertle the Turtle (Seuss) 141

As we read Colato Laine's books, can let's create a list of themes that arise. Document like this—

Title of book.

How, if at there all, are the Family: p.#: "Quotation"
themes sorted Leaving behind: p#: "Quotation"
visually? Family: p.#: "Quotation"
Etc.

Do this for all the books. [Google Doc]